Scotland and
the Flemish People

Scotland and the Flemish People

edited by Alexander Fleming and Roger Mason

First published in Great Britain in 2019 by
John Donald, an imprint of Birlinn Ltd

West Newington House
10 Newington Road
Edinburgh
EH9 1QS

www.birlinn.co.uk

ISBN: 978 1 910900 27 7

British Library Cataloguing-in-Publication Data
A catalogue record for this book is available on request from the British Library

Flanders
State of the Art

The generous support of the General Representation
of the Government of Flanders in the United Kingdom
towards publication of this volume is gratefully acknowledged.

PF Charitable Trust
Wyfold Charitable Trust

The research that underlays this book would not have been possible
without the generosity of the PF and Wyfold Charitable Trusts
and the unwavering support of its trustees.

Typeset in Warnock Pro by James E. Quigley
Printed in Malta by Gutenberg Press

Image on page ii is of Edward Bonkil, Provost of Trinity Collegiate Church,
Edinburgh, portrayed in the Trinity Altarpiece that he commissioned
from the acclaimed Flemish artist Hugo van der Goes (see p. 93).
Royal Collection Trust / © Her Majesty Queen Elizabeth II 2019

For Susan and Ellen—long suffering but ever gracious

Contents

Acknowledgements

This book is the culmination of a major research project on 'Scotland and the Flemish People' hosted by the Institute of Scottish Historical Research at the University of St Andrews and aimed at exploring the relationship between Scotland, Flanders and the Flemish people from the Middle Ages to the present. It would not have been possible without the generous support of the PF and Wyfold charitable trusts, and in particular Adam and Robin Fleming, trustees, who have been a source of great encouragement as the project has unfolded. The Government of Flanders has also provided significant support and we are very grateful to the staff of Flanders House in London, and successive General Representatives of the Government of Flanders, Geert De Proost and Nic Van der Marliere, for their commitment to the project and for making this publication possible.

We have also benefited from the expertise of key members of the Institute of Scottish Historical Research: Professor Michael Brown, Dr Alex Woolf and Dr Katie Stevenson gave much needed advice on the direction of the project. Dr Stevenson also supervised the doctoral research of the two students associated with the project – Dr Amy Eberlin and Dr Morvern French – some of whose findings are detailed in the chapters that follow. We are also greatly indebted to the work of Dr Silke Muylaert, who took time out from her doctoral research at the University of Kent on the Flemish in England to help us explore their migration to Scotland.

Many others with expertise ranging from medieval and early modern Scottish history through to family and local history have contributed to the book. John Irvine deserves special mention for his valued advice, especially in connection with the structuring and development of the project. Among those who have also contributed significantly to the substance of the work, and whose technical advice we have valued, are David Dobson, George English and Charles Rigg.

At an early stage in the project, Alasdair Macdonald of the University of Strathclyde launched a parallel DNA project aimed at exploring whether some Scottish families have Flemish roots. We are grateful to Alasdair as well as co-administrator, Janet Flemming, for their extensive work on the topic. Some of the early finding are summarised in the book.

An important feature in the development of the project was its blog site. This provided a forum for a wide range of people, both inside and outside academia, to make valuable contributions to our understanding of the relationship between Scotland, Flanders and the Flemish people. Many of those blogs formed the basis for contributions to the chapters that follow and we are extremely grateful to their authors, and to a range of additional contributors, for their patience as editorial work has proceeded. Throughout the book, authors are identified by their initials, and fuller biographical information is offered at the end of the volume, but it would be remiss of us not to extend our thanks and appreciation to: Robin Bargmann, Michael Brown, Thomas Clark, David Dobson, Amy Eberlin, George English, Robin Evetts, Elizabeth Ewan, Richard Fawcett, Morvern French, John Irvine, Alasdair Macdonald, Christine McGladdery, Peadar Morgan, Silke Muylaert, Eljas Oksanen, Matthew Price, Elizabeth Rawlings, Charles Rigg, Chris Robinson, and Chris Tabraham.

Finally we would like to acknowledge the fine work of graphic designer James Quigley, who has contributed immensely to the look and the feel of the book.

Alexander Fleming and Roger Mason
January 2019

Introduction

What's in a surname? In some respects, this book is an attempt to answer this question with reference to one particular family name: Fleming. Yet, at the same time, it seeks to unpack the broader and much more complex context in which 'Flemings' — as the people of medieval Flanders were known — came to Scotland. As a surname, Fleming is so common that its geographical and ethnic roots are rarely considered. Yet it is testimony to an enduring relationship between Scotland, Flanders and the Flemish people that spans the centuries from the early Middle Ages to the present. Its most important phase, however, was between the twelfth and sixteenth centuries when migrants from Flanders (now in modern Belgium) first began to settle in Scotland and helped foster commercial, diplomatic and cultural ties with their homeland that proved crucial to the development of the medieval Scottish kingdom. While some Flemish migrants adopted the surname Fleming, many others did not, opting instead for a range of family names unrelated to their country of origin. This has tended to obscure the scale and significance of the Flemish presence in Scotland. In fact, the Flemish were one of the largest and most influential migrant groups to come to Scotland in the Middle Ages and their impact can be traced, not just in the histories of individual families, but in many aspects of Scottish social and cultural life. This book explores this long and complex relationship and seeks to assess the lasting impact it has had on Scotland in a way that is accessible to the general reader as well as useful to students of history.

Part I seeks to provide a broad overview of the extent and nature of Flemish migration to, and settlement in, Scotland. It begins, however, by addressing a vexed question of definition: who are the Flemish people? This turns out to be as much a matter of geography as ethnicity. While the inhabitants of medieval Flanders were generally referred to as Flemish, the political boundaries of Flanders were far from stable and might encompass

Scotland, Flanders and the Benelux region (2019).

not only parts of what are now known as the Benelux countries (Belgium, the Netherlands and Luxemburg), but also parts of northern France. For much of the medieval period Flanders was the economic dynamo and commercial hub of northern Europe, its wealth and population, its industry and urban centres, rivalling those of northern Italy. So why did so many Flemish people leave Flanders for other parts of Europe?

The various 'push' and 'pull' factors at work in this are considered in the remaining chapters in Part I. On the one hand, over-population, and inheritance practices that left younger sons propertyless, were prominent among the factors causing migration from Flanders. On the other hand, the availability of land in Scotland, the development of its wool trade and the establishment of trading burghs on its North Sea coast, all encouraged the settlement of migrants as well as a deepening of commercial relations between the Scottish kingdom and the booming Flanders' economy. Many Flemish migrants, especially those of knightly status, came to Scotland via England and Wales following the Norman Conquest of 1066; but others, notably merchants and craftsmen, made their way directly to the kingdom's east coast ports. Wool production, feeding demand from the textile industry in Flanders, became the lifeblood of the medieval Scottish economy, and commercial links led inevitably to what were often fraught diplomatic relations that became part-and-parcel of wider rivalries and conflicts between Scotland, England and France.

While subject to frequent and severe disruption, commercial ties were never entirely broken and, in the later Middle Ages, when cities such as Bruges and Ghent began producing luxury goods, Scottish kings, nobles and clergymen were among their many customers. Indeed, so highly were Flemish craftsmen valued that, in the late sixteenth century, several attempts were made to have them settle in Scotland as a means of stimulating domestic production, especially in the textile industry. Many of these migrants came via established Flemish communities in England where they had taken refuge from the religious conflict that would result in what amounted to the partitioning of the Low Countries after 1568 into a Catholic south (including Flanders) and a Protestant north, the United Provinces, led by Holland and subsequently known as the Dutch Republic.

The Dutch Revolt and the Eighty Years War that ensued in the Low Countries mark the end of any substantial Flemish migration to Scotland. Some individuals with Flemish (or Dutch) sounding names certainly appear in seventeenth-century records, but there is no further settlement of any note. Part II of this book, therefore, turns from issues of migration and settlement to consider the impact of Flemish people on Scottish culture and society from the Middle Ages to the present. This is evident in a variety of sometimes surprising and intriguing ways. Scotland's built environment, for example, continues to bear witness to the significant impact of Flemish settlement. Flemish migrants were among those who in the twelfth century pioneered the building of motte-and-bailey castles in those areas such as Upper Clydesdale and Moray where they settled most intensively. Flemish influence is also clearly evident not just in the peopling of the many Scottish burghs founded in the twelfth and thirteenth centuries, but even in their street plans, notably in St Andrews, Scotland's ecclesiastical capital. More broadly, the architecture that Scots encountered in Flanders, and the work of Flemish masons and craftsmen in Scotland, can be traced in surviving medieval church buildings and furnishings, while some of the detail — pantile roofs and crow-step gables — that are so characteristic of fishing ports along the Firth of Forth are attributable to later commercial and cultural exchange with the Low Countries.

For late medieval Scots, Flanders and its major cities (especially Bruges and Ghent) was not just a commercial hub, but also a trend-setting cultural marketplace, selling and often manufacturing the luxury goods that it was fashionable for the social elite to possess. Paintings, illuminated manuscripts, Books of Hours, tapestries, silks, glassware, metalwork and so on, were all available and duly purchased by fashion-conscious Scottish kings, nobles and clergymen. While many of these artefacts have been lost or destroyed (not least those items associated with Catholic worship), enough has survived to indicate the central importance of Flemish skilled workmanship to Scottish cultural and religious life before the Protestant Reformation of 1560. Yet another way in which Flemish fashion impacted on Scotland was in the military sphere, including not just the heavy artillery that was a product of Flemish foundries, such as the massive bombard 'Mons Meg', but also chivalric tournaments, such as occurred in 1449 to mark the marriage of James II to Mary of Guelders and that witnessed the comprehensive defeat of the Scottish protagonists by their Flemish opponents. Such occasions had significant political and diplomatic overtones, but there were other recreational activities, such as curling and golf, which were, and still are, contentious for another reason: while long seen as peculiarly Scottish games, they may in reality have been invented in Flanders.

The extent to which the Flemish people, their language and culture, became embedded in Scottish life is the main theme of Part III. In many ways, the process of assimilation and absorption was so successful that it is hard now to recover its full nature and extent. The ways in which the Scots language borrowed Flemish terminology provides a fascinating example. It is often pointed out how the vocabulary of Scots is studded with words of French origin, testifying to the significance of the 'Auld Alliance' with France. Though much less well-known or celebrated, Scots is equally indebted to Flemish and its Dutch cousin for a range of loan words, many of which still have currency. In the same vein, many place-names — most obviously

Flemington — bear witness to their founders' Flemish origins. Yet many Flemish families settled in Scotland without leaving such obvious traces in the landscape and without adopting the Fleming surname. Indeed, modern research has identified a range of surnames besides that of Fleming itself that can, with care, be identified as deriving from the medieval Flemish diaspora.

Scotland is very much a 'mongrel' nation, its people made up of a variety of ethnic groups, many of whom have adapted and assimilated in ways which make them all but invisible in the present. The Flemish are one such people. It is possible to trace the history of prominent noble families of undoubted Flemish descent that played an important role in the political history of medieval and early modern Scotland. The noble house of Fleming itself, Lords of Biggar and Earls of Wigtown, is one such family whose story is intertwined with the history of Scotland from the Wars of Independence to the Jacobite rebellions. But as with other noble families of Flemish origin, the history of the Fleming family is testimony to a process of Scotticisation by which they abandoned any sense of ethnic distinctiveness and were simply absorbed into the ranks of the Scottish aristocracy. Murrays, Sutherlands, Grahams, Lindsays, and even Douglases, may fall into the same category of noble families who were so effectively Scotticised as to obscure their Flemish origins. Of the lower orders of society, however, the merchants and craftsmen who worked and sometimes settled in Scotland, we know much less. Unlike the aristocracy they have left few traces in the historical record. Yet, in the same way as their higher status compatriots, these Flemish migrants were gradually absorbed into Scottish society, becoming indistinguishable from those who hailed from France, England or elsewhere, all of whom thought of themselves simply as Scots.

Thoroughly Scotticised the descendants of these Flemish settlers may now be. Nevertheless, the purpose of this book is to recover the role their forebears played, not just in peopling Scotland, but in shaping its economy and society and even its political and cultural identity. It is not intended to claim that in these respects Flemish influence was paramount or even decisive, though there is good reason to argue that the Flemish people have punched well above their weight in Scottish history. Certainly, there is no denying their historical importance, and the book will have served its purpose if it brings to prominence an aspect of Scotland's interactions with its European neighbours that has received much less attention than it deserves.

Finally, it should be explained that what follows is the product of many hands. While the editors have brought the book together and shaped its contents, they have drawn on the knowledge and expertise of a wide range of contributors. While some chapters are the work of a single expert in the field, others have multiple authors; in each case they are identified by their initials at an appropriate point in the chapter. Fuller biographical sketches of the authors are included at the end of the book, together with a bibliography that indicates the key sources on which they have drawn and which readers may pursue in search of a deeper understanding of Scotland's relationship with Flanders and the Flemish people.

RM/AF

PART I

MIGRATION AND SETTLEMENT

Flanders and the Flemish

Flanders is a region that has for millennia existed at a great European crossroads. Just west of Germany, just north of France and only a short voyage across the sea from Great Britain, its history has been shaped by the perils and opportunities afforded by a position that is simultaneously at the periphery of great western European powers and often at the centre of their geopolitical ambitions.

'Flanders' and 'Flemings' are political, administrative, cultural and social terms that carry both in modern and historical usage several overlapping meanings. Today Flanders is an administrative region of modern Belgium, which only partially maps onto the medieval county of Flanders whence it received the name. Flanders and the Flemish also describe a linguistic and cultural community; again, this identity and its encompassing geographical boundaries have evolved through time. The purpose of this chapter is to examine the political development of Flanders to the beginning of the seventeenth century in order to provide context for the various interactions of the Flemish peoples with Scotland that are the subject of this book.

The Medieval County of Flanders

Following Julius Caesar's conquest of the Gauls in the first century BC the region of modern Flanders formed a part of the Roman province of Gallia Belgica, named after the tribal confederation of the Belgae. Reorganisation and subdivisions of the Roman administrative regions took place over the successive centuries, but by and large the borders of the classical world survived to the Middle Ages only in the form of ecclesiastical provinces. It was in the ninth century, amidst the disintegration of the Carolingian Empire that had dominated western Europe from northern Spain to Germany, that the emergence of the historic county of Flanders took place.

The English Channel coasts had remained an important route of trade and communications through the early medieval period. The name Flanders, as *pagus Flandrensis*, is first mentioned in 745 to designate the area around Bruges, a district a short distance up the North Sea coast from the important but now long abandoned international trading emporium of Quentovic – a stepping stone between the North Sea and the southerly Frankish coast, and between the continent and the British Isles. The broader region gained a measure of infamy in 861 when a local count of Ghent named Baldwin 'Iron Arm' either kidnapped or eloped with Judith, the daughter of King Charles the Bald of West Francia. The pair made their way to Rome and under the auspices of the pope were reconciled with the king in 863. It is from this union that flowed the first dynasty of the counts of Flanders.

Charles granted his son-in-law the *pagus Flandrensis* and other neighbouring lands. These northerly districts would form the political and economic core of the counts' domains for centuries. Later in the ninth century the name 'Flanders' was generally adopted to describe the counts' territories, and it also became an ethnic name used (sometimes erratically) to describe the peoples living in what became the county of Flanders.

The Viking raids of the ninth century opened the door for expansion to Baldwin and his successors by weakening principalities further to the south. By the early tenth century the counts of Flanders had extended their dominion through Boulogne and Artois, closing in on Picardy. It was an overreach: the county of Boulogne passed into the hands of a rival branch of the dynasty and smaller, essentially autonomous principalities formed in southern Artois during the tenth and eleventh centuries. The early political formation of the medieval southern Low Countries was a complex tangle of dynastic politics, but for the present purposes two major threads can be drawn out.

First, the county of Flanders had – more or less – achieved its medieval form by the eleventh century. This included a region south-east of Ghent and east of the River Scheldt that fell into the German Empire. Flanders therefore straddled both the nascent France and Germany, and its counts could perform fealty (ritual political allegiance) to the rulers of both realms. Flanders would never be an exclusively French county but would always possess important ties to the east. Second, the overall political direction in post-Carolingian West Francia had been the loosening of centralised power. This had both benefited and been driven by the ambitions of regional magnates like the counts of Flanders, who carved out essentially independent princedoms from the carcass of

Map 1.1. County of Flanders by the mid-twelfth century.

the old world order, but by the eleventh century the process was beginning to reach the level of minor lordships. A rough linguistic division of medieval Flanders into a Germanic language north and a francophone south was also reflected in political organisation. The bulk of the counts' estates lay in the north, and their influence in the south was mediated by powerful local interests.

This process was arrested and ultimately reversed from the late eleventh century onwards. The central Middle Ages saw the consolidation of the kingdom of France under the Capetian kings based in Paris. It was a long, drawn-out development by no means destined for success, and the counts of Flanders would play a key role in it. On a broader social level the re-emergence of central authority was fuelled by growing economic prosperity and organisation, as well as developments in literacy and administrative practice. The term 'twelfth-century renaissance' is justly deployed to describe this period of extraordinary transformations that, among other achievements, saw the growth of cities and the establishment of new towns that still underlies the urban framework of western Europe. The crown was not the only authority to encourage and seek benefits from these developments. The regional Frankish magnates, especially the rulers of Flanders, were early adopters and sometimes forerunners in developing bureaucratic structures to enhance their governance.

But in the political arena no other event could rival the Norman Conquest of England in 1066 in terms of its impact. At a stroke the union of the kingdom of England and the powerful duchy of Normandy created a new superpower in north-west Europe (see Chapter 3). The rulers of England now possessed a power base and extensive interests in France that they could pursue backed by greatly enhanced economic and military resources. The politically fractured landscape of the region had previously given rise to complex networks of shifting alliances where no single party could dominate the others. Now the sheer presence of the Anglo-Norman union restricted the room for manoeuvre for the other princes. A fault line emerged dividing the interests of the Anglo-Normans and those of the increasingly powerful Capetian rulers of France, with the counts of Flanders siding with now one, now the other in the pursuit of their own dynastic priorities.

The reign of Count Philip 'of Alsace' (1168–91) witnessed probably the highest pinnacle of power and prestige that the counts of Flanders attained relative to their neighbours. Philip's younger brother Matthew became the count of Boulogne, securing the Channel crossing at its narrowest. Philip's sister Margaret married Count Baldwin V of Hainaut, creating a dynastic link with Flanders' often troublesome eastern neighbour. And the veritable master stroke was Philip's marriage to the heiress Elizabeth of Vermandois, a large strategically located county in Picardy between Flanders and the Capetian heartland. With these arrangements in place Philip's power was just a step below that of the French and English kings.

To celebrate and affirm his status the count actively participated in the courtly culture of the time. The late twelfth century was an era of great princely households that sponsored the flowering of chivalric romance literature and ushered in the development of tournament culture. The early tournaments were not merely jousts, for the set piece event consisted of a mock battle in which up to hundreds of lords and knights and potentially thousands of less elevated participants fought. A regular tournament circuit sprung up in northern France attended by lords essentially trailing small armies as their retinues. Shows of military force, conspicuous consumption, elite networking, displays of courtly refinement: Count Philip could be found at the centre of it all.

In no small part this was the reaction by regional magnates against the centralising efforts of their monarchs, and an attempt to cultivate a nexus of aristocratic power

Table 1.1. The counts of Flanders, 862-1206.

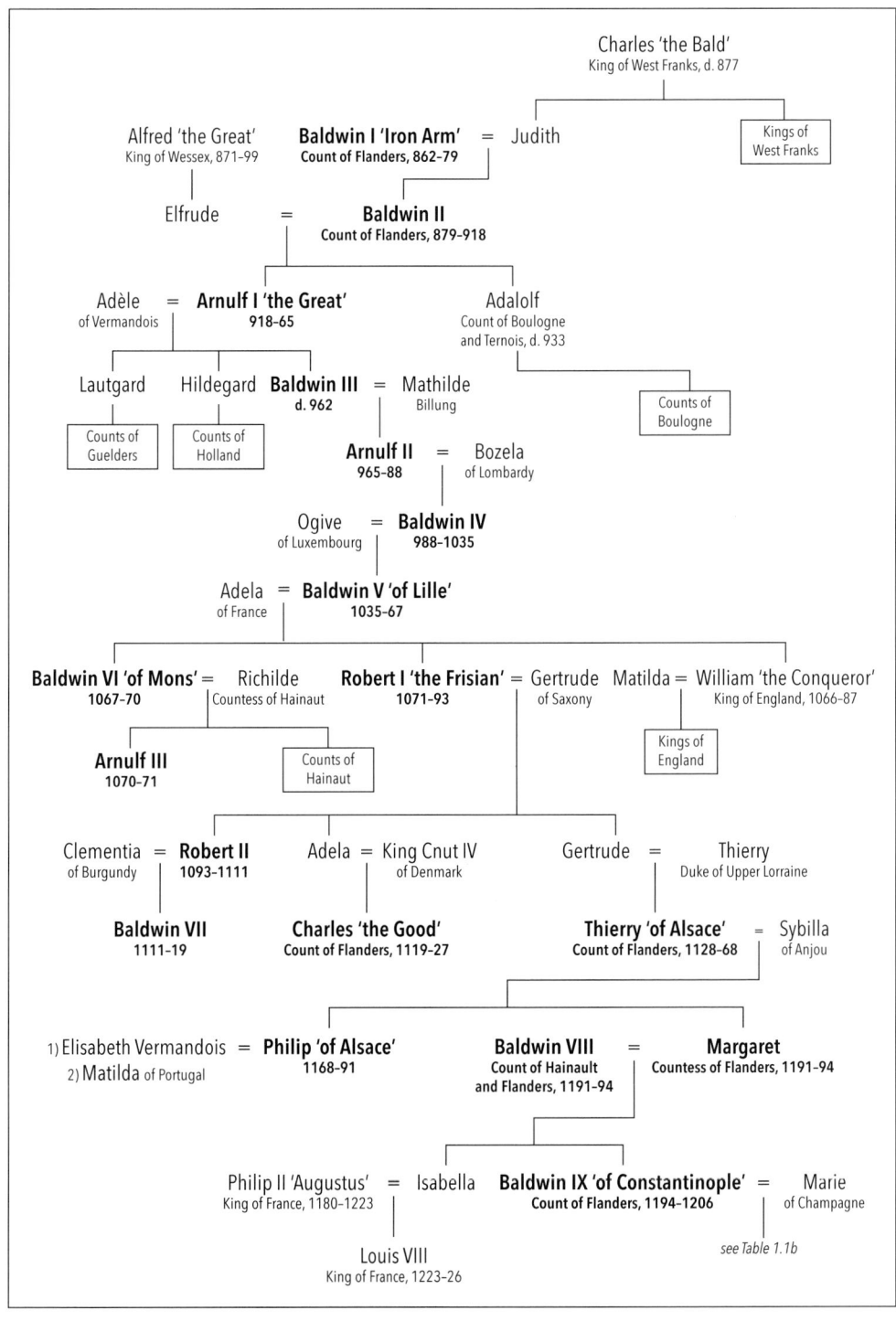

Table 1.2. The counts of Flanders, 1206–1598.

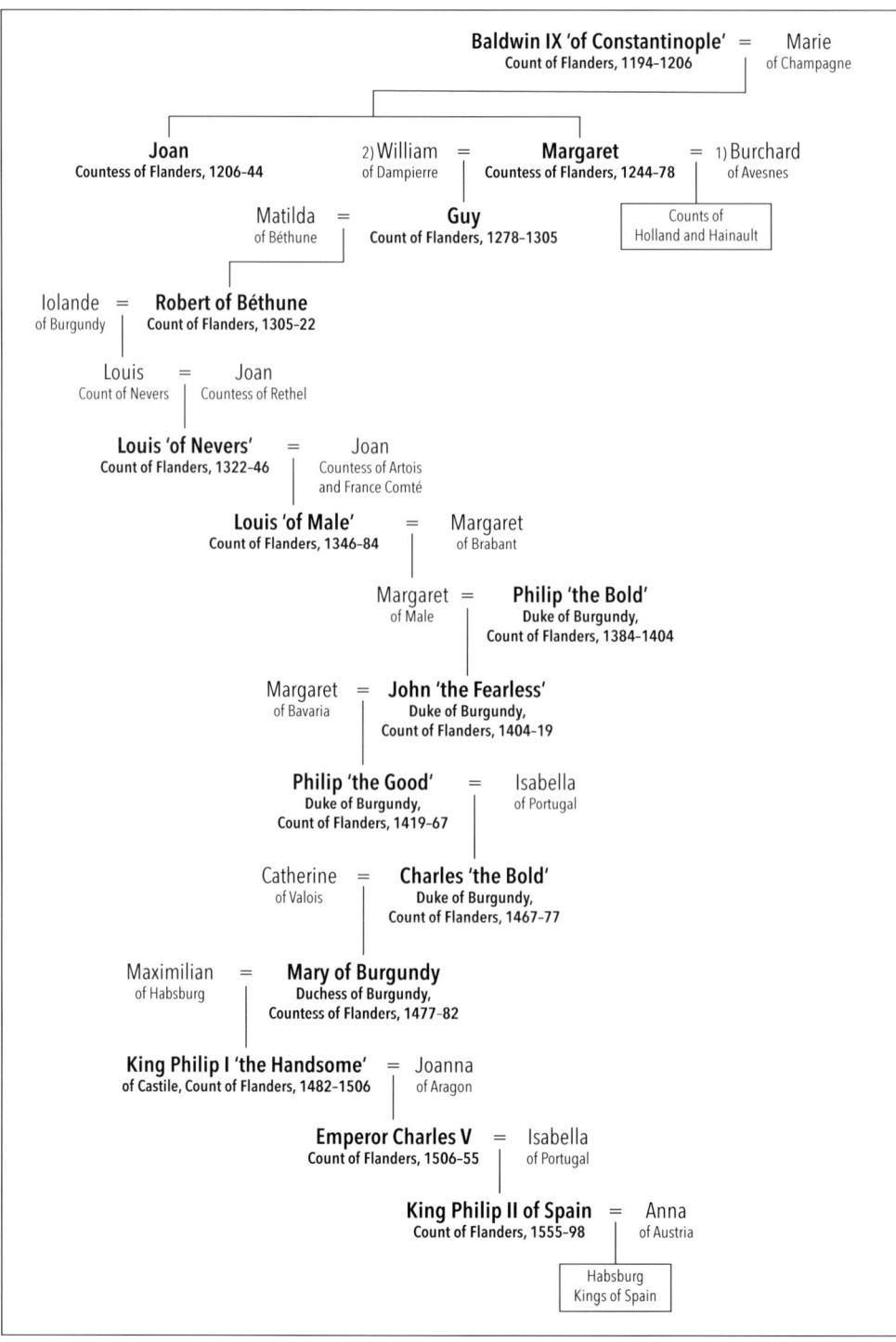

against the looming might of the crown. Philip's efforts undoubtedly paid off in that he was readily acclaimed as a regional power of the first rank. But the gains were transitory. Philip overplayed his hand in attempting to draw the young King Philip II Augustus of France into his dynastic network through marriage with his niece Isabella of Hainaut. As an inducement to the deal Count Philip offered a large section of Artois as Isabella's dowry. This seemingly strange decision effectively to cede key areas of southern Flanders has caused much puzzlement among historians, but it may suggest that he did not consider the south as integrally a part of his domains as northern Flanders.

In any event the count's plans soon lay in ruins. Philip Augustus proved resistant to Flemish machinations and broke off with the count. Count Philip's ultimate failure to consolidate his gains illustrates the potential fragility of dynastic expansion through personal union. After he died without direct issue Vermandois was detached from Flanders and taken over by King Philip, as was much of Artois. The fate of these largely French-speaking regions was subject to a tug-of-war over the next generation, but ultimately the division held and the lost lands of Artois were only brought back together with Flemish Flanders by the Burgundian dukes in the late fourteenth century.

Since Count Philip's brothers had predeceased him the bulk of Flanders passed through Margaret to the counts of Hainaut and a new dynasty. For most ordinary Flemish people the lineal descent of the ruling count would have been, of course, of less immediate concern than their own livelihoods. They were represented in the local political landscape especially through the involvement of urban communities. The huge commercial success of the medieval Flemish towns and their extensive trade links with the British Isles is discussed in later chapters, but it must be sketched out here how their interests shaped regional politics. The greatest – among them Ghent, Bruges, Ypres, Lille, Douai, Arras and St Omer – may have initially grown as regional recon-signment centres for foodstuff trade; several were located by a waterway at the juncture of different agricultural regions. Upon these foundations they had developed by the twelfth century a textile manufacturing industry that was one of the great economic success stories of medieval Europe.

The Flemish urban communities were intensely involved in international commerce: export of cloth across Europe, import of wool from England and Scotland, grain mainly from France, and trade in diverse other goods. It was a source of enormous wealth. The number of silver pennies in circulation in England grew by almost ten-fold in the second half of the twelfth century, and most of the metal is thought to have entered the country through Flemish trade. But the set-up was vulnerable to periods of warfare between the kings of England and France in which the counts found it difficult to remain neutral. The aristocratic rulers of Flanders would ignore mercantile concerns at their peril. Amidst an Anglo-French war in 1196 a trade embargo by King Richard the Lionheart of England pressured Count Baldwin IX to switch sides. During a subsequent conflict in 1208, when the regent of Flanders had sided with Paris, burghers from most of the large cities openly defied him by swearing allegiance to King John of England. At several instances through the Middle Ages the towns effectively ran their own foreign policy initiatives in opposition to those of the counts.

Loss of southern territories to the French crown reduced the number of great urban centres so that by the fourteenth century only Ghent, Bruges and Ypres remained within the county. The towns' power nevertheless remained significant, and they clashed economically, politically and militarily with each other, the counts and foreign powers. The most celebrated triumph of Flemish urban forces took place in 1302 when town militias led by Bruges routed an invading French army at the Battle of the Golden Spurs; the crushing defeat dealt to an aristocratic cavalry-heavy army by primarily infantry forces has been credited as a milestone in the development of the medieval practice of war.

By now the revenues the counts derived from tolls, taxes and administrative duties had long surpassed income from their private landed estates. Urban politics and economics were tightly intertwined. The multifocal political make-up of Flanders gained in formal structures in the 1340s following a revolt led by Jacob van Artevelde, a Ghent merchant, against Count Louis I and the king of France. The urban leadership divided Flanders into four 'quarters' over which the cities exerted considerable administrative power and created the Three Members of Flanders, a corporation consisting of representatives from the three major towns. A fourth Member, the Franc (or castellany) of Bruges, was added in 1386. This institution became the major mechanism by which the Flemish dealt with their aristocratic rulers in the Middle Ages.

Flanders in the Burgundian and Habsburg Realms

The late fourteenth century saw the inception of a powerful new political complex in north-western Europe of which Flanders would be the cornerstone. In 1369 Margaret 'of Male', the daughter and heir of Count Louis II of Flanders, wed Duke Philip the Bold of Burgundy (1363–1404). The marriage was sponsored by the duke's brother, King Charles V of France, who in the context of the Hundred Years War with England (1337–1453) wished to create a friendly power block in this geopolitically central region. Through Margaret the countship of Flanders passed to the dukes of Burgundy. Her and Philip's successors would bring together – by marriage, inheritance, purchase and coercion – an enormous assemblage of principalities that included the duchy of Burgundy, Franche-Comté,

Box 1.1. Languages and villages

Historic Flanders was a crossroads not only politically but linguistically. In the Middle Ages the frontier between the Germanic and Romance languages bisected the county east to west until it arrived to the area roughly between Lille and Ypres. From there it fanned toward the coast to encompass a linguistically heterogeneous region between the rivers Canche and Aa. Southern Flanders, including Artois, was therefore predominantly French speaking. The language frontier more or less coincided with an important divide in historical community organisation. North of the line dispersed settlements predominated: scattered farms with villages acting mostly as service centres. South of the line settlements were nucleated: houses gathered in villages surrounded by belts of fields. This historical pattern still influences the physical organisation of modern rural communities and testifies to the ancient character of the human landscape.

Flanders, Artois, Hainaut, Brabant, Luxemburg, Limburg, Holland, Zeeland, Antwerp and Mechelen; or, in addition to the Burgundian lands, the greater part of the modern Low Countries.

The creation of an over-mighty Burgundian dynasty, even one closely associated with the French crown, was always going to be a risky endeavour with unforeseen consequences. Power struggles fanned by the minority, and later insanity, of King Charles VI soured the Burgundians' relations with the main branch of the French royal family. A moment of rupture came with the assassination of Duke John the Fearless by a rival political faction in 1419 and turned the dukes' alliances away from France. England, as an enemy of the kings of France amidst the Hundred Years War, made for a natural partner. Dukes Philip the Good (1419–67) and Charles the Bold (1467–77) also oriented toward the Holy Roman Empire in which they became, by virtue of their numerous imperial principalities, a leading force. Flanders was now an indispensable part of a multinational Burgundian conglomeration that fully straddled France and Germany. No other principality contributed as much to the treasury of the dukes, and the Flemish lands supplied them with a power base from which they would exert and expand their power.

The emergent Burgundian realm was in the early fifteenth century an assemblage of disparate territories brought together in the person of its princely duke. When

Philip the Bold assumed Flanders through his wife's inheritance in 1384 he had initially done little to replace officials of the former regime. The Burgundian apparatus overlay rather than replaced Flemish institutions; the administrative competence of the Four Members grew rather than diminished under the first dukes. The principalities they ruled maintained their distinctiveness and independent administrations.

Yet by the middle of the fifteenth century this situation was beginning to be drastically revised. Duke Philip the Good successfully pushed administrative initiatives linking his principalities together. In 1433 he reformed the currency, introducing a coinage partially based on the Flemish system. Since the new policy required participation from all the territories in question it has been seen as planting the seed for the development of the parliamentary Estates General of the Burgundian Netherlands. The Estates General were first formally convened in 1464, with annual meetings taking place from 1477 onwards. They provided an important framework within which political cooperation developed. The long-term function of the Burgundian union was therefore not to bind Flanders towards France – as King Charles V might have wished – but rather to link it with the other principalities of the Low Countries into a grander regional complex.

Perhaps paradoxically the success of the Burgundian dukes in forging a composite princely realm owed much to the inherent divisions in their territories. Previously the leadership of the individual principalities had had little by the way of regional cooperation. Political identity and organisation was restricted to regional and local levels, and this meant that rebellions and pushbacks against the policies of the dukes were similarly isolated. Of all the principalities Flanders possessed the most in terms of shared identity and traditions of local autonomy. Serious urban revolts broke out in Ghent and Bruges against the Burgundian administration during the fifteenth century. But here the sheer size of the Burgundian territories came into play: without fully realised cross-regional cooperation the dukes always possessed the greater resources and could deal with internal enemies on a limited basis.

Furthermore, the great Flemish urban communities had entered into long-term economic decline. Competition together with rising labour and raw materials costs meant that by the late fourteenth century the Flemish textile industries were well past their heyday. The cities responded by exploring new market opportunities. Ghent built upon its position as the regional reconsignment hub for the grain trade, which now became an essential economic asset. Bruges developed its service sector, becoming the pre-eminent financial centre of north-western Europe. These developments rested on monopolistic privileges that came at a cost to the rest of the Flemish economy, however, and were ultimately vulnerable to ducal interference.

Map 1.2. Burgundian and Habsburg domains, after D. Nicholas, *Medieval Flanders*, 1992, pp. 444–5.

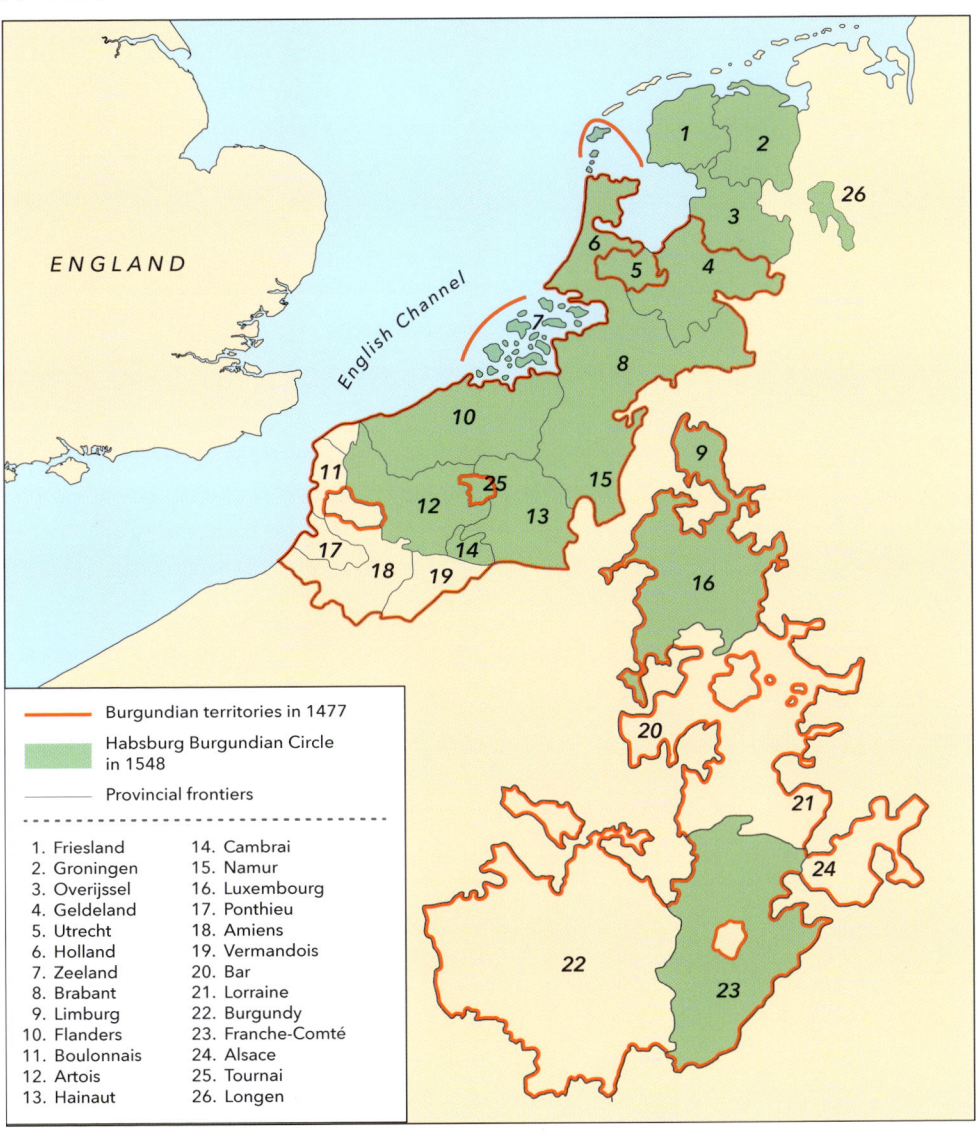

ENGLAND

English Channel

Burgundian territories in 1477

Habsburg Burgundian Circle in 1548

Provincial frontiers

1. Friesland
2. Groningen
3. Overijssel
4. Geldeland
5. Utrecht
6. Holland
7. Zeeland
8. Brabant
9. Limburg
10. Flanders
11. Boulonnais
12. Artois
13. Hainaut
14. Cambrai
15. Namur
16. Luxembourg
17. Ponthieu
18. Amiens
19. Vermandois
20. Bar
21. Lorraine
22. Burgundy
23. Franche-Comté
24. Alsace
25. Tournai
26. Longen

The rule of the dukes of Burgundy came to an end with the death of Charles the Bold at the Battle of Nancy in 1477. Charles had no son, and his nineteen year-old daughter Mary was left in a weakened position. King Louis XI of France annexed the duchy of Burgundy, Franche-Comté, Artois and the Picardian territories. Local communities took the opportunity to exert their muscle and forced Mary to revoke many of the centralising policies of her father and grandfather. In this crisis the communities and principalities nevertheless did not seek the dissolution of the Burgundian-imposed political union, but rather reinforced its existence. In recognising the traditional customs of the regions the 'Great Privilege' of 1477 also affirmed the Estates General as their communal institution. While this is not to say that the Low Countries now possessed political unity and identity, the integration of Flanders and its neighbours as a territorial assemblage had reached a watershed moment.

Later that same year Mary wed archduke Maximilian of Habsburg, the future Holy Roman Emperor, and Flanders passed into the possession of a new international dynasty within which it would remain until 1794. Maximilian's grandson Charles V inherited the Burgundian territories in 1506, became the king of Castile-Aragon in 1516 and the Holy Roman Emperor in 1519. The Burgundian Netherlands were now part of a yet larger multinational conglomeration.

In the context of the wide-flung Spanish Habsburg domains the Low Countries territories were ruled from afar, a fact that contributed to their continuing internal central-isation as well as providing the political context for the split between the northern and the southern Low Countries. The Habsburgs continued Burgundian expansion through

Box 1.2. Names

The term 'Low Countries' we use today to describe the three Benelux countries originated at the Burgundian court in the fifteenth century: 'Pays d'Embas' differentiated these regions from the duchy of Burgundy and Franche-Comté. However, no single universally accepted name for the region existed in the late medieval and early modern periods. Written sources show how authors and administrative authorities, in the Low Countries and abroad, described the region and its inhabitants variously as 'Belgica' and 'Germania Inferior' (from the Roman provinces), 'Bourgogne' (from Burgundy), 'XVII Provinces/Landen' (the Seventeen Provinces of the Burgundian Circle) and 'Nederlanden' (Dutch for 'Low Countries'). In the context of specifically Flemish historical identities it is interesting to note that 'Flameng' or 'Vlaming' (Fleming) had also become a commonly (though again not universally) used supra-regional identity. It was variously assigned to a range of peoples across the Low Countries, from the post-independence Dutch north to the southern French-speaking territories.

the acquisition of several new principalities including Tournai, Utrecht and Frisia. Their administration worked hard to bring the region together. In 1531 Brussels was organised as its new administrative centre. In 1548 Charles V formulated the so-called Seventeen Provinces as the Burgundian Circle of the Empire, and in the following year pushed through his Pragmatic Sanction law that made the Circle an indivisible domain.

In the context of the Protestant Reformation state building became inextricably tied with religious policies. In 1550 Charles' son King Philip II of Spain promulgated a unified heresy law for the Seventeen Provinces and in 1559 lobbied the pope to have most of them detached from their former archbishoprics and ecclesiastically reorganised. The mercantile towns of the Low Countries had become early centres of Protestant activism and intrusive Habsburg policies – whether religious, administrative or fiscal – were poorly received by communities long accustomed to autonomy. Tensions were inflamed by the Iconoclastic Fury of 1566 during which gangs of Protestant image-breakers destroyed Catholic church property and assaulted priests, monks and nuns. Philip's heavy-handed military response and the bloody reprisals of his agent the duke of Alba the following year alienated swathes of the region's political leadership and populace. In 1568 the leading anti-Habsburg rebel William, Prince of Orange, initiated civil war with an invasion of Brabant.

The Eighty Years War (1568–1648) separated the northern from the southern Low Countries and gave rise to the United Provinces, or the Dutch Republic. The Habsburgs could ill afford to lose the coastal territories, which were a crucial military staging point in north-west Europe. But while the crown did re-conquer the south it ultimately failed to crush the United Provinces. To a large extent the emergence of new political associations in the Low Countries was due to the centralising policies initiated by the Burgundians and continued by the Habsburgs. Without the tradition of regional cooperation that had developed over the preceding century the successes of the rebels would surely have been far more meagre.

Towards Modern Flanders

Flanders, along with other principalities mostly falling into modern Belgium and Luxemburg, remained under Spain as the Spanish Netherlands. A series of French conquests annexed the southernmost areas until the Treaty of Utrecht in 1713 largely demarcated the border that now separates France from Belgium. The following year rule over the southern Low Countries passed onto the Austrian branch of the Habsburg family. In 1794 they were fully taken over by the French and in the post-Napoleonic settlement

Map 1.3. Modern Belgium.

of Europe the southern and northern Low Countries were reunited as the Kingdom of the Netherlands. Social and political divisions, however, led to the establishment of the separate Kingdom of Belgium in 1830, and with the full independence of Luxemburg in 1867 the overall composition of the present-day Benelux countries had arrived.

What is today called Flanders was created through a long series of political events born out of the interaction of surrounding powers and regional communities. The concept it now encompasses transcends the borders of the historical county. In 1962 Belgium fixed its internal language borders (affecting the language of the public bodies) by law. State reforms took place from 1970 onwards and in 1993 regional devolution created a multi-layered linguistically based federal structure consisting of three regions: Flemish (Dutch dialect) speaking Flanders, Francophone Wallonia and bilingual Brussels; and three language communities: the Flemish Community, the French Community and the German-speaking Community.

Flanders, past and present, has been defined by many different boundaries. Students of history are therefore advised to bear in mind that the words we use today to define our national or social identities map imperfectly onto past practice and lived historical experience. The English scribes who recorded some of the earliest known *flandriensis* in the Domesday Book of 1086 were describing 'Flemish' settlers in England who hailed from what are now the departments of northern France. Conversely, they would not have used that name for a traveller from Hasselt, today in the Flemish province of Limburg in north-eastern Belgium. The location of Flanders at the crossing point of Europe has bequeathed it a history rich in interactions with peoples across continental Europe and the Atlantic coasts, and also a complex historical identity that reaches deep into the past.

EO

2

Flanders and Scotland

Although Scotland's links with Flanders can be traced back much earlier, it was following the Norman Conquest of England in 1066 that significant numbers of Flemish people made their way to Scotland and that commercial links with Flanders became a primary driver of the Scottish economy. For much of the medieval period Flanders was a rich and prosperous region so there is a fundamental issue as to why people would choose to leave it. Experts on population movement conventionally refer to 'push and pull factors' that effect migration. Pull factors are those that attract migrants to a particular location, including employment opportunities, economic incentives offered by the host government, freedom of religion, and so on. Push factors are those that encourage an individual to leave their place of residence, ranging from economic downturns and lack of employment opportunities to religious persecution. Both push and pull factors are clearly in evidence in the migration of the Flemish to Scotland. The pull factors are addressed in more detail in later chapters; here the focus is, first, on what led the Flemish to leave Flanders and seek their fortunes elsewhere, and second, on the commercial, diplomatic and cultural links that developed between Flanders and Scotland as a result.

Flemings on the Move

The most important incentive for the Flemish to leave Flanders was undoubtedly economic. While there were always adventurous individuals who sought out better economic opportunities elsewhere, there were also times when the Flemish economy experienced difficulties, causing migration to intensify. Largely as a result of its burgeoning textile industry, Flanders became a prominent political and economic player in northwest Europe, while the fast-growing cities of Ghent and Bruges became economic hubs for the region. Between 1000 and 1300, the population more than doubled as Flanders vied with northern Italy as the most urbanised region of Europe. The period thereafter, from 1300 to 1500, brought economic decline and stagnation as political tensions and increasing competition in the textile market undermined the success of the earlier centuries. However, such decline was relative and, under the dukes of Burgundy, Flanders remained an economically powerful region producing art and artefacts at the cutting edge of European culture.

The pressure of overpopulation, though hard to measure, was undoubtedly a significant factor in Flemish migration, not least because of the shortage of land that accompanied it. Although impossible to quantify, emigration from Flanders to all other countries likely ranged from a few hundred people around the eleventh century to perhaps 100,000 in the sixteenth century. Diplomatic tensions, sometimes leading to serious disputes or war, also figured as an occasional push factor, as did the major religious reform movement – the Reformation – in the sixteenth century. Finally, medieval Flanders was also hit by famine, as well as natural disasters such as floods, though the impact of these occasional events on migration is unlikely to have been very significant (see Box 2.1).

Most Flemish migrants who came to Britain went to England in the first instance – only a minority went directly to Scotland. Ironically, the earliest evidence of traffic between Scotland and Flanders involved missionaries travelling from the former to the latter rather than vice versa. Flanders was Christianised around the seventh century at the instigation of the bishops of Tournai who requested the help of Irish, Scottish, and French missionaries. However, these contacts were very limited, and it was trade with nearby England that sustained connections across the North Sea, with some evidence suggesting the presence of Flemish merchants in London in the tenth century. At the same time, Flemish monasteries, notably St-Bertin at St-Omer, maintained connections with England through well-travelled writers such as Drogo of St-Winnocksbergen, and the monk Folcard, who became head of Thorney Abbey in Cambridgeshire shortly after the Norman Conquest of England in 1066. While monasteries were religious communities and centres of culture and learning, they were also, and increasingly, economic hubs with extensive commercial interests. As we will see, in Scotland as in England, monastic foundations played a critical role in the development of the wool trade and in deepening ties with the Flemish textile industry.

Meanwhile, as regards emigration from Flanders during these centuries, the evidence is overwhelmingly concentrated on the elite – that is, the noble classes – and

Box 2.1. Famine and foods

Bad weather and the destruction of crops meant that famines were periodic occurrences in the medieval Low Countries, sometimes causing substantial population movements as people flocked to cities to buy foreign grain. There was, for example, a widespread three-year famine between 1144 and 1147. Most often famines were localised but sometimes the crisis was European-wide, such as the Great Famine of 1315 that particularly impacted on Flanders. There is no evidence that famine caused large-scale migration from the Low Countries, but it is indicative of the problem of feeding an ever-growing population and did contribute to the more general outflow of migrants from Flanders, especially to Germany and England. Although agricultural improvements increased food production, the problem of feeding an ever-growing population remained unresolved, at least until the bubonic plague – the 'Black Death' – led to demographic collapse across Europe in the mid-fourteenth century.

Another explanation that has been used to account for emigration from Flanders from 1000 to 1300 is natural disasters. A thirteenth-century Welsh chronicle, for instance, attributed Flemish migration to England and Wales to devastating floods in Flanders. As Flanders was situated on the coast, the sea inundated parts of the land and forced people to flee, according to the chronicle. This explanation remained popular, even among scholars, until more recent research discredited it. There is evidence of floods that impacted on Flanders – for instance, a large flood in the coastal regions in 1334 – but in terms of migration such events were not of great significance.

their retainers. Given the shortage of land, there were few opportunities for younger nobles and noblewomen within Flanders. As a result, noblewomen in search of a husband were obliged to cross geographical and political boundaries to exploit a wider pool of potential noble matches. By the same token, noblemen sought lands and marriages abroad through military careers as knights, either in the service of their family or in the service of a different magnate. These trends were reinforced by the growing emphasis in Flanders on primogeniture (whereby the eldest son inherited the entirety of their parents' estate). This led to younger sons seeking their fortunes through military activity abroad. As we will see in Chapter 3, this was the case in 1066 when Flemish knights took part in the Battle of Hastings on the side of William the Conqueror who rewarded them with lands in England, an initial settlement that was followed by further waves of colonisation, extending to Wales and Scotland, over the next century and more.

In addition to those non-elite retainers who accompanied the nobility – servants, soldiers and craftsmen – there is also some evidence of skilled agricultural workers leaving Flanders to settle in England and Scotland. Although the cities were increasingly important to the Flemish economy, the region was still predominantly agricultural, but one in which only small pockets of land were arable, and where the supply of land did not keep pace with demand, leading experienced farmers to seek their fortunes abroad. By the end of the twelfth century some parts of the Flemish wetlands had been drained and were being used as pasture. In the following century much of this land was then made arable. Lands were also deforested and cleared for agriculture. Yet, even with improved production techniques, it was still not sufficient to feed the growing population, fuelling further migration. At the same time, population pressure necessitated the conversion of pastureland into arable and, with less land available for domestic sheep farming, Flemish weavers had to look elsewhere for wool. It was this that lay behind the increasing demand for English and subsequently Scottish wool and, conversely, for experienced Flemish sheep-farmers to find work in Britain.

As this suggests, urbanisation in Flanders created opportunities for buying and selling merchandise on an ever-increasing scale. This encouraged merchants to look beyond the domestic economy and seek products and markets in other countries. The expanding Flemish fishing fleet, for example, exploited the rich fishing grounds on Britain's eastern seaboard, often landing catches in English and Scottish ports, and ferrying passengers – merchants and craftsmen, clerics and diplomats – to and fro across the North Sea. Although little is known about individuals, groups of Flemish merchants existed in both England and Scotland for much of the medieval and early modern period. As we will see in later chapters, while Scottish merchants took advantage of the increasingly diverse range of high quality merchandise available in Flanders (wines, spices, textiles and manufactured goods), Flemish merchants were chiefly interested in Scottish wool.

Scotland and the wool trade

In comparison to Flanders, the Scottish economy in the twelfth and thirteenth centuries was rudimentary and primarily reliant on the production and export of wool and woollen

Table 2.1. Kings of Scots, 1058-1286.

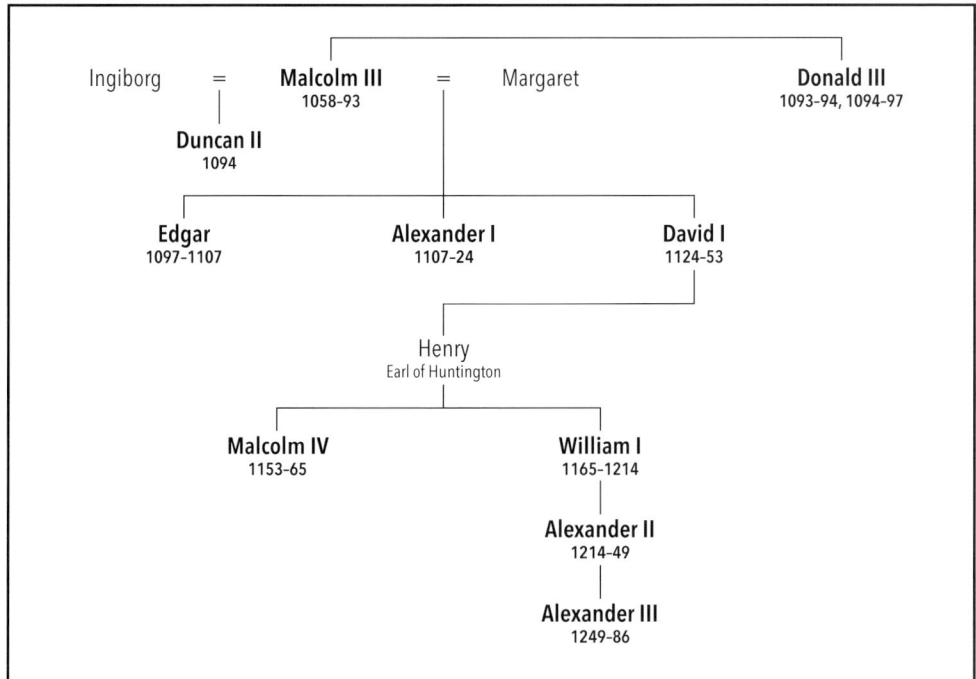

products (sheep skins and woolfells or fleeces). A small kingdom on the periphery of Europe, Scotland had nevertheless emerged as a distinct entity by the eleventh century and, under the rulership of the descendants of Mael Coluim III (1058–93), better known as Malcolm III Canmore, began to establish close commercial links with the Flemish weaving industry through sheep farming and wool production. The early development of the wool trade was boosted by two critical innovations, often associated with the reign of Malcolm's third son, David I (1124–53), but equally promoted by his royal successors: first, the introduction of new monastic orders to Scotland, and second, the foundation of royal burghs with exclusive trading privileges.

As noted above, monasteries played a key role as commercial corporations as well as religious communities and, in Scotland as in England, many developed extensive sheep farms in response to demand from Flanders (see Map 2.1). In Scotland, it was in the Tweed Valley, with relatively easy access to the port at Berwick-upon-Tweed, where abbeys like the Cistercian community at Melrose (1136) and the Premonstratensians at Dryburgh (1152) first introduced large-scale sheep farming and wool production. The Cistercians established further houses at Coupar Angus (c.1162) and Balmerino (c.1229), while other orders, such as the Benedictines of Coldingham Priory (c.1147), were also active in the trade. Lay merchants and farmers were not excluded, but the religious orders played a dominant role in what rapidly became Scotland's primary export and the backbone of its economic development. The Cistercians, for example, had their own warehouses at Berwick and Perth, bypassing local merchants, and dealing directly with Flemish buyers.

Berwick and Perth were two of some twenty royal burghs founded by David I – a further thirty or so would be created by 1300 – with the exclusive right to trade overseas. This generated customs' dues for the crown, but also encouraged greater commercial activity in more settled and privileged communities. Many of the new foundations – Aberdeen, Montrose, Dundee, Perth, St Andrews, Edinburgh and Berwick – were on the country's eastern seaboard and well-placed to take advantage of the trade with Flanders (see Map 2.1). Wool and wool products predominated, but the growing populations of cities like Ghent and Bruges also created demand for foodstuffs with herring, salmon, cod and wheat all being exported from Scottish ports. At the same time, Flemish merchants and craftsmen were encouraged to settle in the Scottish burghs (see Chapter 4) and, in the case of St Andrews, it was a Fleming who was responsible for the burgh's layout (see Chapter 6).

Long-standing commercial ties not surprisingly led to diplomatic links and alliances that in the Middle Ages were normally secured through arranged marriages. For example, in 1282 Alexander, the son and heir of the Scottish king Alexander III (1241–86), was married to Margaret of Flanders, daughter of Guy de Dampierre, Count of Flanders. The marriage was short-lived – Alexander died aged only twenty in 1284 – but it is nonetheless indicative of the growing stature of Scotland as a wool producer and trading partner. It is an intriguing question what might have happened had Alexander outlived his father and his marriage to Margaret produced male heirs. However, as it happened, Alexander III died in 1286 without a direct male heir precipitating a succession crisis that would in turn lead to a series of conflicts with England – known as the Wars of Independence (Box 2.2) – as the English king Edward I attempted to assert age-old claims to lordship over Scotland by force. While Robert Bruce eventually emerged victorious from these conflicts, and Scotland's status as an independent kingdom was vindicated, the economic costs of war were huge. In 1296, Edward I sacked and seized Berwick-upon-Tweed, the key to the Scottish wool trade, with long-established links to Flanders. The burgh subsequently changed hands several times before it finally fell to England in 1482, but it had long since lost its status as the jewel in Scotland's economic crown.

The disruption of trading patterns caused by Scotland's wars with England were complicated still further by England's wars with France. As a result of Edward I's invasion

Box 2.2. The Wars of Independence

Between 1296 and 1357 Scotland was engaged in an ongoing struggle with England to maintain its independence. English kings had long claimed rights of feudal superiority over their Scottish counterparts and, in the succession dispute that followed the death of Alexander III in 1286, Edward I agreed to adjudicate on condition that whoever was chosen as king of Scots would pay homage to him.

However, when Edward's appointee, John Balliol, began resisting the English king's demands, it led in 1296 to the invasion of Scotland and the sack of Berwick-upon-Tweed. Thereafter, Scottish resistance to English occupation was led, first, by William Wallace, who was brutally executed for treason against the English crown in 1305, and then by Robert Bruce, who seized the throne in 1306 and led a series of military campaigns that culminated in a major victory over the English at the Battle of Bannockburn in 1314. In the year of his death in 1328, Robert was formally recognised as a fully independent monarch by the Treaty of Edinburgh-Northampton.

The conflict was renewed in 1333, however, when Edward Balliol, the son of King John, with the backing of the English king Edward III, challenged the right of Robert Bruce's son, David II, to the throne. The conflict was finally ended by the Treaty of Berwick in 1357 that recognised David II as king of Scots and brought an end to what had been a long and debilitating conflict. While Scotland's independence had been won, its economy had suffered badly. Wool production and trade with Flanders were seriously disrupted by the conflict and infant craft industries in the burghs were snuffed out. Nevertheless, allied to France, and with improved access to Flemish ports, the export of wool products continued to sustain the Scottish economy.

of Scotland in 1296, the Scots had entered into what would come to be called the 'Auld Alliance' with France. A key motive for this was the fact that the Count of Flanders owed allegiance to the French monarch, Philip IV, who the previous year had closed Scottish access to markets in his domains. They were re-opened on the understanding that Scotland entered into a full alliance with France against England – an alliance that

Map 2.1. Abbeys and burghs in the reign of David I.

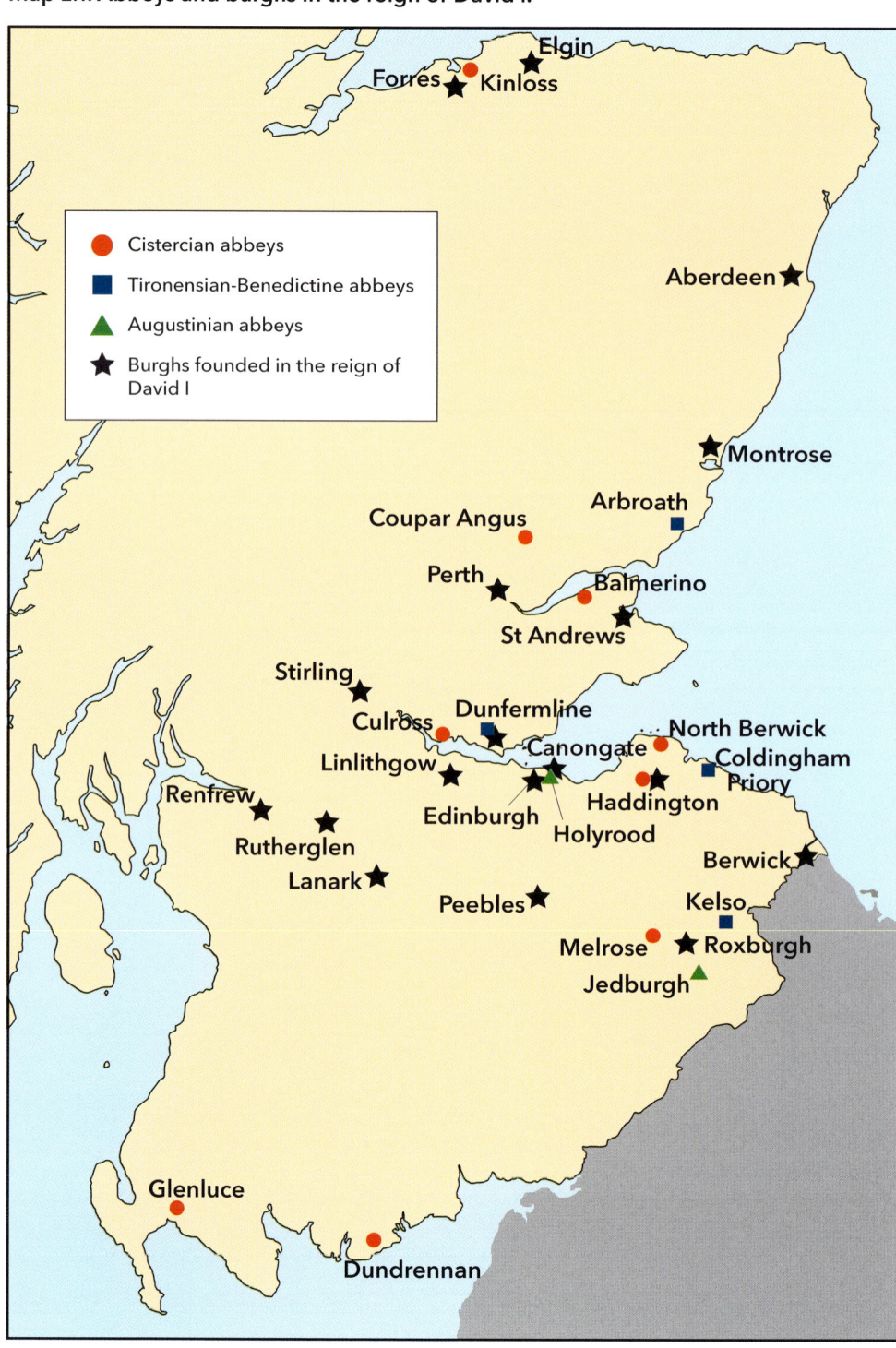

would continue throughout the Hundred Years War (1337–1453) and beyond. Ongoing military conflict certainly disrupted trade and led to a marked downturn in the Scottish economy, but producers and merchants adapted to changing conditions. The loss of Berwick led to the development of ports on the River Forth, especially Leith near Edinburgh, but also smaller coastal burghs such as Crail and Kinghorn. Perth gave way to Dundee as the major port on the River Tay, while Aberdeen retained its position in the north-east.

However, it was not just in Scotland that the economic boom of the previous two centuries gave way to stagnation and adaptation. In Flanders itself the textile industry as a whole was in decline. Ironically, its very prosperity, and its increasing reliance on the import of wool as well as foreign grain to feed its burgeoning urban population, made it politically and diplomatically vulnerable. War between France and England may have benefited Scotland, but it had serious implications for the Flemish economy. In 1336, for example, Edward III of England forbade trade with Flanders, preventing both the export of English wool and the import of Flemish textiles. England was rapidly developing its own textile industry, stimulated in part by skilled Flemish immigrants, so the cessation of trade with Flanders boosted local production, while proving disastrous for the Flemish economy. The result was a period of turmoil and crisis that proved a major turning-point as concentration on woollen textiles gave way to a more diverse economy based on a greater range of more specialised products.

However, so long as Flemish weavers needed wool, and supplies from England remained uncertain, Scotland was a valuable source of raw materials. The merchants and cloth manufacturers of Bruges were particularly keen to secure a monopoly of Scottish supplies and, at some uncertain date before 1347, an agreement was reached that designated Bruges as the sole entry point for Scottish wool to Flanders in return for offering Scottish merchants a range of coveted trading privileges. Bruges was still a major centre of textile production as well as international banking and its designation as the Scottish 'Staple' – the term used for these arrangements – formalised a trading relationship that was already of long-standing and that is still evident in the Schottendyk, the only wharf in the city named for foreigners. Bruges remained a key marketplace for Scottish merchants until the later fifteenth century when the silting up of the River Zwin made access to the city's docks increasingly difficult. But competition – both economic and political – meant that at various times the Scottish Staple was moved to Middelburg and Veere before, in 1508, Bruges was finally abandoned in favour of Veere's more accessible deep-water harbour.

Box 2.3. Anselm Adornes

Anselm Adornes (1424–83) was a merchant from Bruges, where his family (an offshoot of the Adorno of Genoa) had been settled since the thirteenth century and where they were wealthy and respected members of the mercantile community. Anselm first visited Scotland in 1468 on what amounted to a trade mission, but appears to have made an instant impression on the young James III who personally knighted him in 1469 and made him a member of his privy council.

The Adornes family had a tradition of going on pilgrimage to the Holy Land and the family chapel in Bruges (the Jerusalem Chapel) was modelled on the Church of the Holy Sepulchre in Jerusalem. Anselm was apparently already making plans to travel to the Holy Land before his visit to Scotland, but James III probably encouraged him. Certainly, this is the impression given in the account of the journey – which took place in 1470–71 – written up by Anselm's son, John, and dedicated to James III.

The pilgrimage took Anselm and his retinue to Italy (Rome and Genoa), Tunis and Egypt before they arrived in Palestine. In Jerusalem, they visited the church of the Holy Sepulchre as well as other sites in the vicinity. They then returned via Damascus and Beirut, sailing to southern Italy via Rhodes, and arriving back in Bruges in April 1471, and making their way to the Scottish court in October 1471, when their account of the pilgrimage was presented to the king. Anselm was rewarded with grants of land in Scotland and the office of conservator of the privileges of Scottish merchants in the territories of the duke of Burgundy. He returned to Bruges in the summer of 1472.

However, political problems in Bruges saw Anselm being excluded from public office in 1477, whereupon he returned to the court of James III and quickly re-established himself as one of the king's close companions and was appointed keeper of the king's palace at Linlithgow. Although he attracted unfavourable comment from James's enemies, he was not one of the victims of a rebellion against the king in 1482. Rather he was murdered the following year (in circumstances that remain obscure), his body buried at Linlithgow and his heart taken to Bruges and placed in an elaborate tomb in the Jerusalem Chapel, where it remains to this day.

Table 2.2. Bruce-Stewart royal line, 1306-1603.

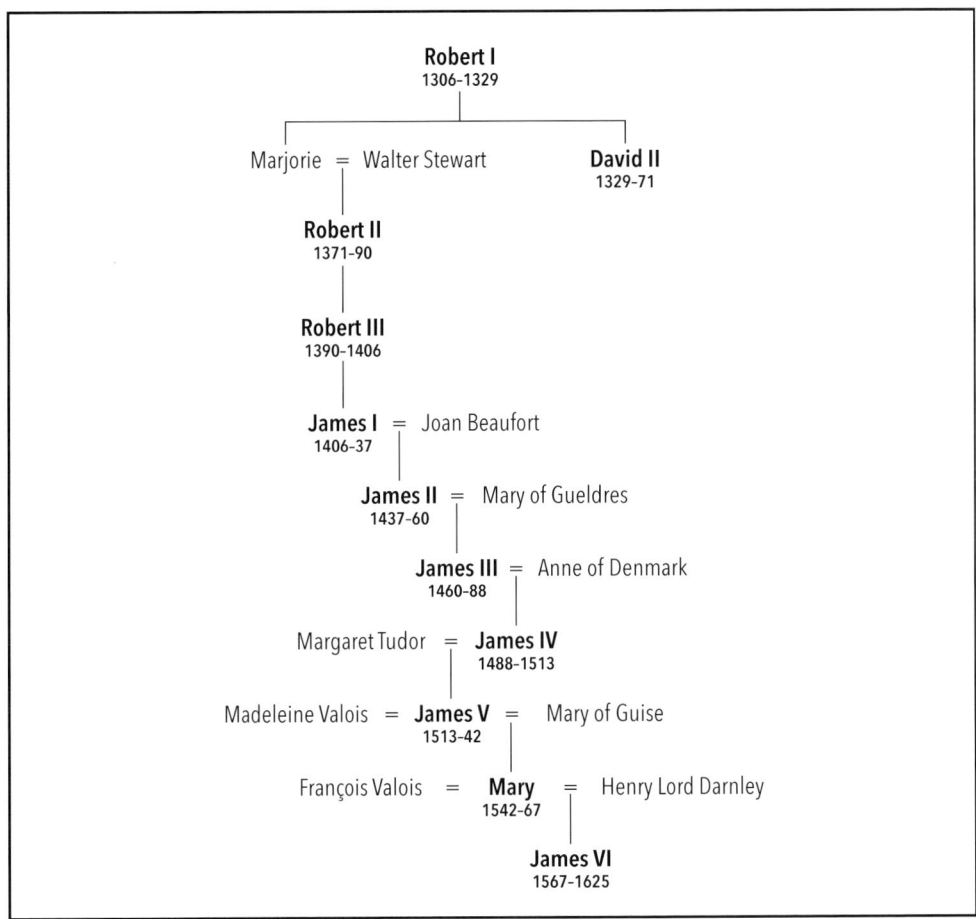

Renaissance and Reformation

The adaptation of the Flanders' economy to changing circumstances was facilitated by the rule of the dukes of Burgundy over the region from 1384 to 1482 and the increasing importance of the Burgundian court as a model of ostentatious princely display. Renaissance ideas of 'magnificence' encouraged lavish displays of wealth by kings, princes and nobles in the form of elaborate pageantry, ritualised knightly conduct in chivalric tournaments, luxuriously bejewelled clothing, rich tapestries and paintings, and finely wrought jewellery and metalwork. The resources of the Burgundian dukes enabled them to spend lavishly and, in the process, to encourage the development of specialised crafts for which cities like Bruges and Ghent became by-words. Rivalling the city-states of Renaissance Italy, Bruges played host to renowned artists such as Jan van Eyck (c.1390–1441), but also to a host of lesser known but highly skilled illuminators, jewellers, goldsmiths, armourers, spinners, dyers and weavers. Flemish luxury goods dominated the 'high fashion' industry of Northern Europe and marketplaces like Bruges were where the Northern European elite went shopping.

Among them were Scottish kings, nobles and high-ranking clergy. The emergence of the Stewarts as kings of Scots in the fifteenth century coincided with the rule of the dukes of Burgundy and deeply influenced both courtly and elite Scottish culture. Perhaps the highpoint of the diplomatic relationship between Scotland and Burgundy was the marriage of James II to Duke Philip the Good's grand-niece, Mary of Guelders, in 1449, a match that was preceded by a spectacular tournament featuring Scottish and Burgundian knights (described in detail in chapter 8). Mary was the founder of Trinity Collegiate Church in Edinburgh which, though now demolished, housed the renowned Trinity Altarpiece by Brugeois artist, Hugo van der Goes (see Chapter 6); while her son, James III, had among his close familiars another citizen of Bruges, Anselm Adornes, whose murder near Linlithgow in 1483 remains something of a mystery (see Box 2.3). As this suggests, despite the annexation of the Burgundian dukedom by the French crown in 1477, and the passing of Flanders into the hands of the Spanish Habsburg monarchy, Scottish kings continued to look to the Low Countries for the art and artefacts through which to display their kingly authority. James IV, for example, made extensive use of Flemish merchants in purchasing the rich textiles, tapestries and illuminated manuscripts that were part-and-parcel of courtly culture (see Chapter 7), while the survival of one of the ledgers of the Scottish merchant Andrew Halyburton, based in Middelburg in the early years of the sixteenth century, gives us a unique insight into the wide range of goods purchased by a cross-section of elite Scottish society (see Chapter 4).

In many ways, the reign of James IV (1488–1513) was the highpoint of Scotto-Flemish commercial and cultural exchange. The sixteenth century witnessed major upheaval that led to the partitioning of the Low Countries and a severing of Scotland's historic ties with Flanders. What lay behind this was first and foremost the Reformation, the religious schism initiated by Martin Luther in 1517 that divided Europe into warring Catholic and Protestant camps. The Habsburg rulers of the Low Countries, Charles V and his son Philip II, were militant defenders of the Catholic faith and from the 1540s onwards their persecution of Protestants was as cruel as anywhere in Europe. Many Protestants – men, women and children – were burned at the stake, while many others fled the country, seeking refuge in more hospitable lands (see also Chapter 4). England was a favoured destination following Henry VIII's repudiation of the pope's authority in the 1530s and the more overt commitment to Protestantism of his son and successor,

Box 2.4. Mary Queen of Scots and the 'Rough Wooing'

The untimely death of James V in 1542 led to a major conflict between England and France for control of Scotland. The king's sole legitimate heir was a week-old baby girl, Mary, who immediately became the focus of intense dynastic interest. The long-standing enmity between France and England was worsened by Henry VIII's break with Rome and his attempts to persuade James V to follow his example. James chose instead to maintain his ties, not only with the Catholic church, but with his 'Auld Ally' the French king. His marriage to Mary of Guise, the mother of Mary Queen of Scots, was part of this strategy.

The deteriorating relationship between James V and Henry VIII had led to the outbreak of war in 1542. However, the Scottish king's death presented Henry with an opportunity to bring Scotland to heel by dynastic rather than military means: the betrothal of the infant Queen of Scots to his own son and heir, Prince Edward, would unite the kingdoms and put an end to centuries of conflict. While the Scots initially agreed to this proposal, they almost immediately reneged, and set in motion a series of military conflicts known as Henry's 'Rough Wooing' of Mary. The wooing was unsuccessful. The Scots turned once again to France for aid, and in 1548 the six year-old queen was shipped off to France and a future marriage to the Dauphin François, the heir to the French throne.

The marriage finally took place in 1558 and a year later Mary became queen of France when her husband was crowned François II in July 1559. However, not only did the sickly François die aged only sixteen in 1560, but the same year witnessed a successful Protestant Reformation in Scotland. When Mary returned to her native kingdom in 1561, therefore, she did so as the Catholic ruler of a formally Protestant kingdom. It proved an unsustainable combination. While her Catholic marriage to Henry Stewart, Lord Darnley, produced a male heir, James, her husband's assassination triggered a major constitutional crisis. In 1567 Mary was forced to abdicate in favour of her son. While Mary fled to England, and eventual execution, James VI was brought up in Scotland as a Protestant, becoming also in 1603 James I of England on the death of the childless Elizabeth Tudor.

Edward VI (1547–1553). The first flow of refugees to England in the late 1540s was briefly stemmed by the reign of the Catholic Mary Tudor (1553–1558), but was resumed and gained increasing force under Mary's Protestant half-sister Elizabeth (1558–1603). At the same time, following three decades of religious and diplomatic tension, including the brutal war with England known as the 'Rough Wooing' (see Box 2.4), Scotland in 1560 formally adopted the Protestant religion. While the brief personal rule of the Catholic Mary Queen of Scots (1561–1567) proved a highly unsettling interlude, the long reign of her son James VI (1567–1625) saw Scotland adopting and adapting a particularly rigorous brand of Protestantism.

The early years of Elizabeth's reign in England, and the emergence of a Protestant Scotland, coincided with a deepening of the religious crisis in the Low Countries. A marked economic downturn, and the collapse of the weaving industry, was already prompting Flemish migration to England drawn by the pull of greater economic opportunity. These numbers were now swollen by the push of religious persecution on a massive scale. Following the Iconoclastic Fury of 1566 – during which Protestants across the Low Countries destroyed the hated religious icons and imagery associated with Catholicism – what amounted to a prolonged religious war wreaked havoc with the Flemish economy and prompted a major challenge to Habsburg rule. The Dutch Revolt or Eighty Years War (1568–1648) effectively partitioned the Low Countries between the Catholic Spanish Netherlands to the south and the Protestant United Provinces or Dutch Republic to the north. Up to and beyond 1585, when the key town of Antwerp fell to Catholic troops, Flemish Protestants moved north in large numbers to the United Provinces – perhaps as many as 100,000 were displaced by the warfare – and many of these pushed on to Germany, England or Scotland.

As we will see in Chapter 4, it is impossible to quantify the number of Flemish migrants to Scotland in the latter part of the sixteenth century, whether directly or via England. However, we do know that the Scottish government was keen to recruit skilled weavers and other craftsmen who might contribute to the kingdom's economic development. Push and pull factors continued to interact in ways that linked the Scottish and Flemish economies. Yet direct links with Flanders, now part of the Spanish Catholic Netherlands, gradually weakened, while ties to the northern and Protestant United Provinces gathered strength. As Scotland in 1603 entered a regal union with England through the accession of James VI to Elizabeth Tudor's throne, so Scottish traders, churchmen and diplomats sought new opportunities in the Dutch Republic rather than the Spanish Netherlands.

SM/AE/DD/RM

3

Flemish Migration I:
Knights and Mercenaries

As the previous chapters have shown, the two key moments in the migration of Flemish people to Great Britain in general and Scotland in particular were the Norman Conquest of England in 1066 and the reign of David I in Scotland from 1124. This chapter focuses first on the extent of Flemish involvement in the Norman Conquest and the subsequent settlement of Flemish knights in England and Wales in the late eleventh and twelfth centuries. It then goes on to examine how David I's innovations in Scotland encouraged further migration north during his and his successors' reigns and the establishment of communities of elite Flemings in areas of Scotland such as Moray and Clydesdale.

Flanders and the Conquest of England

On 5 January 1066 the English king, Edward the Confessor (1042–1066), died without leaving a direct heir. The result was a succession crisis that was finally settled in favour of William Duke of Normandy (1028–1087) at the Battle of Hastings on 14 October. While known as the Norman Conquest of England, the role of the Flemish in the succession crisis should not be overlooked. The then Count of Flanders, Baldwin V (1035–1067), had a keen interest in the outcome since his domains not only bordered Normandy but lay close to England across the North Sea. On Edward's death, the English throne was immediately seized by Harold Godwinson, the late king's brother-in-law, who asserted that Edward had promised him the throne on his deathbed. However, Harold's claim was quickly challenged by William of Normandy and King Harald III of Norway (1046–1066), both of whom also claimed they had been promised the throne by Edward. Edward's mother was Emma of Normandy, William's aunt, so dynastic ties between England and Normandy were already close. But equally significant, William's wife Matilda was the daughter of Baldwin Count of Flanders.

Nevertheless, Baldwin did not immediately or openly support his son-in-law's claim. In fact, he offered indirect help to William's rival King Harald through his support for the husband of his half-sister Judith, Tostig Godwinson (1026–1066), Harold Godwinson's exiled brother. Baldwin allowed Tostig to recruit a band of mercenaries in Flanders in order to raid England. Seeking to regain his former position there, Tostig joined forces with King Harald of Norway when the latter attacked Harold Godwinson in a bid to claim the throne. Together they raided parts of the eastern coast of England, but they were heavily defeated by Harold at the Battle of Stamford Bridge on 25 September 1066, at which both Harald and Tostig were killed.

Baldwin's reluctance to come out openly in support of either side was due to the complex political landscape of northwest Europe. A united England and Normandy would create a powerful new realm abutting the count's territories, while also reshaping relations between Normandy and the French king. At the time, Baldwin was guardian and co-regent to the fourteen year-old Philip I of France (1052–1108) to whom he owed allegiance as his vassal (Baldwin was married to Adèle, a daughter of Philip's grand-father, Henry I). Baldwin may therefore have attempted to stay neutral, allowing both parties to recruit mercenaries in Flanders, but not otherwise taking sides. However, while some argue that he had little direct involvement in the Conquest, it seems more likely that he lent troops as well as counsel to his son-in-law.

If Baldwin's involvement remains uncertain, there is no doubt that his vassal, Eustace II of Boulogne (1015/1049–1087), supported William's invasion and took part in the Battle of Hastings. The county of Boulogne, wedged between Flanders and Normandy, is now part of France, but in the eleventh century was part of French-speaking Flanders. Although ruled by a junior line of the house of Flanders, it had attained a great deal of political independence since the second half of the tenth century and relations between Baldwin V and Eustace II were often strained. This rivalry may explain Eustace's enlistment in William's invasion force that landed in England just days after Harold's victory at Stamford Bridge. Harold hurried south and confronted William's army at Hastings on 14 October. While Harold's army was primarily made up of foot soldiers, William had a large number of mounted knights – perhaps as many as 2,000 – as well as archers. The centre of his army was the Norman contingent, while Bretons were on the left flank and Flemish and Frankish fighters, including Eustace, on the right. The English defended stoutly, but when a group of Bretons seemed to flee and Harold's men raced after them, their battle lines were broken and the Normans prevailed. The English

Figure 3.1. William of Normandy and Eustace II of Boulogne at the Battle of Hastings from the Bayeux Tapestry (respectively second and third figure from the left).

defeat was confirmed by Harold's death on the battlefield, reportedly when an arrow pierced his eye.

William was crowned king of England on Christmas Day 1066, and over the next two decades combined stabilising his power over the English with rewarding the knights and mercenaries who had fought for him. Many became his tenants-in-chief (holding lands directly from the king). As we saw in Chapter 2, the Flemish knights were often landless younger sons of nobility seeking career opportunities and adventure. The Domesday Book of 1086 – the great survey of landholding in England and Wales compiled at the end of William's reign – records at least fifteen Flemish tenants-in-chief, and a number of other Flemish under-tenants (see Box 3.1). Out of 9,500 landed estates recorded, some 760 were in the hands of tenants hailing from Flanders or its neighbouring regions in the southern Low Countries.

The best-known of these was Eustace II of Boulogne. Arnold of Ardres fought under his banner and was also generously rewarded with several estates. Another prominent beneficiary was William's niece Judith de Lens from Artois, the region covering southern Flanders. Judith brought a Flemish entourage and became a considerable landholder. Most Flemish estates (shaded turquoise in Map 3.1) were concentrated in Hertfordshire, Bedfordshire, Northampton, Yorkshire, Lincolnshire, and Somerset. Those controlled by Count Eustace lay largely in Essex.

While details of the elite knightly class can be found in Domesday Book and other documentary records, making it possible to identify their Flemish origins, virtually

Map 3.1. Landholding and immigration from the southern Low Countries to England (c.1086) and Wales (c.1093).

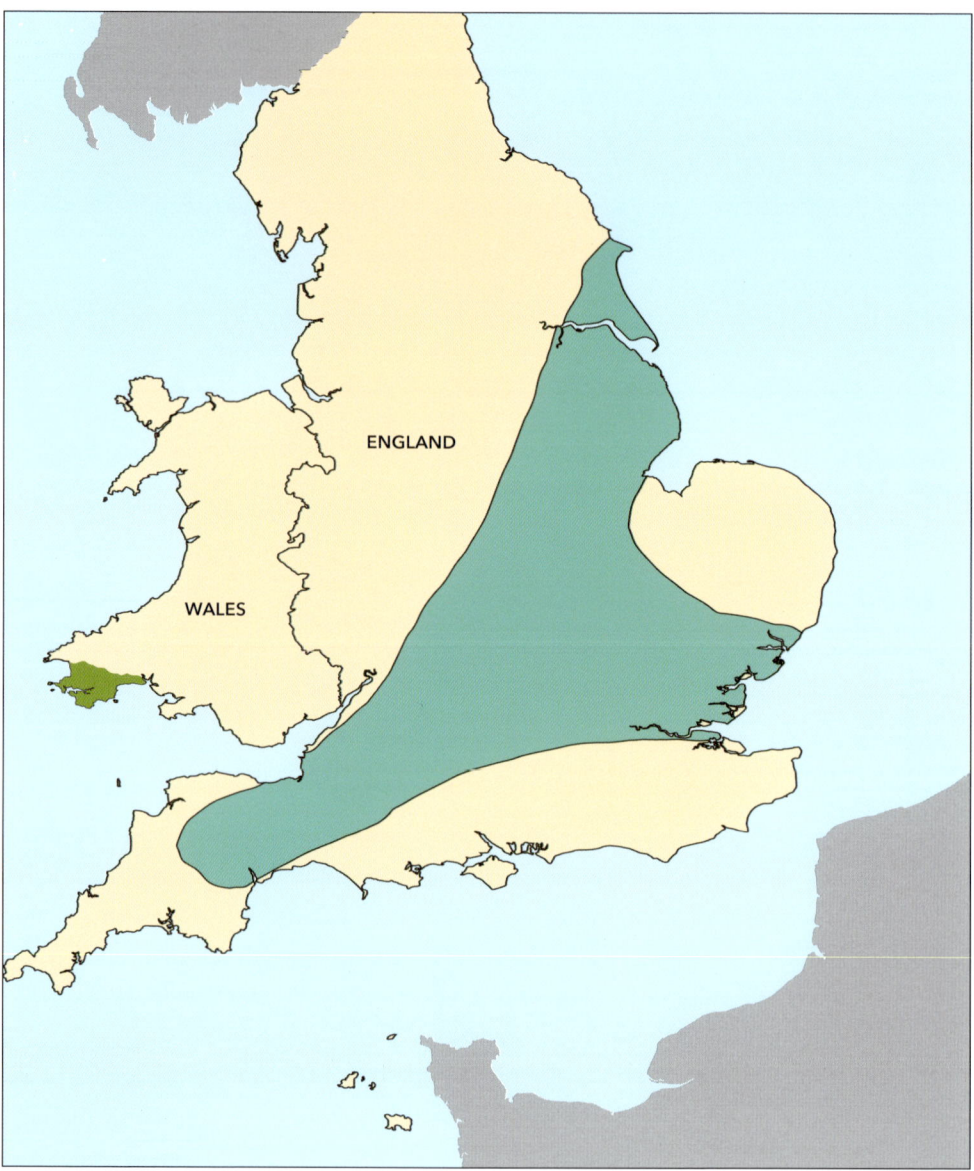

nothing is known of the lesser status retainers and mercenaries who accompanied them. All that can be said with certainty is that there were significant numbers of them and that the Flemish were considered particularly tough and reliable fighters. Indeed, given their fearsome reputation, it may be that mercenaries sought to identify themselves as

Box 3.1. Flemish tenants in the Domesday Book

Some of the names of the Flemish tenants were derived from a particular place of origin, such as Arnold of Hesdin or Gunfrid of Chocques, part of medieval Flanders but today in northern France. Others were identified more broadly as being from Flanders (*flandrensis*) such as Odo the Fleming, Walter the Fleming, and Winemar the Fleming. Some of the chief landholders from the southern Low Countries, most notably Count Eustace II, arrived from adjoining independent counties such as Boulogne, over which the Count of Flanders had little control.

Relatively few Flemings from the Flemish-speaking part of Flanders can be found in the Domesday Book as tenants-in-chief. The most prominent one was Gilbert of Ghent, who became governor of York. Gilbert descended from the Lord of Alost in Flanders and was the younger son of the family. One of his descendants became Earl of Lincoln in the thirteenth century, while his sons migrated to Scotland and founded the Lindsay family (see Chapter 10). Gilbert's family helped administer another Flemish landholder, St Peter's Abbey in Ghent. The Abbey of St Peter in Ghent held properties near London in Lewisham, Greenwich, and Woolwich, both before and after the 1066 Conquest. Church institutions in Flanders and England were well connected to one another before and after the Conquest, which facilitated the migration of clerics. Another landholder originating from Flemish-speaking Flanders, near Ghent, was Gerbod of Oosterzele, who most likely fought at Hastings and became Earl of Chester.

Flemish whatever their actual origins. The descriptor 'Flemish', therefore, may well have been a more generic label for mercenaries from the Low Countries and France.

SM

The Flemish in Wales

In William I's reign, Flemish settlement in Britain was confined to England. Under his successors, however, William II (1087–1100) and especially Henry I (1100–1135), it was extended to Wales over which the English crown wished to exert control. Thus in 1093

Flemish mercenaries took part in a major invasion of South Wales, while later, around 1107, Henry I established Flemish settlements in Pembrokeshire in the south-west of the country. This solved two problems for Henry. First, it enabled the removal from England of Flemish settlers who had become a source of concern for him. At this time the relationship with Flanders had soured and Henry was fearful that the Flemish in England – even though they were first or second generation descendants of the original migrants – might become subversive. Second, the native Welsh were in a state of constant revolt against the expansionist English crown. By relocating numbers of the Flemish to south-west Wales, Henry believed that he would be able to contain the rebellious Welsh.

Map 3.2 shows the main areas of Flemish settlement. Fortifications were built along what is called the Landsker line with the Flemish/Norman settlers in the south, and the indigenous Welsh driven to the more mountainous areas to the north. The size of the Flemish settlements is difficult to gauge, but it has been estimated that a population of 2,500 arrived in Pembrokeshire in several waves. The Flemish were therefore numerous enough to constitute a substantial fighting force, and throughout the twelfth and early

Map 3.2. South West Wales and the Landsker Line.

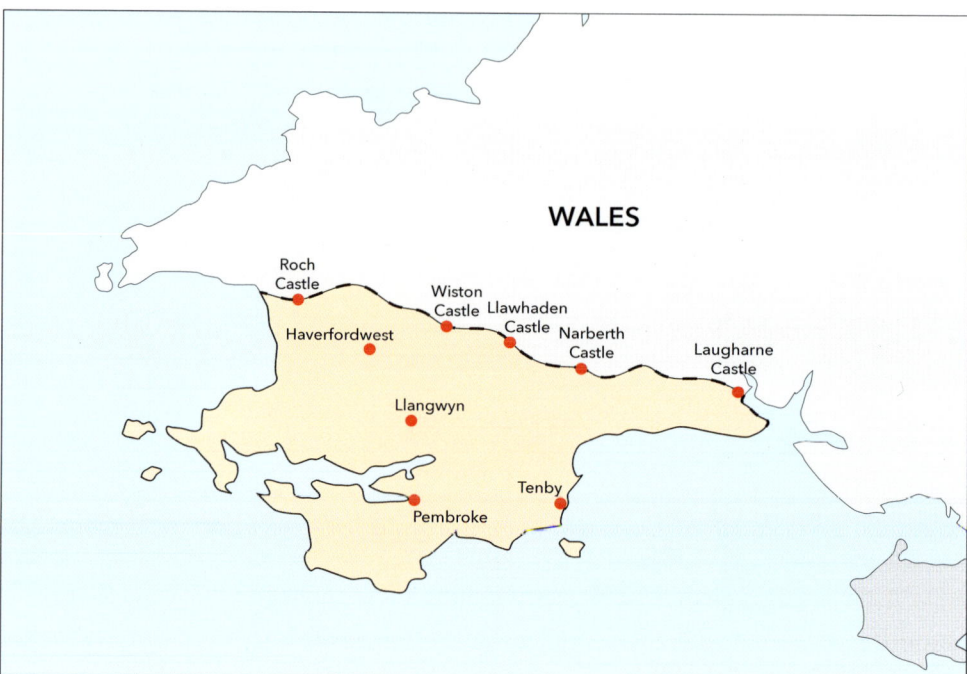

Box 3.2. Llangwm and the De La Roche family

The renowned De La Roche family has long been associated with the village of Llangwm (shown in Map 3.2). This family has Flemish roots and is descended from Godebertus Flandrensis (Godebert the Fleming). Godebert was born in Pembroke Castle, around 1095. His ancestors are not known with certainty, but it is conjectured that either his father – or perhaps his grandfather – was part of William the Conqueror's invading force in 1066 and his father was part of the mercenary force that came to Wales in 1093.

Godebert had two sons, Richard and Rodebert, and they took the topographical surname De La Roche (of the rock) from the rocky outcrop on which was built Roch Castle. Both sons took part in the invasion of Ireland in 1167, were knighted, and received vast grants of land there as a result.

The Llangwm Heritage Project (www.heritagellangwm.org.uk) examined the impact of the Flemish on Llangwm with a particular focus on the De La Roche family.

thirteenth centuries there were repeated skirmishes between the Flemish incomers and the native Welsh. Among the notable Flemish leaders of the Welsh settlements were William of Brabant, Letard (the Little King) and Tancred who became the governor of the castle at Haverfordwest, a key town for the colonists. One leader who came directly from Flanders to Pembrokeshire was Wizo the Fleming who arrived in about 1112 and built a castle in Wiston. His arrival raises the interesting possibility of a direct connection between the Welsh settlements and Flanders itself.

The later settlers were not solely there as a garrison force but came with families and applied their skills in farming, cloth making and other crafts. The Flemish influence continued right through to the end of the sixteenth century with reports of the Flemish language still being spoken in the region up to that point. Certain words of Flemish origin are still in the local dialect and used by older members of the communities. Also place names in Pembrokeshire, for example Flemingston, Wiston, Walwyn West and Tancredston, reflect the county's Flemish heritage.

ER

The Flemish in Scotland

The reign of David I was a critical time in the movement of Flemish people to Scotland. The new Scottish king was very much part of the post-Conquest Anglo-Norman world: his sister Matilda was married to the English king Henry I and David himself spent much of his time at his brother-in-law's court, marrying Matilda, Countess of Huntingdon, in 1113 (see Box 3.3). On becoming king of Scots in 1124, it was to his English estates that he looked to recruit the Norman and Flemish settlers that he brought to Scotland as part of the same process of social and economic transformation that witnessed the foundation of royal burghs and the development of the wool trade with Flanders. The flow of migrants to Scotland was almost certainly augmented by the decision of Henry II on coming to the English throne in 1154 to expel the foreign mercenaries – many of them Flemish – who had ravaged the kingdom during the civil wars that disfigured the reign of his predecessor, Stephen (1135–54). As a result, there is likely to have been significant movement

---

Box 3.3. The marriage of Matilda and David I

David pursued the marriage of Matilda Countess of Huntingdon and Northampton after her husband Simon of Senlis died in 1111. In this David benefited from the support of his sister the English queen and in 1113 Henry I granted David's marriage wish.

Matilda was a rich widow who had inherited her father's Midland estates, and through this marriage David gained the earldom of Huntingdon and the lands that went with it. These were scattered over at least ten counties but mainly concentrated in the shires of Huntingdon, Cambridge, Bedford and Northampton. After David became king, these lands provided a source to recruit younger sons of families of knightly status to move north and settle permanently in Scotland.

Matilda was of Flemish extraction and it is thought she brought with her numbers of Flemish kinsmen to the royal court after David became king. They had only one child, Henry, and he married into the de Warenne family which held estates in East Anglia, an area characterised by a large number of Flemish settlements. The de Warennes had inter-married with leading Flemish families on both sides of the channel and Henry's marriage to Ada de Warenne may have provided a direct link to men of Flemish ancestry who later moved to Scotland.

of Flemish men-at-arms from northern England to south-east Scotland, though there are few traces of this in the historical record.

However, we are on firm ground in identifying two groups of Flemish colonists who settled in Moray and Clydesdale during the reigns of David I and his successor Malcolm IV. One of the most prominent and important of these Flemish incomers was *Fresechinus* (the Latin form of his name), the progenitor of several important Flemish origin Scottish families. He was later referred to as Freskin or Freskyn of Moray (Latin: *de Moravia*). We do not know for certain where Freskin lived prior to his coming north to Scotland. The presence of a Freskin in Wales is attested by a document showing that he owed the Exchequer the sum of 20 shillings, a debt that was fully paid by September 1130. However, we cannot be certain that this is the same Freskin as appears in Scotland.

Freskin's impressive castle at Duffus on the Moray Firth is examined in Chapter 5, but he also held other lands nearby, including Rossisle as well as the now vanished nearby settlements of Inchkell, Machar and Kintrae. Freskin was also given land further south in Uphall, Broxburn, and Strathbroc, West Lothian. A charter of King William I given to Freskin's son, 'Willelmo Filio Freskin', confirmed the original grant to Freskin of all the places noted above. Freskin's grandson, Hugo Friskin de Moravia, was granted the title of Lord of Sutherland in 1214. Later, in 1237, Hugo's son, William de Moravia, was made Earl of Sutherland. The family had a highly influential place among the Scottish nobility: while the senior line remained Earls of Sutherland, a separate branch

Map 3.3. Freskin's lands around the Moray Firth.

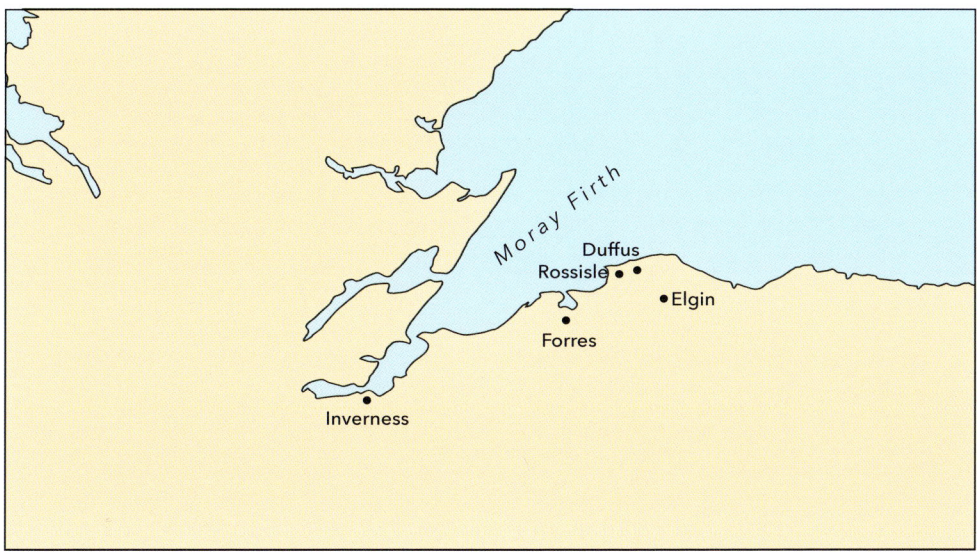

Map 3.4. Freskin's lands in West Lothian.

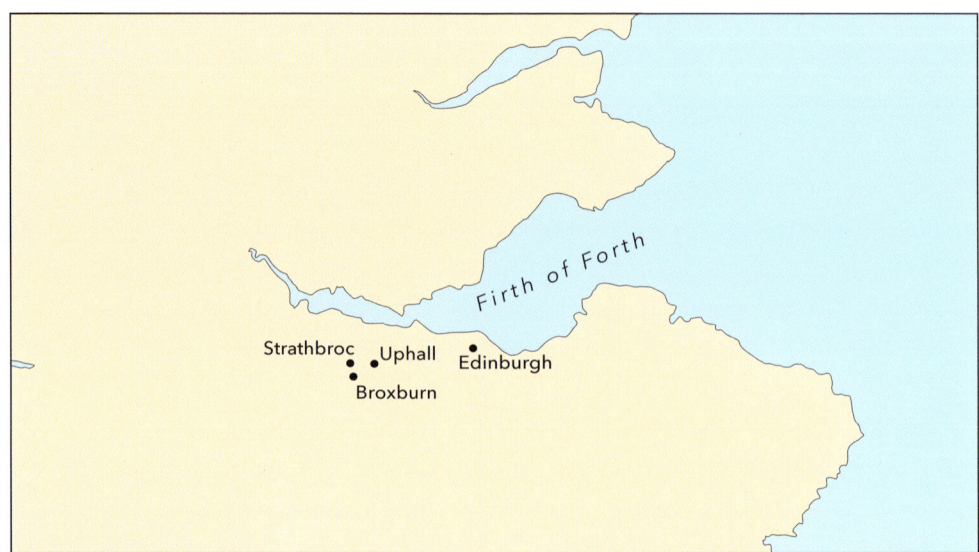

of the family became the Murray Earls of Atholl, while another, the De Kerdale family, developed links with the Stirling and Douglas families.

It is believed that Freskin assisted David in bringing parts of northern Scotland under royal control. However, David's strategy for extending the crown's reach was not simply to use brute force, but to foster economic, social and religious improvement as well. Some historians have speculated that David copied a practice common in other parts of Europe where a so-called *locator* was used to find colonists to settle and make improvements to the land. Freskin's role in Moray may well fit this description, but given the paucity of documentary evidence, it is impossible to say for sure. Similarly, it is not known whether another Fleming associated with Moray, Berowald, had any association with Freskin. Berowald also held land in West Lothian, giving his name to Bo'ness (Berowald's-toun-ness). In 1160 Malcolm IV granted to Berowald the lands of Innes and Nether Urquhart in the sheriffdom of Elgin. He subsequently took the family name Innes.

Another notable Fleming who came to Scotland during Malcolm's reign (1153–65) was Baldwin of Biggar. Little is known for certain about Baldwin's origins but there is a possibility that he may have arrived from Yorkshire (see Box 3.4). He first appears in a Scottish charter dated to around 1150 when the name 'Baldwinus flam' is listed next to Hugh son of Freskin as one of forty witnesses. The fact that the scribe identified 'Baldwin' as Flemish ('flam') gives us the clearest indication of Baldwin's ancestry. It is not until

Box 3.4. Baldwin's origins

It is most likely that Baldwin did not come directly from Flanders to Scotland, but rather via England. One theory has it that he came from the south-west of England. Erkenbald the Fleming arrived there in 1086; he held several holdings in Devon and Cornwall of which Bratton was the largest. These acquisitions may have been Erkenbald's reward for supporting William the Conqueror in putting down the 1068 rebellion in that area. Erkenbald's eldest son, Stephen fitz Erkenbald, was in possession of the family estates by 1139 and his third son was named Baldwin. Genealogists have long argued that it was this grandson of Erkenbald who came to Upper Clydesdale. This theory was based, however, on an unreferenced nineteenth-century genealogical history.

Perhaps the most likely origin for Baldwin is Yorkshire. There is a possible connection with Alan, Earl of Richmond and Count of Brittany, who held lands in Yorkshire and whose son was to marry Malcolm IV's sister in 1160. A tantalising piece of evidence relates to a Baldewino de Multon (Malton) who witnessed a gift by Alan between 1136 and 1145. The subsequent absence of Baldewino's name from the English Pipe Rolls (financial records) of Henry II offers the possibility that it was this Baldwin who moved to Scotland sometime after Alan died in 1147.

about 1154 that he appears under the title 'Baldwin of Bigre', a witness to a charter relating to lands given to another Fleming – Theobald – in Douglas Water. It is not known whether this Theobald was related to the William son of Arkenbald (or Erkenbald) who is thought to have adopted the surname Douglas from the same place (see Chapter 10). Baldwin's landed interests extended beyond Biggar to Inverkip and Houston in Renfrew under Walter fitz Alan – David I's steward in Scotland – and Pettinain near Lanark.

By May 1159 Baldwin was being described as a *vicecomite*, in other words, a sheriff; and three years later as holding that office for Lanark and Clydesdale. The position of sheriff was an important royal administrative office that required him to supervise the collection of revenues, the administration of justice and the raising of military forces on behalf of the crown. To be given such a position reflects the high regard Malcolm had for him and it would appear that he repaid his king's faith in him in 1164. In that year Somerled – Lord of Argyll – threatened to take over Walter fitz Alan's lands in Renfrew and, in Walter's absence, the responsibility for facing this attack most likely fell to Baldwin as sheriff. In addition, Somerled's fleet would have passed Baldwin's coastal properties in Inverkip and Houston. There is no detailed contemporary account that specifically names Baldwin as leader of this armed band, but it is recorded that Somerled and his son were killed by 'men of the surrounding area' led by an unnamed leader, who may well have been Baldwin.

Baldwin is also believed to have brought skilled incomers of Flemish origin to Upper Clydesdale. However, as with Freskin, the evidence that he played the role of locator is at best circumstantial. What we do know is that the decision to colonise Clydesdale was a deliberate act of royal policy and included the grant of some lands taken from the cathedral church of Glasgow, such as Wandell and Wiston. Upper Clydesdale was an area of strategic importance where routes north from Carlisle and west from Tweeddale converged near Lanark, but the primary purpose behind its colonisation was to develop the area economically rather than to fulfil a specific military function. Upper Clydesdale was attractive as sheep farming land at a time when, as we saw in Chapter 2, Scottish merchants and religious houses were exploiting the huge demand for wool from the burgeoning textile industry in Flanders. Evidence that the settlers had close connections to Kelso Abbey has led some historians to postulate that the incomers in effect became Kelso Abbey's middlemen in the wool industry.

Among the Flemish incomers brought to join Baldwin in Upper Clydesdale we know the names of Lambin, his brother Robert, Simon Loccard, Wizo and Tancred. These men gave their names respectively to Lamington, Roberton, Symington, Wiston and Thankerton (Map 3.4). In addition, there is a 'John stepson of Baldwin' at what became known as Crawfordjohn. Their new estates were relatively small and of almost equal size, though most of them also had landed interests elsewhere: Lambin Asa of Lamington, for example, farmed land owned by Kelso Abbey at Draffan and Dardarach in the district of Lesmahagow, while his son James held Loudon. Another example is Simon Loccard who also gave his name to lands he held in Ayrshire; in addition, either he or his brother Stephen gave his name to Lockerbie in Dumfriesshire.

The most likely origin of Upper Clydesdale's twelfth-century incomers is Yorkshire. The Domesday Book throws up the familiar sounding names of 'Baldwin the Fleming' and 'Wico' who formed part of the post-Conquest Flemish settlement at Holderness. They were probably brought there by Drogo of Beuvrière, from his lands near Béthune, in German-speaking Flanders. This Flemish settlement at Holderness was relatively short-lived but a Flemish presence continued there through the families of Gant and the Alosts. There is also evidence of significant Flemish settlement in Cleveland, north Yorkshire, where a Tancred the Fleming sold his towns to the monks of Whitby during the reign of Henry I (1100–35). Robert de Brus, lord of Cleveland, was a witness to

Map 3.4. Upper Clydesdale.

that charter and by 1124 had been invited by David I to Annandale, south of Upper Clydesdale. It has been argued that the Brus lords of Annandale brought many of their knights and feudal dependents from Cleveland and the Upper Clydesdale settlers may have come from the same area. A possible link between the Bruces of Cleveland and the Upper Clydesdale settlement is provided in a charter that names Agnes de Brus as being in possession of a knight's fee at Thankerton about 1185. The exact relationship of Agnes to the Brus family is not known, but an Agnes de Brus appears on the Yorkshire Pipe Roll for 1156, suggesting that she too came from Yorkshire.

The various possible origins of these Flemish incomers to Scotland inevitably raises the question of how Flemish they actually were. Baldwin and the other named settlers in Clydesdale were clearly not direct migrants from Flanders, but second or third generation re-settlers from England. Lambin the Fleming provides an interesting example of this as he is also named in another charter as Lambin Asa, an unusual name in a Flemish context. The Flemish origins of Baldwin, Lambin and his brother Robert were sufficiently well known for them to be identified in charters as 'Fleming', and in the case of Wizo and Tancred their names alone indicate their Flemish heritage. Similarly, with Simon Loccard who, either through himself or his brother, gave his name to Lockerbie in Annandale, it is his name that hints at strong Flemish roots.

Box 3.5. Wizo and Tancred

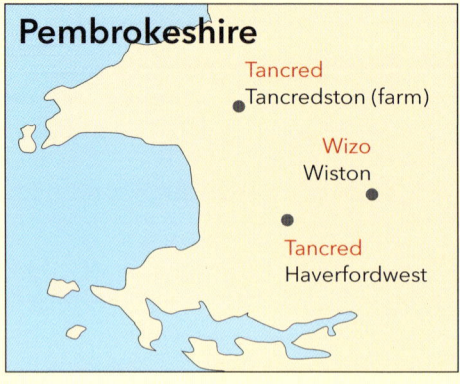
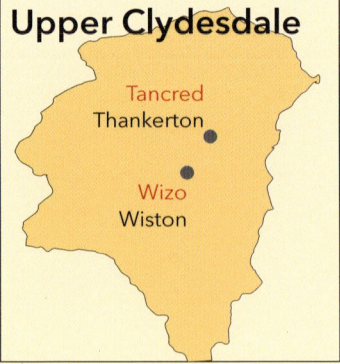

Did all these incomers to Upper Clydesdale come with Baldwin from Yorkshire? Some writers have suggested that two incomers, Wizo and Tancred, came north from Pembrokeshire, but this was not the case. It is true that place-names derived from the name Wizo and Tancred appear in both regions and this gives the theory a certain appeal. However, we know from the Cartulary of Worcester Cathedral Priory that the Pembrokeshire Wizo, who built the impressive motte-and-bailey castle of Daugleddau in the 1110s, was dead by 1130. Similarly, the Pembrokeshire Tancred, who was castellan of Haverfordwest, died around the same time. Any suggestion that the Pembrokeshire Wizo and Tancred were the same people who settled in Upper Clydesdale has therefore to be discounted. Scottish charter evidence points to Wizo being in Scotland between 1153 and 1159 and Tancred some years later. It is a reminder that names like Wizo and Tancred were in fact common Flemish names for the time.

The last we hear of Baldwin is around 1174 when he appears in records during the reign of William I (1165–1214). His son Walter (Waldevus) was with William during the Scottish king's ill-fated campaign to reclaim lands in England. At the siege of Alnwick in 1174 William's army – largely made up of Flemish mercenaries – was overpowered, many being slain and only those likely to fetch a ransom taken prisoner. Walter of Biggar was one of these men and he may well have suffered the same indignity as the king: taken away with his legs tied under the belly of his horse. Exactly when and under what terms Walter was released we do not know but it was by 1180. His descendants can be traced down to Sir Nicholas of Biggar, either a great-great-grandson of Baldwin or a great-great-great-grandson, who by the end of the thirteenth century held lands as far north as Garioch in Aberdeenshire, another area noted as having a large number of Flemish settlers. Whether or not Baldwin can lay claim to being the progenitor of the Fleming family that was later to become associated with Biggar, Cumbernauld and the earldom of Wigtown is examined in Box 3.6.

In addition to Baldwin and Freskin, and the families associated with them, we know of other Flemish families of elite status who migrated from England to Scotland

Box 3.6. Baldwin – The progenitor of the Fleming family?

The original source of this speculation was George Chalmers who wrote in 1824 that the descendants of Baldwin decided at the beginning of the fourteenth century to abandon the name they received from the locality (Biggar) and adopt the one derived from their nationality (Fleming). What Chalmers failed to appreciate was that between 1290 and 1292 the male line traceable back to Baldwin had come to an end with the death of Sir Nicholas of Biggar.

What exactly happened after the death of Nicholas is unclear. The most likely explanation is that Marjorie, his eldest daughter, married a member of the Fleming family that rose to prominence during the first half of the fourteenth century. So it is to this Fleming family that we must look to find the progenitor of the noble Scottish Fleming family (see Chapter 12).

Table 3.1. Descendants of Baldwin.

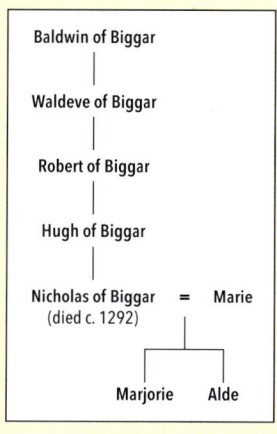

Table 3.2. The Flemings.

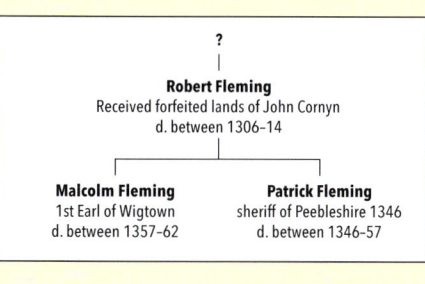

in the twelfth century. Some of these are discussed further in Chapter 5, among them the de Quincys. Robert de Quincy originated in Cuinchy, to the east of Béthune in French Flanders and may have come to England as a follower of William the Conqueror. He brought several other French Flemings to Scotland, including Alan de Courrières, Hugh de Lens, Robert de Béthune, Robert de Carvin, and Roger de Orchies. Other elite Flemish people settled in north-east Scotland. As noted already, at Garioch in Aberdeenshire there was a significant Flemish population in the early thirteenth century, when 'Bartholomew Flandrensis' granted 'to the church of St Drostan of Inchemabani [Insch] a toft and two acres of arable land adjoining the toft in his vill of Ravengille'. This Flemish settlement left its name at the farms of New Flinder, Old Flinder, and Little Flinder; and it is thought that Bartholomew also held Flemington near Forfar.

A number of Flemish people took the family name 'Fleming' because it designated their land of origin. As a result, there were likely a number of elite families, perhaps a dozen or more, who came to Scotland and took the name Fleming, but were not otherwise related. It is not clear where in England these various Fleming families originated or when they arrived in Scotland. As we have seen, even the English origins of the noble Fleming family, that included the Earls of Wigtown and Lords Fleming of Biggar and Cumbernauld, is not known. Meanwhile, the next chapter explores the settlement in Scotland of a range of Flemish people of lesser social status, including merchants, craftsmen, labourers and, in the sixteenth century, religious refugees.

AF/CLR

Flemish Migration II: Merchants and Craftsmen

The trading relationship between Scotland and Flanders from the twelfth to fifteenth centuries would not have developed as it did without the catalytic role played by Flemish, and subsequently Scottish, merchants in facilitating the exchange of goods. Flemish labourers and skilled craftsmen also came to Scotland at various times in the Middle Ages, pushed by over-population in Flanders and pulled by the growth of the wool trade and the foundation of the Scottish burghs as centres of economic development. Later, towards the end of the sixteenth century, Flemish craftsmen were specifically targeted by Scottish legislation that provided inducements for skilled workers to come to the country, taking advantage of religious persecution in the Low Countries that led to further migration of Flemish craftsmen to Scotland, primarily via England. This chapter seeks to explore in more detail the causes and consequences of these migrant journeys and the interactions with the Scottish people that they entailed.

Flemish and Scottish Merchants

Flemish merchants, engaged primarily in the wool trade, played an important role in developing economic ties between Scotland and Flanders from the eleventh to the fourteenth century. These merchants acted on their own account, sourcing produce, organising and financing its shipment, and delivering it to market in Flanders. From the middle of the fourteenth century Scottish merchants largely supplanted Flemish merchants in conducting this trade, exporting wool and related products (such as hides, fleeces and woolfells) and importing manufactured and luxury goods from Flanders.

Box 4.1. John Crabbe, merchant, military man, and privateer

The distinction between legal and illegal trade in the medieval period could be an ambiguous one, especially when rulers benefited from a merchant's piratical activities. John Crabbe (c.1280–c.1352), provides an excellent example. He combined his skills in trade and piracy, serving three different leaders. Probably born in Muiden, Flanders, from 1306 he earned a reputation as a successful privateer, preying on Dutch and then English shipping, and helping Scottish allies during the First Scottish War of Independence (1296–1328). It suited the Count of Flanders to ignore his illegal activities, despite the English king's protests, as Flanders benefited. Crabbe supplied food through piracy for the population during the 1315–16 famine. He moved to Aberdeen sometime after 1310, setting up as a merchant after selling off pirated goods in Flanders. In 1318 Crabbe and his family moved to Berwick. Turning his privateering skills to urban activities, he organised the town's defences and, as a merchant, sold provisions to the Scottish crown. Robert I rewarded his contributions by compensating victims of his earlier piracy.

A leading townsman, Crabbe served as Berwick's constable in 1331. When the Second War of Independence broke out, he turned again to his sea-faring skills, leading a fleet of ten ships to besiege the English-supported king, Edward Balliol, in Perth in 1332. However, the fleet was burned and Crabbe later captured. Edward III, like the rulers of Flanders and Scotland, saw his value, recruiting him by paying his ransom and protecting him from punishment for his piracy. With his intimate knowledge of Berwick's defences, Crabbe helped direct the successful English siege of the town in 1333, although at great personal price as the townspeople killed his son. Swearing allegiance to Edward III, he was rewarded with valuable properties in Berwick in 1334. However, when given the life position of constable of Somerton Castle in Sowerton, Lincolnshire, he left the town. He proved a loyal English subject until his death c.1352, providing military supplies for the war against Scotland, and, ironically, protecting English merchant ships from Flemish piracy.

EE

One of the earliest references to trade between Scotland and Europe occurs in Bishop Turgot of St Andrews' biography of St Margaret, queen of Malcolm III (1058–1093), who recorded that:

> It was due to her that the merchants who came by land and sea from various countries brought along with them for sale different kinds of precious wares which until then were unknown in Scotland. And it was at her instigation that the natives of Scotland purchased from these traders clothing of various colours, with ornaments to wear.

Many of these merchants were from Flanders and the establishment of trading burghs on Scotland's east coast by Margaret's twelfth-century descendants led to significant Flemish settlement. St Andrews, for example, was said in a charter of 1164 to be peopled by 'Scots, French, Flemish, and English, both within and without the burgh'. Foreign residents clearly made up a significant proportion of its inhabitants. Mainard the Fleming, provost of the town (see Chapter 6), may have brought in some of these new inhabitants from his native Flanders, or more likely from his previous residence in Berwick-upon-Tweed, settling merchants and craftsmen in the burgh to develop its commercial potential. Many of the new Scottish burghs were peopled in this way with the skills of foreign migrants playing a critical role in their development.

Perhaps the best-known evidence of Flemish merchant activity in Scotland relates to Berwick-upon-Tweed, the hub of the early wool trade and the country's most important trading port before it was sacked and seized by an English army in 1296 (see Chapter 2). Wealthy Flemish merchants had been established in the burgh since the reign of King Alexander II (1214–49) and were granted a substantial property known as the Red Hall from which to transact their business, apparently in exchange for a pledge to defend the town against the English. When in the opening shots of the Wars of Independence, Edward I attacked Berwick in 1296, butchering many of its inhabitants, thirty Flemish merchants are said to have held the Red Hall for a day before it was burnt to the ground, killing all of them.

While some Flemish merchants, such as John Crabbe, earned considerable notoriety for their colourful careers (see Box 4.1), most were presumably hard-working entrepreneurs whose names are largely lost to history. Nonetheless, based in the east coast burghs, they acted as a critical bridge between the religious orders and other wool-producers in Scotland's rural hinterland and the textile manufacturers in their homeland. Such evidence as there is suggests that the process of assimilation into burgh communities was relatively easy and uncontentious and that those Flemish merchants who chose to

Figure 4.1. Edward III counting the dead after the Battle of Crécy in 1346, from Jean Froissart's *Chroniques* (1410).

stay in Scotland were rapidly Scotticised (see Chapter 11). In fact, by the mid-fourteenth century, Scottish merchants were beginning to supplant them in the on-going trade with Flanders. As we saw in Chapter 2, commerce between the two countries was subject to the vagaries of diplomacy and, in the 1340s, the relationship was especially fraught as Scottish trade was threatened by both war with England and an anti-French alliance between England and Flanders. The year 1346 witnessed not only the English victory over France at the Battle of Crécy, but also the capture of the Scottish king, David II, following his defeat at the Battle of Neville's Cross. One response to the crisis that ensued was an act passed by the Scottish Parliament in 1347 expelling all Flemish people from Scotland. The descendants of the Flemish elite who had come to Scotland in the first half of the twelfth century were not affected by this sweeping edict as they were by then so well embedded in society as to be taken as Scots. However, Flemish merchants, craftsmen and labourers, who contributed so much to the Scottish economy, presumably did suffer. Certainly, even when trade with Flanders was restored in the later fourteenth century, there was a marked decrease in the number of Flemish merchants in Scotland and a steady increase in the number of Scots engaged in overseas trade. Only a handful of Scots were involved in pre-1347 trade with Flanders, compared with several hundred in the period from 1347 to 1513.

As a result, Scottish merchants became increasingly powerful politically with a significant voice in Scotland's diplomatic ties, not least with Flanders, where negotiating terms for a renewal of trade or establishing mercantile privileges and protections were crucial to successful commerce. Just as Bruges became the 'Scottish Staple' in Flanders (see Chapter 2), so Scottish merchants established a thriving community there, with their own church, taking advantage of the privileged trading position that the Bruges' authorities had granted them. The Mercer family provides a good example of a successful Scottish merchant dynasty of the fourteenth century (see Box 4.2), its wealth and position derived from the Flanders' wool trade and their network of contacts in Bruges and elsewhere. But there was a wide range of lesser folk who as merchants and sailors criss-crossed the North Sea between Scotland and Flanders making their living from trade between the two countries.

Another example that spans the fourteenth and fifteenth centuries is the various branches of the extended Lauder family who maintained strong mercantile links with Flanders while also, in the person of William Lauder, Bishop of Glasgow, scaling the

Box 4.2. The Mercer family of Scottish merchants

While Scotland's merchant elite was made up of many prominent families, the Mercers were amongst the most influential in local and national politics. John Mercer, burgess of Perth, was the wealthiest man in fourteenth-century Scotland, perpetuating his fortune through a continued investment and interest in trade. The earliest record of John Mercer is in a payment of customs made by his wife, on his behalf, while he was in Flanders in 1328. A member of the elite in Perth, Mercer held positions in local government and trade. John Mercer's significance, and the influence inherited by his son, Andrew Mercer, was a result of Mercer's successful commercial activity and his service to the Scottish crown. It was only after John Mercer acted as an ambassador in the negotiations for David II's release in 1357, and in 1360 was named the deputy of the king of Scots in Flanders, that the Mercer family rose into the ranks of the lesser nobility of Scotland. Elevated in social and political standing by grants of lands and their associated titles, John Mercer received the lands of Kyncarrochy from the abbot and convent of Scone in 1358, and in 1362 he was granted the barony of Meiklour from Maurice, lord Drummond. While following the receipt of Meiklour, the Mercer family had become members of the lesser nobility, the elevation of status did not fundamentally change their roles in Perth or Scotland's overseas trade.

ecclesiastical hierarchy and becoming a key figure in Scotto-Flemish diplomacy on behalf of James I (1424–37). Such contacts multiplied in the late medieval period and, just as diplomatic ties with the Burgundian dukes grew closer in the fifteenth century, so high quality Flemish goods and the skilled craftsmen who made them became more evident in Scotland.

Craftsmen and Labourers

In 1188 Gerald of Wales described the Flemish as:

> a brave and sturdy people … a people skilled at working in wool, experienced in trade, ready to face any effort or danger at land or sea in pursuit of gain; according to the demands of time and place quick to turn to the plough or to arms; a brave and fortunate people.

Box 4.3. Engineering and construction skills

The pressure on land resources in Flanders during the medieval period led to significant efforts at land reclamation. Some, but not all of this effort has been attributed to religious orders within Flanders. From an engineering perspective the reclamation required the dyking and draining of wetland areas. Areas where such reclamation has been attributed to the Flemish include the salt marshes of the North Sea coast and the wetland interior of Holland.

It is feasible that Flemish labourers, skilled in land reclamation, were brought to Scotland during or just after the reign of David I. One theory suggests that over a period of about a century land along the shore of the Moray Firth (the Laich of Moray) was subject to reclamation and intensification of exploitation. This may have permitted sheep farming to take place on a large scale.

Flemish involvement in engineering design (the layout of St Andrews) and the erection of domestic buildings in the style of the Low Countries (the coastal towns of Fife) point to the import of a skill set that was important for Scotland. The fabric of some buildings incorporating Flemish pantiles and the 'Flemish bond' in brick structures is evidence of Flemish masons at work (see Chapter 6).

From the twelfth century onwards Scotland undoubtedly benefited from the migration and settlement of Flemish craftsmen and farmers as well as the elite fighting men and merchants already discussed. These lesser, and less easily identified, incomers brought with them a range of skills in sheep farming and related trades but also more unique experience in projects such as land reclamation (Box 4.3). When in the mid-fourteenth century the Flemish cloth industry suffered a sharp contraction, skilled weavers joined the migrant trail, while towns in Flanders such as Bruges and Ghent and Arras in Artois sought to diversify into luxury goods.

The taste of Scottish kings and noblemen for Flemish art and artefacts (detailed more fully in Chapter 7) often led to the temporary settlement of Flemish craftsmen in Scotland. The town of Arras, for example, was particularly famed for its production of high quality tapestries to the extent that the town became synonymous with the luxurious 'Arras' that were used to decorate the walls of royal and aristocratic residences. The 'Matthieu de Araz' who was present in Scotland in 1312 may well have been a tapestry maker, while 'Egidius Gremar de Arras' was employed by James I in 1435, being paid £6 10s for his work, and in the following year an 'Egidius tapisario', possibly the same person, was paid £7. There is evidence also that the painter Willem Wallinc, master of the Bruges guild of painters in October 1506, was resident for a time in Scotland. He may have been the same William Wallanch or Wallange employed by George Brown, Bishop of Dunkeld, between 1505 and 1516, as well as the artist who painted the portrait of Bishop William Elphinstone of Aberdeen in the early sixteenth century, a copy of which bears the label 'William of Bruges'.

Evidence of Scottish royal patronage of Flemish artists includes James IV in 1502 receiving the painter Meynnart Wewyck who had previously worked for Henry VII of England; while in September 1505 Scottish conservator in the Low Countries Andrew Halyburton (Box 4.4) – a key figure in Scotto-Flemish commercial and cultural exchange – sent to James IV a 'Piers the painter'. Piers remained at the Scottish court until 1508, painting

61

> **Box 4.4. Andrew Halyburton**
>
> Andrew Halyburton played a crucial role in fostering the trade rela-
> tionship between Scotland and Flanders towards the end of the fifteenth
> century. As conservator of Scottish privileges in the Low Countries he had
> a political role as well as being a factor acting on behalf of clients in the
> purchase and sale of goods. While he was often based in Middelburg,
> he also had close business contacts with merchants from Bruges and
> Antwerp. On behalf of his clientèle, Halyburton purchased or sold wool,
> cloth, books, salmon, trout, wine, fruit, spices (particularly pepper and
> ginger), and skins. In addition to trade, Halyburton was situated at the
> centre of a Scotto-Flemish artistic network through his marriage to
> Cornelia Bening, a daughter of the Scotto-Flemish illuminator Alexander
> Bening. The Benings were at the heart of northern Renaissance painting,
> and Alexander was married to a relative of the painter Hugo van der
> Goes. Halyburton represented James Stewart, Duke of Ross, William
> Elphinstone, Bishop of Aberdeen, and William Scheves, Archbishop of St
> Andrews, as well as members of prominent Edinburgh merchant families,
> including the Patersons, Halkerstons and Turings.

courtly and chivalric items such as tournament banners and standards. James V employed a Peter Flemisman to carve the figures adorning the canopied buttress niches on the south front of Falkland Palace chapel. The Flemish brought other luxuries to Scotland. Examples include children's toys (dolls were known as 'Flanders babies'), Flemish '*pendens*' or curtains, and lace. During the fourteenth century the commonest head covering was a large Flemish beaver hat made from waste wool compressed with some adhesive.

MF/AE

The Settlement of Skilled Migrants

The late sixteenth century saw renewed efforts to encourage the migration and settlement of skilled Flemish weavers. The pull of economic incentives was facilitated by the push of conflict and religious persecution in the Low Countries where the outbreak of the Eighty Years War led to substantial population displacement and the flight of many Flemish and Walloon Protestants to England. There was already by the early 1550s a significant

Flemish settlement in London, including both Dutch- and French-speaking 'strangers' churches, and this was supplemented in the 1560s and 1570s by further settlements in east coast trading and weaving towns such as Sandwich and Norwich. It is possible that some of these migrants headed north to Scotland, perhaps encouraged by moneys sent by the Scottish church to the 'needful' refugees in England and the personal networks developed over the long history of commercial and cultural ties between the two regions. Certainly, there is clear evidence of attempts by the Scottish government and burghs to stimulate a homegrown textile industry by luring skilled migrants both direct from the Low Countries and from their English communities.

In 1581, for example, the Scottish Parliament granted Robert Dickson of Perth permission:

> ... to learn within this realm the art of the making and working of silks, to be as good and sufficient as the same is made within the countries of France or Flanders and to be sold within the same cheaper than the like silks are sold within this realm brought here out of other countries.

In return Dickson was granted the sole privilege of silk weaving in Scotland as well as custom-free imports of raw and finished materials and the position of burgess in Perth, 'or such other places where he shall please to plant'. While it is not clear that Dickson recruited Flemish experts for his enterprise, a few years later, in 1587, three Flemish weavers, John Garden, Philip Fermant, and John Banko, successfully appealed to the Scottish Parliament to allow them:

> ... to exercise their craft and occupation in making of serges, grograms, fustians, bombasines, stemmings, baize, coverings of beds and others appertaining to their said craft [of weaving] and for instruction of the said lieges in the exercise of the making of the works, and have offered to our said sovereign lord and whole common-wealth of this realm the experience and sure knowledge of their labours.

It was considered 'for the common good of the realm' that these three should bring with them a further thirty weavers, fullers, and other textile workers, and that they should take on Scottish boys and girls as apprentices to be taught the Flemish art of cloth production. Significantly, Garden, Fermant, and Banko were granted 'the liberty and privilege of naturalisation and to be as free within this realm during their remaining as if they were born within the same, and that their lawful bairns shall possess the said privileges as if they were naturalised or born Scotsmen.'

It is not clear whether this initiative bore fruit, and no evidence that a 1594 act authorising the establishment of a 'strangers' church' in Scotland had any impact – it may be that the migrant population was too small and dispersed to warrant its own place of worship, though there is also evidence to suggest that the newcomers were adaptable enough to worship along with their Scottish host communities. More effective was a government initiative of 1600 authorising the migration to Scotland of a hundred 'stranger' families with textile skills, the masters of the families to be made naturalised citizens of the realm. The following year, the Convention of Royal Burghs (a powerful lobby of Scottish trading burghs) was actively recruiting Flemish weavers in Flanders and England. Thus, in accordance with the Convention's policy, Edinburgh town council immediately dispatched the merchant Alexander Hunter to Norwich to persuade Flemish cloth makers to settle in Scotland. In June 1601 he returned with seven Flemish weavers, six to make 'seyis' (a type of worsted) and the seventh to make broadcloth. One immediately decided to return home; others were allocated to work in Dundee, Perth, Ayr, and Edinburgh. A further twelve Flemish families from Norwich arrived in Edinburgh in July. These were led by a Gabriel Bischop, a manufacturer of broadcloth and stuff, and brought their 'wives, children, gear, and work looms'. Those based in Edinburgh were allocated premises by the Nor' Loch, but later the house of correction was used. The poor people living there were taught skills in textile manufacturing.

These later Flemish migrants largely carried Dutch surnames (rather than the French origin surnames carried by many of the early Flemish elite). Many of them settled in and around Edinburgh, the nation's capital, and with its associated port of Leith, a key centre of commercial activity. For example, a number of Flemish merchants and craftsmen set up business in the Canongate, where the aristocracy and major landowners had their town houses so they could be near to the Palace of Holyroodhouse and the royal court (see Box 4.5). Similarly, the portrait painters, Arnold von Bronckhorst and Adrian Vanson, possibly Dutch but referred to as Flemish in contemporary records, were active at the court of James VI. The latter was appointed the King's Painter in 1584 and was made a burgess of Edinburgh the following year in the hope that he would teach apprentices his craft.

Flemish craftsmen were also employed in the maintenance or construction of royal buildings such as Edinburgh Castle, but whether they remained there is not clear. For example, in 1599 Edinburgh town council, faced with a major repair to the roof of St Giles' Cathedral, sent to Flanders for skilled workmen and material, while a Bartholomew Fleming was a mason employed in Edinburgh Castle in 1639. As the case of Vanson suggests, to operate a business in a Scottish burgh it was necessary to become a burgess and some Flemish immigrants can be identified through burgess rolls. For example, Abraham van Soun, a goldsmith from Flanders, was admitted as a burgess of Edinburgh in 1587. Another was Philipe van der Straeten, a merchant from Bruges, who was admitted as a burgess in 1684.

Further afield, there is more or less convincing evidence of a Flemish presence in the towns and villages bordering the Forth and Tay estuaries. Local tradition holds that some of the foreign wrights hired by James IV to help build his ships at Newhaven on the Forth were Flemish and that they settled and intermarried with the

Figure 4.3. James VI c.1595 by the Netherlandish artist Adrian Vanson.

local fisherfolk. More convincingly, on the north shore of the Forth, a number of towns and villages – Crail, Cellardyke, Anstruther, Pittenweem and Culross – were engaged in trade with the Low Countries in the seventeenth century, hosting Flemish skippers and seamen and often adopting distinctive architectural styles of Dutch and Flemish provenance (see Chapter 6). As the size of trading vessels grew and larger harbours were required, other Fife towns such as Kirkcaldy, Burntisland, and Dysart joined the Low Countries' trade. Dutch origin names suggest also that Flemish weavers were settled in Burntisland, Dunfermline, Anstruther, Crail and St Andrews.

There is similar evidence of a Flemish presence in the Tay estuary, especially in Dundee, but also upriver in Perth, an important port in the earlier medieval period. In Dundee, for example, late medieval lists of its provosts and bailies – key local officials – point to a number of Flemish occupying these prestigious positions. Subsequently, in the sixteenth and seventeenth centuries, there is evidence of a Flemish presence in a range of trades, such as bonnet makers, tailors, weavers and masons. A list of Dundee burgesses from the mid-sixteenth century has fourteen with possible Flemish origin names. It is not clear

Box 4.5. The Flemish presence in Edinburgh and Leith

Among the people found in Edinburgh and Leith who were most likely Flemish were David Jonking, a merchant, 1610; Jacob Jamart, a merchant, 1674; Andrew Grosser, a burgess, 1599; and William Yungar, a cordiner, 1573. Clement Toures was a glass-wright in Edinburgh in 1616; Peter Frank, a smith in Edinburgh Castle, 1625; and Francis van Gent a burgess of the Canongate in 1702.

In 1681 Peter Bruce, a German engineer resident in Scotland, established a playing card and carver making business in Leith. He went to Holland and Flanders to recruit skilled workmen then successfully petitioned the privy council to prohibit the import of playing cards.

Flemish mercenary soldiers are known to have served in Scotland in the later medieval period – James IV's ship *The Great Michael* had both French and Flemish gunners aboard in 1513. Robert Hector, a gun-maker in Edinburgh, sent his son to Flanders in 1541 to serve an apprenticeship as a gun-maker. Other possible Flemish artisans in the same calling were Josias Rikker, a gunner in Edinburgh Castle in 1540, and Peter Sochan, a gunsmith in Edinburgh around 1680.

whether these people are new migrants or descendants of earlier Flemish arrivals. Under the Convention of Royal Burghs' 1601 initiative to recruit skilled Flemish tradesmen Dundee was allocated Claus Lossier, a shearer, Cornelius Dermis, a weaver, and Henri de Turk, a cloth maker who had been in Norwich before coming north. The settlement of Flemish craftsmen in Dundee was not confined to the weaving trade, however, but extended to malting where, in 1623, Flemish settlers were involved in the establishment of the Maltman Incorporation.

There is also evidence of a Flemish presence in Perth where merchants from Flanders had settled in the early fourteenth century. In the sixteenth and seventeenth centuries, the burgh records indicate the presence of substantial numbers of skilled tradesmen with Flemish surnames. The 1601 recruitment drive led to the further settlement of Jacques de la Rudge, a camber and a spinner; Jacob Peterson, a shearer; and Abigail van Hort or Houte, a spinner, and one of the few Flemish women identified by name in the records. Flemish migrants can also be found in rural Perthshire: John Drummond, second Earl of Perth, brought Flemish weavers into Strathearn between 1611 and 1662. Flemish migrants

Map 4.1. The Flemish presence in the Forth and Tay estuaries.

may also have settled in Crieff in the early seventeenth century, while if oral tradition is to be believed the ruins of a settlement in Glenshee testify to a Flemish presence in an area that a Flemish origin family, the Spaldings, had peopled in the medieval period.

AF/DD/JI/SM/GE

PART II

IMPACT AND INFLUENCE

5

Castles

As we have seen, in the course of the twelfth century, Flemish knights were settled in both Wales and Scotland. However, the circumstances could not have been more different. The Flemish who arrived in Pembrokeshire c.1107 were despatched thence by Henry I of England to cow the indigenous population into submission – one chronicler dubbed them *Lupi Flandrensis*, 'Flemish wolves'. By contrast, the Flemish who settled in Scotland after 1114 came not as invaders but at the invitation of the king – circumstances almost unknown elsewhere in the Anglo-Norman world. In Pembrokeshire the new arrivals had no recourse other than to build strong castles to help protect themselves and their armed retinues, and from which they could lord it over the native populace. But did their countrymen settling in Scotland build castles also? This chapter explores the caputs, or chief seats, of these pioneering Flemish settlers, and of their descendants thereafter.

Settling in

The Flemish who arrived in Scotland were part of a more wide-ranging settlement involving other continental elites, emanating chiefly from Normandy, Brittany, France and Picardy. The process was incremental, beginning in south-eastern Scotland after David I's return from the court of his brother-in-law, Henry I, in 1114, and gradually filtering north during his reign (1124–53) and those of his grandsons, Malcolm IV (1153–65) and William I (1165–1214). The introduction of continental knights was part of the wider crown-led process of modernisation that we have encountered in earlier chapters. This involved the comprehensive reform of the church (including not just the introduction of new monastic orders but the creation of the local parish system) and the widespread establishment of burghs to facilitate trade and economic development. In addition to these major changes, the system of land holding was also radically altered through the introduction of feudal tenure, whereby landlords held their estates in return for 'knight service'. Alongside the new parish churches and towns arose castles, to house the new baronial class, and from where they could carry out governance, justice and military service. These fortified residences were built not so much for defence but as status symbols, outwardly displaying the power and might of their lords within.

In the twelfth century, the majority of 'Norman' castles were of earthwork-and-timber construction. They were hierarchically zoned, to permit the lord greater privacy and security. The most obvious castle form today is the motte-and-bailey, because the high mound of earth forming the motte, on which stood the lord's private residence, has generally survived the rigours of time. Their associated baileys – mostly simple ditched and banked enclosures housing feasting halls and ancillary buildings – have largely disappeared. There are around three hundred known mottes in Scotland (Map 5.1). The vast majority were in areas peripheral to the crown's power-bases in Tweeddale, Lothian and Fife, thus reinforcing our perception of them as symbols of authority imposed by militant, non-native rulers.

As well as mottes there were what archaeologists call 'ringworks', where the zoned castle area remained on the same level as the surrounding ground but was defended by a raised earthen bank fronted by a ditch. Although not as visually impressive as motte-and-baileys, they would nevertheless have provided lords with perfectly adequate fortified residences. Only a handful are known in Scotland, in contrast to the situation in Pembrokeshire where they are on a par with mottes. It is possible that many have been lost to agricultural improvements and urban development down the centuries, but they may well have been the 'residence of choice' for barons living in the heart of the realm.

Whilst the digging of ditches and forming of banks may have taken little time but a great deal of effort, the use of timber rather than stone as the prime building material does not necessarily imply inferiority. For example, the three-storey timber keep that Arnold II, Lord of Ardres, near Calais (France), built on the top of his motte c.1120 was extolled by contemporaries as 'a marvellous example of the carpenter's craft', and comprised storage cellars, residential apartments, living quarters, a kitchen, chapel and servants' quarters all under the one roof. The stunning twelfth century stave church at Nes (Norway), fully recorded before its demolition in 1864, graphically demonstrates the potential size and complexity of medieval timber buildings.

There was nothing unusual about the incoming Flemish lords that set them apart from their fellow knights. The Flemish had, as we have seen, been an integral part of the

Map 5.1. Distribution of mottes and castles in Scotland.

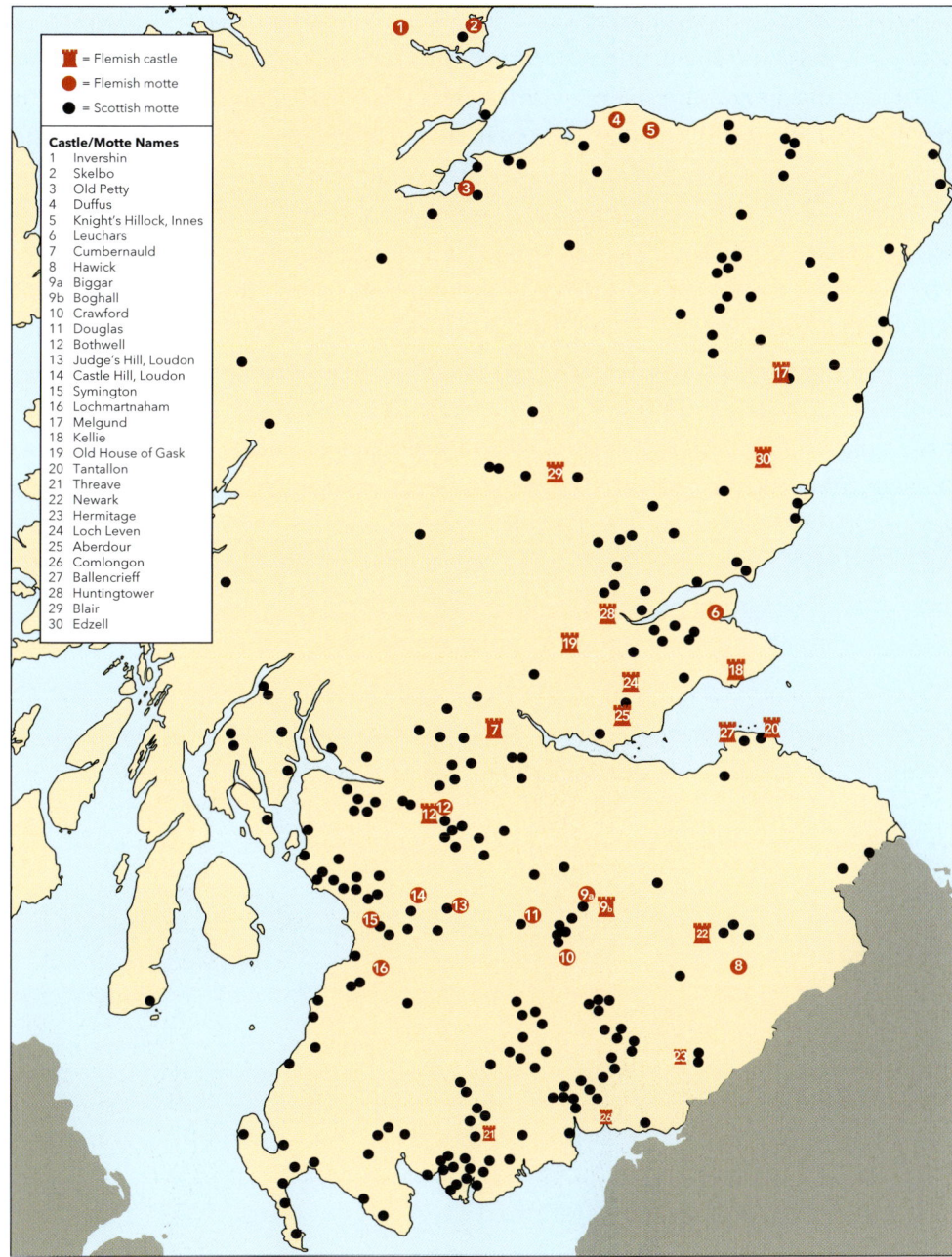

Legend:

- ▉ = Flemish castle
- ● (red) = Flemish motte
- ● (black) = Scottish motte

Castle/Motte Names
1 Invershin
2 Skelbo
3 Old Petty
4 Duffus
5 Knight's Hillock, Innes
6 Leuchars
7 Cumbernauld
8 Hawick
9a Biggar
9b Boghall
10 Crawford
11 Douglas
12 Bothwell
13 Judge's Hill, Loudon
14 Castle Hill, Loudon
15 Symington
16 Lochmartnaham
17 Melgund
18 Kellie
19 Old House of Gask
20 Tantallon
21 Threave
22 Newark
23 Hermitage
24 Loch Leven
25 Aberdour
26 Comlongon
27 Ballencrieff
28 Huntingtower
29 Blair
30 Edzell

Norman fighting machine since William the Conqueror married Matilda of Flanders in 1052. Like many of their companions in arms, the majority came to Scotland via estates in Anglo-Norman England, rather than direct from Flanders. Take Henry Lovel, for example, who acquired the barony of Hawick c.1170 and doubtless built the fine motte there (Figure 5.1). He had relocated from distant Somerset, where his father, Ralph, had been castellan of Cary Castle for Robert of Bampton, son of Walter of Douai, one of William the Conqueror's right-hand men. Both Cary and Bampton castles were motte-and-baileys, and although Hawick motte has no evidence for an accompanying bailey, there almost certainly was one that now lies beneath the grass surrounding the motte.

A number of Flemish came north from David I's own English Honour of Huntingdon and were most probably personally acquainted with him. Among them were David Olifard, founder of the Oliphants, Walter de Lindsay, progenitor of the Clan Lindsay, and Robert de Quincy. Of David Olifard's caput at Smailholm (Roxburghshire) there is now no trace, whilst Walter de Lindsay's motte-castle at Crawford, in Clydesdale, now supports the crumbling remains of their later tower house. However, one of de Quincy's two caputs does survive reasonably intact. The question is – did he build it?

Figure 5.1 Hawick motte.

Robert de Quincy was scion of a seigneurial family hailing from Cuinchy, near Béthune in French Flanders. His father Saher was married to David I's step-daughter and lord of Long Buckby (Northants), where he built a castle comprising an oval ringwork enclosed within a triangular bailey. By David I's death, Robert, their younger son, had come north and been granted an extensive estate in Lothian, centred on Tranent. However, no trace of an early castle survives there, and we can only assume that it was a ringwork such as he had been born and raised in. However, we are on firmer ground when we track Robert as he crosses into Fife to marry Orabilis, native heiress of Ness, lord of Leuchars. Within bow-shot of Leuchars' fine Romanesque church, dated to the mid-twelfth century, is a motte-and-bailey castle, albeit much eroded by cultivation; indeed, the bailey is visible only as cropmarks from the air. Whether it was built by Ness or Robert de Quincy has yet to be resolved.

Robert de Quincy's elevated status as kinsman of the king meant he had a knightly retinue of his own, which he doubtless brought with him from England. They appear as witnesses to his charters, and to judge by their names, most were Flemish also; they included Robert de Béthune, founder of the Beatons. These too were probably granted smaller baronies by their lord, and will have built castles, albeit not on the same scale, but here again we lack physical evidence.

Another Fleming who doubtless knew David I personally was Freskin, whose origins and settlement in Scotland are discussed in Chapter 3. We find him early in David's reign holding the compact barony of Strathbrock, beside Uphall (West Lothian), but in the 1140s he acquired a much larger lordship centred on Duffus, near Elgin in the Laich of Moray. His caput in Uphall has long disappeared (although nearby Houston Castle perpetuates the name of one of his grandsons), but his motte-and-bailey at Duffus remains. The motte itself measures 50 metres in diameter and 14 metres high, and its oval bailey 60 metres by 75 metres. It is one of the finest surviving in Scotland (Figure 5.2).

As we have seen, it has been suggested that Freskin was a *locator*, or entrepreneur, working with the crown to bring like-minded men to Moray and, though there is no hard evidence for this, it is possible that 'Berowald the Fleming' was brought north in this way (see Chapter 3). He was granted the barony of Innes and Urquhart, east of Elgin, by Malcolm IV for the service of one knight in Elgin Castle; his duty of 'castle-ward' is the first of its kind recorded in Scotland. It is not known whether Berowald was a kinsman of Freskin, or one of his knights, but he too came north from West Lothian, from 'Berowald's-toun-ness' – now Bo'ness. Nothing remains of his Lowland caput, but near the later Innes House stands a low conical flat-topped mound about 30 metres in diameter known locally as the 'Knight's Hillock' that could well have been his base in Moray.

Figure 5.2. Duffus Castle.

Undoubtedly the region where the Flemish were most prominent in the twelfth century was Clydesdale. Here Malcolm IV and William I made the running, feuing out much of their royal demesne, as well as lands belonging to Glasgow Cathedral, to bolster the crown's presence in the west of their realm. David I had earlier granted large fiefdoms bordering the Firth of Clyde to some of his leading magnates, and Malcolm IV may have seen a strong knightly presence in Clydesdale as reinforcing that particular 'postern gate' into his kingdom. He was right to be so concerned for in 1164 Somerled, lord of the Isles, led a huge armada into the Clyde, intent it seems on overthrowing the twenty-three year-old king of Scots; he died in the attempt.

A select handful of Flemish incomers to Clydesdale were elite barons already settled elsewhere in Scotland. They included David Olifard of Smailholm, granted Bothwell. His caput there lay not at the later castle (discussed below) but in the heart of the town, beside the parish church. Sadly, it was swept away during the Industrial Revolution, but not before Major-General William Roy had depicted its motte on his 'Great Map' surveyed c.1752. It was massive – twice the diameter of the motte at the royal castle of Lanark (which still exists) – and the ovoid shape of the eighteenth-century 'toun' of Bothwell to its south-west hints that this had once been the bailey. The great size should come as no surprise given that David Olifard's godfather was David I himself.

Another significant player in Clydesdale, almost certainly Flemish, was William, son of Erkenbald (or Arkenbald), who settled in Douglasdale. Little now remains of Douglas Castle, sited 800 metres north-east of Douglas itself, but William's caput, like David Olifard's at Bothwell, may well have lain at the heart of the settlement, on the prominent knoll overlooking Main Street, where the ruined nave of the late-twelfth-century St Bride's Church still stands.

As we have seen in Chapter 3, in the train of these leading lords came a host of lesser knights with Flemish-sounding names – among them Bard, Folcard, Loccard, Thancard (Tancred) and Wice (Wizo). This influx of Flemish settlers from the later 1150s on may well be linked to Henry II of England's expulsion of many Flemish men-at-arms from the north of England in 1156; a few fled to Wales, but many crossed into Scotland. The only two definite Flemish settlers in Clydesdale, however, were Robert and his brother 'Lambeen Fleeming' or 'Lambin Asa', who gave their names to Roberton and Lamington respectively. They have long been linked with Baldwin 'of Biggar', who appears on record in 1162 as sheriff of Lanark and castellan of the royal castle there, and whose Flemish roots are considered in Chapter 3. His own caput at Biggar survives in part – a large motte, 32 metres by 20 metres, overlooking the Biggar Burn, which stood 12 metres high in 1854. The bailey has not survived but most probably lay immediately to the north of the motte, with the parish church immediately beyond, and the associated settlement to their east and south.

One reason for linking Robert and Lambin with Baldwin is the rate of assessment of castle-ward for their baronies due at Lanark Castle in 1359, for it was the same – 20 shillings. Other probable Flemish baronies with an identical evaluation were Symington (Simon Loccard) and Wiston (Wizo). Such a uniform evaluation hints at the symmetrical character of the Flemish plantation of Upper Clydesdale two centuries earlier, possibly with Sheriff Baldwin acting as Malcolm's *locator*, much as Freskin may have acted for David I in Moray. If this were indeed the case, then other Clydesdale barons associated with him can be brought into the mix, including his step-son John of Crawford, lord of Crawfordjohn, and two of his vassals – Hugh 'of Pettinain', and Richard Bard, who held Strathaven.

Where, then, did these lesser barons have their caputs? Only a handful of mottes, in addition to Biggar, are recorded in Upper Clydesdale and no obvious ringworks. An understandable assumption has linked those in the parishes of Crawfordjohn, Lamington and Roberton with John of Crawford, Lambin Asa and Robert. However, none of them lies adjacent to its respective medieval church and settlement – Lamington motte is 1.2 km distant, Roberton is 1.6 km and Crawfordjohn 5.5 km – which is highly unusual. The probable answer to this riddle came with the excavation of the motte at Moat Farm, in Roberton parish, in 1979, for a sherd of an imported watering-pot, recovered from the

Box 5.1. Moving house

Sometime around 1400, the Flemings of Biggar moved house. They had been living in the motte-and-bailey beside the town for some two hundred years, and decided to relocate. They were not alone. Motte-castles had served their purpose in those pioneering days of the 1100s, but by the 1300s they were becoming unfashionable. They were not easy to access and were cramped too.

The Flemings of Biggar selected a level piece of ground to the south of the motte, suitably distanced from the noise and smells of the settlement they had created, and there they built a fine stone castle — Boghall — from which to carry out their feudal obligations. Little remains of Boghall today, but eighteenth-century depictions of it show a hugely impressive curtain-walled castle with an eye-catching entrance, projecting corner towers and noble buildings rising up within.

Figure 5.3. Boghall Castle.

From an etching by John Clerk Esqr of Eldin.   Schenck & Son. Lithog.^{rs} Edin.^r

BOGHALL   CASTLE.

primary construction layer at the centre of the motte, demonstrated that the earthwork could not have been built earlier than c.1300, a date supported by the pottery from the motte's summit and ditch. Far from being Robert's caput, the motte must have been built during the civil war between the Balliols and the Bruces, a fact supported by the documentary evidence, for in 1346 its Balliol lord gave it to David II, son of 'The Bruce', in return for clemency. Robert the Fleming's caput may well have been in the village of Roberton itself, at Castledykes, a late Iron-Age fort with signs of re-use. Only excavation will determine whether the other three mottes – Crawfordjohn, Culter and Lamington – share a similar history.

Spreading out

It was not long before these first Flemish settlers were spreading out. Prominent among them were those who originally settled in Clydesdale, who mostly expanded west into Renfrewshire and Ayrshire. Baldwin of Biggar seems to have been particularly favoured, holding Houston (named after his vassal Hugh of Pettinain) and Inverkip of the hereditary Stewarts. However, there is no obvious trace of an early castle in either place. About the only candidates for Flemish castles in Ayrshire are two indeterminate sites in Loudon parish – Judge's Hill, east of the later Loudon Castle and another simply called Castle Hill, overlooking the Glen Water north of Darvel – and a small motte in Symington parish 800 metres from the town and church. Loudon was held by Lambin of Lamington's son, James, whilst Symington takes its name from its lord, Simon Loccard, Lambin's neighbour in Clydesdale. However, James, son of Lambin, also held the barony of Lochmartnaham, near Ayr, and in that loch is an island that may have served as his caput before the Campbells of Loudon built a stone castle on it in the 1500s.

Undoubtedly the most successful Flemish lords to spread out were the offspring of Freskin of Moray and William of Douglas. Both families have bequeathed some of Scotland's finest castles.

Following Freskin's death c.1171, his son William inherited, and became so powerful in the region that by 1200 he had taken the surname 'of Moray', now Murray. Of his two sons, Hugh, the younger, became lord of most of Sutherland, and the motte-castles at Invershin and Skelbo were most likely built either by him or his kinsman, Gilbert, to whom he sub-let them. Hugh's own seat at Dunrobin has since transmogrified into the Victorian château we see today, but the ancient stone tower entombed deep within may well have been built by Hugh, or his son William, created Earl of Sutherland c.1235.

Figure 5.4 Bothwell Castle Donjon.

Meanwhile, Hugh's elder brother William remained in Moray and most probably built the impressive motte-castle at Old Petty, in the shadow of the seventeenth-century Castle Stuart, east of Inverness; it may well have been the birthplace of that great Scottish patriot, Andrew Murray, who with William Wallace led the Scots to victory over the English at Stirling Bridge in 1297. However, it is the castle that William's son Walter built far from Moray that claims our attention the most.

In 1242 Walter inherited the rich lordship of Bothwell in Clydesdale on the death of his father-in-law, Walter Olifard. However, rather than make do with David Olifard's century-old motte-castle beside the church, Walter Murray created a new stone castle of enclosure a little to the west. It was still not finished at his death in 1278, and it fell to his son William to complete it. William's by-name 'the Rich' says it all, for the new Bothwell Castle, even in its ruined state, powerfully impresses. The huge polygonal-shaped courtyard covered almost two acres, putting it on a par with Edward I of England's Caernarfon, and at its heart stood a great circular keep housing his private residence (Figure 5.4). Still remarkably intact, despite the vicissitudes of war and time, it is today justly recognised as the grandest piece of medieval secular architecture surviving in Scotland.

The Douglases, unlike the Murrays, remained in relative obscurity in Clydesdale through the thirteenth century, well-connected but minor lords nonetheless. Their rise was down to one man, the 'Good Sir James' of Douglas, Robert Bruce's right-hand man. Sir James was too busy fighting the English to build castles. That was left to his descendants, the 'Black Douglases', who benefited greatly from the vast estates he accumulated, mostly forfeited by the Balliols and Comyns. By the time his natural son Archibald 'the

Box 5.2. Later Flemish castles

The descendants of those early Flemish settlers went on to build some significant castles. They included the infamous Cardinal Beaton, descended from Robert de Béthune, who built the impressive tower-house castle at Melgund, in Angus, shortly before his murder in St Andrews Castle in 1546. David Olifard's descendants, the Oliphants, have bequeathed Kellie Castle, in Fife, and the Old House of Gask, in Perthshire, a large seventeenth-century courtyard house that sits atop its thirteenth-century predecessor. The Crawford Lindsays moved north to Edzell, in Angus, where they built one of Scotland's best-preserved tower-house castles, including its beguiling and unique 'pleasance', or walled garden, added in 1604 by Sir David Lindsay, son of the ninth Earl of Crawford. Sadly, little remains of the chief seat of the Flemings of Biggar in Cumbernauld other than a couple of grim vaulted cellars in the eighteenth-century Cumbernauld House.

The descendants of William son of Arkenbald and Freskin of Duffus created some of the finest castles Scotland can offer. The Douglases built not only mighty Bothwell and Tantallon but also the great tower-houses at Threave, in Galloway, Newark, in the Yarrow Valley, Hermitage, in Liddesdale, Lochleven, near Kinross, and the fascinating complex at Aberdour, in Fife, overlooking the Firth of Forth. The Murrays of Cockpool built the massive five-storey tower at Comlongon south-east of Dumfries, c.1400, and the Murrays of Elibank the pretty late-sixteenth-century tower-house at Ballencrieff, in East Lothian, whilst the Murrays of Tullibardine (later Earls, Marquises and Dukes of Atholl) had a hand in creating two impressive Perthshire castles – Huntingtower, beside Perth, and Blair, that brilliant-white battlemented baronial castle majestically set within an awesome Highland landscape.

Grim', third Earl of Douglas, died in 1400, at his tower-house residence on Threave Island, in Galloway, the family held lordships across the length and breadth of Scotland, from Wigtown in Galloway to Avoch in the Black Isle. Their castles are too numerous to treat with here in detail. However, two merit special attention.

Archibald the Grim's cousin, William, was created first Earl of Douglas in 1358, and celebrated his ennoblement by building a great castle on the cliffs overlooking the

North Sea in his newly-acquired North Berwick barony. Tantallon was the last great castle of enclosure built in Scotland (Figure 5.5). Its most conspicuous element was the awesome curtain wall of red sandstone drawn across the neck of the headland. Three lofty towers projected from it. The tallest of them, the 'Douglas Tower', was his private residence and originally stood seven storeys high. Even after Oliver Cromwell's devastating bombardment of 1650, the castle still impresses, as it was intended to do from the outset.

In 1362, whilst Earl William was building anew at Tantallon, his cousin Archibald was marrying Lady Joanna, heiress of the Murrays' vast estates, thus uniting two great Flemish families and in the process inheriting the rich lordship of Bothwell. He set about rebuilding the great thirteenth-century castle there that had suffered much damage during the bitter Wars of Independence (1296–1356) and lain derelict since a devastating siege in 1337. He downgraded Walter of Moray's shattered keep and built a new, even loftier, rectangular tower house at the opposite side of the vast courtyard. In its shadow arose other impressive structures, including a great hall, chapel and lodgings for his large retinue and honoured guests.

Quite how Flemish Lord Archibald Douglas and Lady Joanna Murray felt when they wed in 1352 is not recorded. Two hundred years had elapsed since William of Douglas

Figure 5.5. Tantallon Castle.

Figure 5.6. Bothwell Castle.

and Freskin of Duffus had settled in Scotland, and although Flemish blood still coursed through their veins, it is doubtful if either felt anything other than the odd twinge of nostalgia for the homeland of their distant forebears. The Wars of Independence had finally decided the nationality of the descendants of those pioneering 'Anglo-Norman' lords, forcing them to decide, once and for all, whether they were Scottish or English. Among those opting for English allegiance were the Quincys and the Lovels of Hawick. But there was no doubting where the Douglases' and Murrays' loyalties lay at this critical watershed. Their great keep at Bothwell is tangible proof of that, for in 1337 it had been reduced to a shattered shell not by Edward III of England but by its owner Sir Andrew Murray, son of the patriot, to prevent it being held again by the enemy, the English.

CJT

Towns and Churches

The Flemish had skills that were not generally available in Scotland in the twelfth century. Such skills included engineering – as evidenced by land reclamation in the lowland areas of Flanders around this time – as well as associated experience in the laying out of planned villages and towns on reclaimed sites. There is clear evidence that this experience was brought to bear in Scotland, notably in St Andrews. But Flemish influence extended beyond the basic layout of towns. By the fifteenth century, for example, the design of Scottish churches was being shaped by Flemish examples, and their interiors were often furnished with the products of Flemish workshops. Subsequently, the distinctive Flemish and Dutch features of 'crow-stepped' gables (sixteenth century) and pantiles (seventeenth century) were incorporated into the design of houses built along parts of Scotland's east coast.

Town Planning

As we have seen in earlier chapters, one of the most important developments in twelfth-century Scotland was the establishment of urban centres – royal burghs – that were given trading privileges by the crown to stimulate economic growth and prosperity. The expansion of the Flemish weaving industry, and its insatiable demand for wool, was one of the reasons behind this and many of the thirty or so burghs that date from this period are located on the east coast and were soon engaged in trade with Flanders. Indeed, many of them were initially populated by Flemish colonists. Most of these individuals are lost to history, but the names of two Flemish experts, engaged in what we would now call town planning, have come down to us. One Ranulf, for instance, believed to be Flemish, is said to have laid out the street plans of Haddington and Glasgow. More convincing, however, is Mainard the Fleming, who was placed by David I in Berwick-upon-Tweed and is credited with having laid out its plan and who was then moved to St Andrews, an ancient religious site on the Fife coast that was emerging as Scotland's ecclesiastical capital. The historic architecture of St Andrews comprises ecclesiastical ruins, churches, university buildings of various types, and houses and other buildings of differing sizes, styles and dates, all contained within and governed by the distinctive wedge-shaped town plan of today. But such a town plan did not always exist. The settlement to which Mainard the Fleming came in the mid-twelfth century – the older monastic community of Culdees known as Kilrimund – had been in existence since at least the eighth century, and the monastic and adjoining lay settlements were at that time on a north-south axis at the eastern end of the promontory on which the town developed.

The origin of the town's more familiar east-west axis dates to 1124−44 during the reign of David I. Bishop Robert (episcopate 1124−59) was appointed by the king from the Augustinian house at Scone to re-organise the existing monastic community on Augustinian lines, and to establish a burgh of St Andrews. Mainard was appointed the town's first 'grieve' or provost and granted three 'tofts' of land to the east end of what is now South Street. Thus began the development of South and North Street westwards, both probably following existing tracks but providing appropriately wide and impressive processional routes to the new Cathedral, perhaps planned by Robert but begun by his successor Arnold in 1160. From this time the name St Andrews – based on the relics of the Apostle that had long been in possession of the religious community of Kilrimund – came to be used for both monastic and lay settlements.

By the later sixteenth century, when John Geddy drew his famous bird's eye view of the city (Figure 6.1), St Andrews had reached the peak of its medieval development and was one of the great historic cities of Europe. Houses for the populace were laid out in distinctive burgage plots or rigs, as initiated by Mainard in the twelfth century. All this was encompassed within perimeter walls, boundaries and ports (gates), which if not defensive were at least protective, and close to the harbour, vital for communication and trade, not least with Flemish ports in the Low Countries. The fifteenth-century Bishop of St Andrews, James Kennedy, a frequent visitor to Bruges, possessed a ship – 'the biggest that had been seen to sail upon the Ocean', according to a later description – to take personal advantage of the constant commercial traffic between Scotland and Flanders.

One of the remarkable features of St Andrews is that the plan with which Mainard is so closely associated, and its subsequent extension, has survived virtually intact. Moreover, many of the most significant historic buildings, or substantial parts of

Figure 6.1. John Geddy's Map of St Andrews – although remarkably accurate in detail, Geddy oddly has North and South Street in parallel rather than converging on the cathedral precinct.

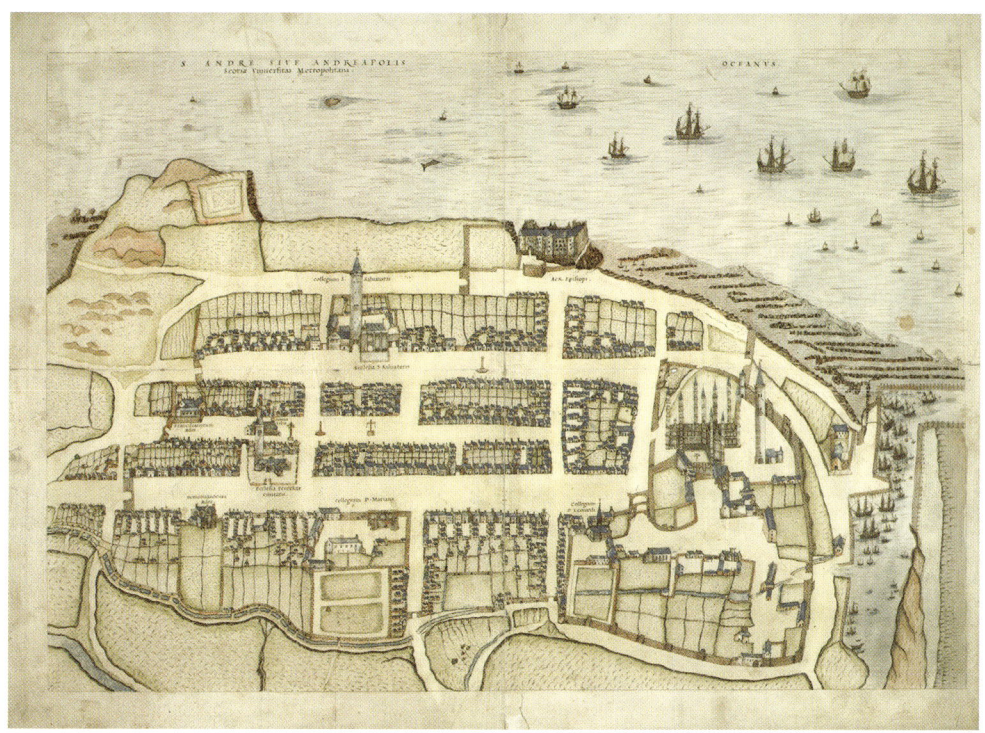

them, remain. Mainard's great contribution, in association with Bishop Robert, was to initiate a formula or template whereby a rich mix of buildings could be appropriately and handsomely accommodated, as if to a master plan, while retaining the dominance of the cathedral and its precinct. This east-west, wedge-shaped plan has become one of the town's defining characteristics. As for Mainard himself, there is evidence that he and his family remained influential members of the St Andrews' community for generations – several of his direct descendants in the twelfth and thirteenth centuries acted as the town's grieve – before being fully assimilated into local society. While the name 'Fleming' was dropped, a century later one Robert Mainard honoured his famous progenitor by adopting the Mainard surname.

RE

Church Architecture

Later medieval church architecture in Scotland – so well represented in St Andrews – is the result of a synthesis of ideas brought together from a wide range of sources. The long wars with England that had such a devastating impact on Scottish creativity for much of the fourteenth century resulted in a reluctance to re-establish the close architectural links that had existed between the two countries throughout the twelfth and thirteenth centuries. Instead, Scottish patrons and their masons looked to those parts of Continental Europe – including Flanders – with which they had the closest ongoing contacts for at least some of their inspiration, as they worked out a fresh approach to meeting their architectural needs.

The contributions of masons from the Low Countries, and from Flanders in particular, are not well documented. Nevertheless, the architectural evidence suggests that their buildings were a significant factor in the melting pot of ideas, and some masons were evidently brought to Scotland to work. We know, for example, that a craftsman named Peter Flemisman carved statues for the exterior of Falkland Palace in 1538–39, while in 1599 Lawrence the Fleming was one of two masons recruited by the municipality of Edinburgh at Middelburg after being heavily plied with drink.

So far as architecture is concerned, a taste for Netherlandish works is apparent in a number of features in Scotland's major late medieval churches, presumably in many instances the result of patrons and their masons observing buildings while travelling through the Low Countries. Those admired buildings were located not only in Flanders, but in the neighbouring counties of Zeeland and Holland, and possibly further afield as well. This is not surprising given how often Scots clerics travelled to the Low Countries. We have already seen how Bishop James Kennedy of St Andrews was a frequent visitor to Bruges, but he had also been a student at the University of Louvain in Brabant along with William Turnbull, the future Bishop of Glasgow. The heavy Scottish presence in fifteenth-century Bruges in particular is evident in the endowment by Scottish artisans of two altars in the church of St Giles as well as a chapel dedicated to St Ninian in the Carmelite friary. William Elphinstone, Bishop of Aberdeen, was so at home in Bruges that at Easter 1495 he stood in for the bishop of Tournai in performing his ceremonial duties. It is possible that the fine portrait of Elphinstone owned by his university foundation at Aberdeen, and believed to be of Flemish provenance, is a memento of these visits (see Figure 4.2). Certainly, in 1491, his contemporary William Scheves, Archbishop of St Andrews, commissioned a magnificent bronze portrait medal from the distinguished artist Quintin Metsys, then working in Louvain, where Scheves had himself studied.

It was not of course just high quality portraiture that Scottish clerics commissioned in the Low Countries. As we will see, many types of church furnishings were purchased there too, while there are not surprisingly many echoes of Netherlandish architecture in Scottish church buildings. For example, a feature that was favoured in a number of later Scottish churches, and whose adoption was probably a result of contacts with the Low Countries, was a renewed taste for arcade piers of cylindrical form. An early case of the revived use of such piers in the Netherlands is the choir of Mechelen Cathedral as rebuilt after a fire in 1342, and since Mechelen had been acquired by the counts of Flanders in 1333 it can be regarded as to some extent Flemish. However, the city was enveloped within the duchy of Brabant, and it was perhaps from churches in that duchy that the idea was imported into Scotland. The reason for this suggestion lies in the fact that, in one of the earliest cases of the use of such piers in Scotland, at Aberdeen Cathedral, there are also crossing piers of a type that is particularly associated with Brabant. Those piers have a large cylindrical core, to which four substantial semi-cylindrical shafts are attached, and they find one of their closest reflections in the tower piers of Brussels Cathedral.

Figure 6.2. Cylindrical piers at Aberdeen (left) and Brussels (right) Cathedrals.

There are a number of other Scottish churches where there are elements that are derived more obviously from Flanders. Two examples are the ceiling of King's College Chapel in Aberdeen and the west front of the collegiate church of Haddington St Mary. King's College has one of two almost identical timber barrel ceilings in Aberdeen, the other, which is now lost, having been at St Nicholas' parish church in New Aberdeen. The former dates from around 1506, and the latter from about 1495. These ceilings are of arched profile, with a decorative cross-pattern of ribs that imitates structural ribs in stone vaulting.

What marks out the Aberdeen ceilings as different from other Scottish timber ceilings is the use of bosses at the rib junctions in the form of long sprigs of foliage, a type of boss that was particularly favoured in Flanders. Amongst the earliest examples are those on the timber vault of the town hall in Bruges, which was constructed in 1402. But they continued in vogue for an extended period, and they can also be seen in simpler form on the timber ceilings of St Giles' Church in Bruges, where Scottish artisans had their chapel. The patron of both Aberdeen ceilings was none other than William Elphinstone and, given his familiarity with Bruges, and the fact that he also imported equipment for use in building King's College Chapel from the Low Countries, the likelihood of borrowings seems clear.

The west front of Haddington Church stands out amongst the entrance façades of the great burgh churches for its unusual sophistication. The central part of the front

Figure 6.3. Timber ceilings from King's College, Aberdeen (left) and St Giles Church Bruges (right).

is framed by strong buttresses capped by pinnacles, and the processional entrance is through a pair of round-arched doorways within a round-headed embracing arch. Immediately above this is a large window that is subdivided into two parts by unusually massive sub-arches, and running over the window, at the base of the gable, is a traceried parapet.

Apart from the doorway and window, a noteworthy feature of the west front is the arcaded parapet in front of the walkway at the base of the wall-head gable. Such a parapet is again a feature that finds parallels in façade design in the Low Countries, whether at the base of the gable or

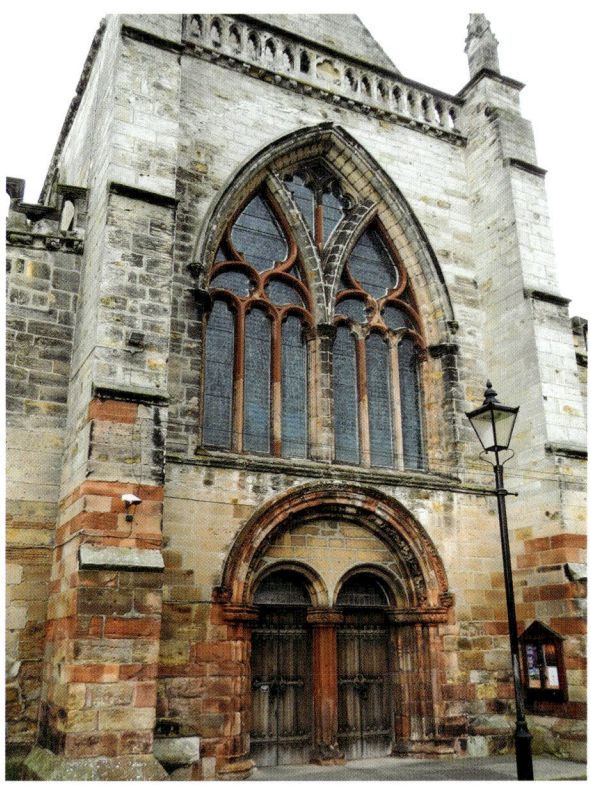

Figure 6.4. The west front of St Mary's Church, Haddington.

running over the doorway. Amongst many parallels that might be cited is the west front of the lost Dominican Church in Bruges, which probably dated from around 1500. Only a few fragments of this survive, incorporated into a modern building, but its form is known from a number of engravings. On the basis of these engravings (Figure 6.5) it appears to have been of a significantly similar design to Haddington in the form and inter-relationship of the round-arched double doorway and the sub-arched window, and also in the presence of an arcaded balustrade, albeit in this case the balustrade runs above the doorway rather than at the base of the gable. It is attractive to consider that a building of this kind, which must have been familiar to many Scots visiting or resident in Bruges, could have been one source of inspiration for the burgesses of Haddington as they sought to give the frontispiece of their church the greatest visual impact that could be contrived.

More examples of likely Scottish architectural debts to the Low Countries include the use of certain types of window tracery, such as a type composed of uncusped

Figure 6.5. The Dominican Church, Bruges, published by J. Beerblock in 1716.

loop-like forms. The process of building up these debts appears to have involved copying individual elements that presumably had been admired in the course of travels, and of grafting them onto the native stock. There was, however, clearly no intention of attempting to adopt the ecclesiastical architectural repertoire of another nation in its entirety. Inspiration drawn from the Low Countries, including Flanders, can thus be regarded as a significant contributor to the pool of ideas underlying the formation of Scottish ecclesiastical architecture in the period before the Reformation.

RF

Church Furnishings

Leaving aside personal items such as Books of Hours which were often purchased in Flanders, there is ample evidence of Flemish artists and artisans being directly involved in the fitting out of Scottish church interiors. The most famous surviving example is the Altarpiece commissioned for the Church of the Holy Trinity in Edinburgh in the 1460s. The church itself (surviving now only as a rebuilt fragment) was founded by Mary of Guelders, recently widowed by the death of her husband James II, but the Altarpiece appears to have been commissioned by the collegiate church's first provost, Edward Bonkil, who is depicted kneeling in prayer in one of the panels. Bonkil also procured an organ for the church, perhaps like the one depicted in the background of his portrait, but it is not known where the organ was made.

The Altarpiece, however, is the work of Hugo van der Goes, one of the leading artists of the Bruges-Ghent school in the 1460s and 1470s, and a friend of the Ghent-based Scottish artist Alexander Bening, who married Van der Goes' cousin, and whose son, Simon Bening, had a distinguished career as an illuminator (see Chapter 7). The Altarpiece does not survive as a whole. The central panel, possibly depicting the Virgin and Child, has been lost, and the two wings probably only survive because they feature portraits of James III and his wife Margaret of Denmark kneeling in prayer. The portraiture is uneven in quality and it is likely that Van der Goes, or members of his workshop, were working from drawings of the sitters, though the life-like features of Edward Bonkil's face perhaps suggest that he was among the many Scottish clerics who were regular visitors to Flanders.

Figure 6.6. The four surviving panels of the Trinity Altarpiece by Hugo van der Goes. The two on the right depict James III flanked by St Andrew with his son, the future James IV, and his wife Margaret of Denmark. The donor, Edward Bonkil, is portrayed in the panel second to left.

Such was the thoroughness with which Scottish churches were stripped of their furnishings during and after the Reformation that little survives intact. However, there are a few tantalising references in documentary sources that indicate that churches up and down the land turned to Flanders for the more ornate church furnishings that were not produced in Scotland to the same high quality. For example, in 1508 Bishop George Brown of Dunkeld imported from Flanders, through a Haddington merchant David Fourous, a tabernacle for the high altar in Dunkeld Cathedral and another for the church in Dundee. In the same year Pluscarden Abbey granted fishing rights in the River Spey to Robert Innes, John Dunbar, and Alexander Catour for installing two tabernacles in the abbey, one for the high altar and one for the altar of Our Lady, both made in Flanders. Brass pillars were erected around the high altar from the fifteenth century to support the riddel curtains which flanked the altar. Typically their tops were decorated with candelabra or statues of angels, who sometimes held the Instruments of the Passion. The goldsmiths' altar in St Giles' collegiate church in Edinburgh contained 'brass pillars' sent from Flanders, and in 1498 Archdeacon Robert Wells of St Andrews purchased via Andrew Halyburton 24 brass pillars weighing 592 lbs at a total cost of £11 2s.

Figure 6.7. Chandelier, St John's Kirk, Perth.

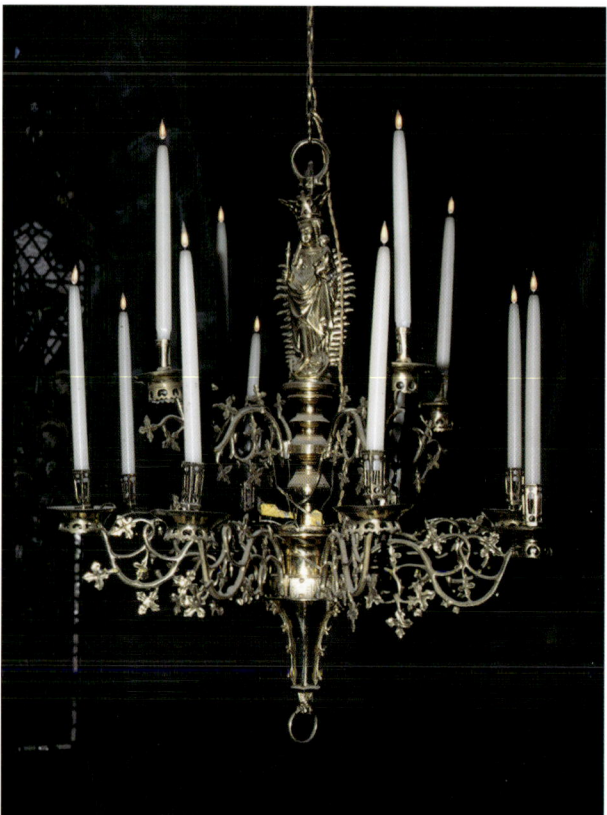

A notable example of Flemish metalwork that has survived is the gilded brass chandelier of St John's parish church, Perth, made in the late fifteenth or early sixteenth century (Figure 6.7). The curved, branch-like brackets featuring vine leaves and tendrils were typical motifs of Flemish metalwork. At the top is the figure of Our Lady in the Sun, a popular Marian image of the period. Flemish chandeliers produced for export were sold in pieces and assembled on arrival at their destination. In 1464 Piero de' Medici of Florence imported from Bruges a 'large brass chandelier with twelve candle-holders with numerous branches, figures and foliage'. His agent Tommaso Portinari wrote: 'I should dearly like to know how it pleases you. Here it was held to be the most beautiful that had been seen for a long time. Be sure that whoever reassembles it takes good care, because as you will see, it is in many pieces, and they are marked'. It is possible that the Perth chandelier was exported from Flanders in a similar state.

Many church bells in Scotland also originated in the Low Countries, particularly from Mechelen, a metalworking town in the duchy of Brabant. The region was known internationally for its bells. The Roman chaplain Antonio de Beatis noted that in Flanders:

> Everywhere there are tall and very narrow bell towers, with fine bells. Their clocks go by twelve hours and twelve, starting from noon, and before they sound the hour certain small bells play three part and well harmonised motets by way of warning; in many places these bells also signal the half-hour.

Examples of bells from Mechelen can be found in east coast towns such as Perth and Aberdeen, as well as more isolated locations such as Fearn Abbey and Iona Abbey. Many were manufactured by the Van den Ghein or Waghevens workshops, as stated on their inscriptions. For example, the 1506 bell of St John's parish church in Perth has the Latin inscription 'In Mechelen Peter Waghevens made me'. Several of the known bells bear inscriptions in the Dutch language that do not refer to the institutions or towns for which they were made, suggesting that they were produced on speculation rather than specially commissioned.

As well as bells, the southern Low Countries exported grave markers – tombstones and plates – to elite Scottish consumers. Bruges, Ghent, and Tournai were leading centres of memorial brass production. Their skilled craftsmen provided figural and textual brasses to international aristocrats, burgesses, merchants, and clergy. The region also exported the stone component of graves. In 1373 a group of Edinburgh burgesses was sent to Flanders to purchase 'diverse black stones for the tomb of David II' at Holyrood Abbey. These are likely to have been Tournai marble, which was imported into Flemish cities to be manufactured into grave slabs. Such marble was used for the tomb of Bishop James Kennedy of St Andrews (d.1465) at his foundation of St Salvator's Chapel (Figure 6.8). The tomb is composed of a thick slab of the black stone within a recess made up of intricate tabernacle, vaulting, and arch motifs. Some such stones had inset memorial brasses. Elite consumers including William Scheves, Archbishop of St Andrews (d.1497) and his

Figure 6.8. Bishop Kennedy's tomb St Salvator's Chapel, St Andrews.

successor in the archbishopric, James, Duke of Ross (d.1504) imported their brasses from Flanders. Scheves and Ross both did so through Andrew Halyburton, who recorded the brass plates as being 'bought in Bruges'. Halyburton paid 28s. for the pattern or design of the monumental brass for the Duke of Ross, which was once one of the largest in Europe.

Another form of church furnishing that we know was brought from Flanders are carved wooden choir stalls. One of the most fully documented is a set purchased for the Cistercian abbey of Melrose. They were ordered from the carpenter Cornelius van Aeltre of Bruges in about 1433, with the specification that they were to be modelled on those of the Flemish Cistercian abbeys of Ter Duinen and Ter Doest, suggesting at least some knowledge of appropriate models on the part of Melrose's monks. Although nothing has survived of them, we may suspect that the Melrose stalls were similar to those still surviving in the cathedral church of St Salvator in Bruges, which date from the second quarter of the fifteenth century. The completion and delivery of the stalls to Melrose were dogged by difficulties, though it is clear that Cornelius expected he would have to travel to Scotland to fit them himself. It is surely likely that a number of craftsmen similarly found their way to Scotland either to install works manufactured in Flanders or to initiate and carry out works in Scotland.

A set of choir stalls that has survived the rigours of time is in William Elphinstone's King's College Chapel in Aberdeen. Constructed in the early 1500s, they bear a

Figure 6.9. The elaborate tracery in the canopies of the choir stalls, King's College Chapel, Aberdeen.

distinctly Flemish Gothic aesthetic, with linenfold, blind fenestrated, and flamboyant tracery characteristic of the Low Countries. They are thought to have been carved by a team under John Fendour who also worked for Bishop George Brown of Dunkeld and James IV, as well as the burgh council of Aberdeen at St Nicholas' parish church. Whether Fendour was working from a Flemish design, or had experience of working with Flemish craftsmen, is unknown. However, in keeping with other aspects of Elphinstone's legacy, the choir stalls seem redolent of Flemish example and inspiration.

RF/MF

Domestic Architecture

A Flemish, or more broadly a Low Countries', influence can still be seen today in the architecture of houses in the East of Scotland. Fife provides an excellent case study. A

Figure 6.10. A seventeenth century house, Pittenweem harbour.

characteristic feature of many of Fife's domestic buildings is the corbie or 'crow-stepped' gable that is often seen combined with a clay pantile roof, particularly in the picturesque East Neuk fishing villages. As we have seen, these historic burgh ports had a long tradition of contact and trade with the Low Countries. As is so often the case, this was accompanied by an exchange of ideas, skills and even building materials. The interchange of peoples and materials between ports such as Bruges in Flanders and Middleburg and Veere in Zeeland and those in Fife undoubtedly led to a Low Countries' imprint on Fife architecture.

Fife did not have a tradition of building in brick but had an abundance of building stone. Stone, being less easy to fashion into intricate gable shapes than brick and render, lent itself to the simpler stepped style of gable. However, the old, narrow form of stepped gable which developed in Scotland had its own distinctive character, different from that seen on the continent. Also known as 'crawstep' or 'crowstep' gables, the breadth is no more than between 150mm and 200mm. Steps are on average 250mm high and the depth will vary, according to the roof pitch, between 150mm and 180mm. A variation can be found in Orkney that has examples of gables with diminishing sized steps.

Figure 6.11. A typical crow-stepped gable.

Another factor that may have contributed to the prevalence of the distinctive Flemish-style stepped gable in Fife was the increasing availability and use of pantiles for roofs that occurred at about the same time. Also known as Flemish tiles, this type of tile had developed in the Low Countries in the fifteenth and sixteenth centuries from the earlier Roman forms of roof tile. '*Pan*' is Dutch for tile, although it is also suggested that the derivation may be from the Finnish '*paan*' meaning shingle. At the beginning, in the sixteenth century, they were used only on high status buildings, but later, as the cost came down, assisted by better roads and larger scale local production, they occur on ever more modest buildings, until they reached a peak in the nineteenth century.

Figure 6.12. A mixture of red and grey pantiles.

Pantiles were known in Scotland from 1669. Customs records and correspondence confirm that they were imported to this part of Scotland from Rotterdam in the last quarter of the seventeenth century. It is claimed they were imported as ballast in boats from the Low Countries, making the crossing to Fife for coal, salt and wool, but there is no evidence of

Box 6.1. First pantile works in Scotland

A significant event in the story of the development of this characteristic style of roof was when in 1714 William Adam, mason, entrepreneur and renowned architect, started the first pantile works in Scotland, at Linktown of Abbotshall, Kirkcaldy, Fife. He had been forced to return home to Kirkcaldy from his studies at university in the Low Countries, to take over the family business on the death of his father. As well as his academic studies he had studied the manufacture of bricks and pantiles and no doubt been influenced by the houses he saw with shaped gables, built of brick and with pantiled roofs. He started the works in partnership with William Robertson of Gladney, his future father-in-law, and by 1716 was calling himself 'Master of the Tyle Manufactory in the Links of Kirkcaldy'. Gladney House that he built in 1711 used imported pantiles and with its shaped gables would have had a consciously Dutch aspect.

this. Conversely, there is evidence to suggest that pantiles were a valuable commodity, carefully stored on board.

As early as 1709 a consent was granted for digging clay for the manufacture of bricks and tiles, across the Forth from Fife, where the nearby town of Linlithgow was already importing pantiles (see Box 6.1). At first pantiles were used mostly on prestige buildings. As the works became established and techniques improved, the price fell. An early building was nearby Aberdour Manse that was roofed in 1722. It was still a luxury item and most roofs remained thatch or turf. However, tiles continued to be shipped from Flanders and Holland.

MP

Art, Artefacts
and Artillery

The fifteenth and early sixteenth centuries witnessed Scotto-Flemish trade in luxury goods reaching its peak. What in shorthand we call material culture – that is, manufactured objects that can be used to tell historians about the values of a particular society – demonstrates that Flemish products were held in high regard by those Scots who could afford to buy them.

As we have seen in earlier chapters, by the late Middle Ages, Flanders had emerged as one of the most urbanised and populous areas of Europe. Among its residents were merchants and artisans, administrative and bureaucratic elites, and the wealthy court and courtiers of the powerful dukes of Burgundy. Such a population created consumer demand for luxury products, stimulating production in Flanders and consumer demand abroad. However, it can be difficult to assign an object or type of object to one specific town or county in the southern Low Countries due to the dominance of a particular style – the Flemish aesthetic – throughout the region and the lack of clarity in documentary sources regarding the origin of objects. While this chapter concentrates on Flemish art and artefacts, therefore, it also includes those of the nearby regions of Artois, Brabant, and Hainaut.

The international trade links of Flanders made it a flourishing centre for the production of a vast array of commodities including textiles, tapestries, metalwork, woodwork, painting, and manuscripts. In the fifteenth century the Flemish economy was increasingly geared towards luxury products, prompted partly by the decline of its textile industry, but initiating a new era of commercial prosperity and an unprecedented boom in artistic production. The Flemish diplomat Philippe de Commynes wrote in the late fifteenth century that, '[these] lands are best able to be called the promised lands of all other principalities which are on the earth. They are so full of riches …, the meals and banquets greater and more lavish than in any other place that I know'. This perception undoubtedly added to the prestige of Flemish material culture, along with its association with the sophisticated dukes of Burgundy. In an aristocratic context, Flemish luxuries became the 'gold standard' for princely courts and courtiers, status symbols that elevated Flemish craftsmanship to the height of fashion.

Flanders held great international fairs at Bruges, Ypres, Torhout, Lille, and Mesen. During fair time goods were displayed and sold from specialised *hallen* ('halls'), market squares, shops, stalls, workshops, and public buildings such as churches. Members of certain crafts tended to congregate in specific areas of town. In Bruges Philipstockstraat was identified with goldsmiths, illuminators, and scriptoria, Wapenmakersstraat with armourers, and Minderbroedersstraat with woodworkers. In 1482 the Bruges *pandt* was established. This was an exhibition gallery and marketplace within the Franciscan monastery of the Minderbroederklooster, in an open courtyard enclosed by 187 stalls. These could be rented during fair time by artisans, dealers, and merchants.

Of the wealth of Flemish artefacts imported by Scots in this period, only a fraction survives. As we saw in the previous chapter, Scotland's rich medieval devotional culture suffered particularly from the effects of the Reformation of 1560 when much was destroyed in waves of Protestant iconoclasm. However, much has also been lost due to the nature of certain types of object. Tapestries, for example, suffer wear and tear and many were destroyed in order to extract the precious metal from their gold and silver threads. Consequently, no tapestry with a history of medieval Scottish ownership is known to exist. Precious metal objects, including jewellery and gold and silver plate, were likewise melted down and re-used. Manuscripts, on the other hand, tend to have survived quite well due to their small size and the personal, private nature of their usage. Generally, high status luxury objects tend to have survived better than 'everyday' objects, which are more likely to have been used to the point of disintegration and then discarded. As a result, much less is known about the material culture of ordinary people. However, while much has been lost, surviving artefacts such as the Trinity Altarpiece (discussed in Chapter 6), together with documentary evidence, allows us to build up a picture of the range of Flemish luxuries imported into Scotland in the late medieval period.

Illuminated Manuscripts

Late medieval Flemish manuscripts were highly prestigious objects known for their richly coloured illuminations – that is, the painted initials, borders and illustrations that decorate the hand-written text. Highly decorated Books of Hours – personal devotional texts including a calendar of saints' days with appropriate prayers, psalms and readings – were especially popular with the clerical and aristocratic elites. Typical elements included illusionistic borders of flowers, acanthus leaves, insects, jewels, and shells. The use of bright colours, realistic shadows, and other optical illusions or *trompe l'oeil* effects became a speciality of Flemish workshops in the fifteenth century. Illuminators shared designs and compositions for illustrations, leading to a fairly uniform style of illumination throughout the southern Low Countries and the relatively speedy production of manuscripts.

Manuscripts produced for a generalised market did not diminish the perceived value of these products but widened their appeal by making them accessible and relatively inexpensive. Some were owned by Scots and show evidence of standardised production. An example is the Aberdeen Book of Hours (National Art Library, London), produced in the southern Low Countries between 1440 and 1450. The calendar and illumination are conventional, suggesting serial production for a generalised market. However, on one of its pages, a rubric and prayer in the Scots language have been added: 'Qwha sa says yis orison dayly devoutly he sal hafe ful remissione of al hys synnys' ('Whoever says this prayer daily and devoutly, he shall have full remission of all his sins'). It is likely that such manuscripts were produced using patterns then sold in workshops or at the *pandt*.

Flemish manuscripts were also commissioned by individual buyers. Dean James Brown of Aberdeen Cathedral travelled via the Low Countries to Rome in 1497 to secure the Archbishopric of St Andrews for James, Duke of Ross (King James IV's younger brother). On his return Brown was in the Low Countries from May to October 1498, as recorded by Andrew Halyburton, conservator of Scottish trading privileges (see Box 4.4). While there he commissioned a Book of Hours with naturalistic floral borders of violets, roses, daisies, and other plants. The manuscript also contains a full-page illumination depicting Brown kneeling in prayer before an altarpiece accompanied by an episcopal patron saint, perhaps Machar or Ninian (see Figure 7.1). The text was clearly customised as the calendar contains over thirty-five Scottish saints, obituaries for members of Brown's family, and a memorandum on the promotion of the Duke of Ross to the see of St Andrews.

The best known Flemish manuscript imported into late medieval Scotland is the Book of Hours of James IV and Margaret Tudor. It was given by James to Margaret on their marriage in 1503. The marriage was held at Holyrood Abbey, and the presentation of the lavishly illuminated Book of Hours was an appropriate addition to Margaret's spectacular entry into Edinburgh, the feasting and tournaments that accompanied it, and the king's extravagant expenditure on the event. The book is a recognisable

Figure 7.1. Dean Brown's Book of Hours, NLS, MS 10270, ff. 17v-18r.

product of the prestigious workshops of Flanders. The miniatures were executed by artists including Simon Bening (c.1483–1561) and Gerard Horenbout (c.1465–1540/1). From 1500 Bening belonged to the Bruges image makers' guild of St Luke and from 1508 the book makers' guild of St John the Evangelist, but he continued to reside in Ghent, receiving commissions from elite patrons including Portuguese royalty. His father Alexander, who originated in Scotland, was also a prominent illuminator. Gerard Horenbout joined the Ghent painters' guild in 1487. From 1515 to 1522 he was the court painter of Margaret of Austria at Mechelen, shortly after which he entered the service of Henry VIII of England.

James IV's Book of Hours does not contain any reference to the royal couple in the text, and most of the images in the manuscript represent typical marital and devotional themes such as the Annunciation, the Nativity, and the Adoration of the Magi. However, several references to James and Margaret, such as their arms and initials, are included in the imagery, while two full-page depictions of the king and queen at prayer before altar-pieces are its most striking illuminations. James is presented by St James and Margaret by an unknown male saint, while both images portray the royal couples' armorial bearings. By commissioning these portraits from the skilled illuminators of Flanders, James IV was asserting his status as a culturally refined prince aware of the prestige associated with Flemish manuscripts.

Figure 7.2. Portraits of James IV and Margaret Tudor from the James IV Book of Hours

This prestige continued into the sixteenth century, undiminished by the advent of printing around 1450, and it was during these decades that Flemish illumination reached its peak of realism, illusion and vivid colour. Nonetheless, printing presses were soon being established in Flanders, at Aalst and Bruges by 1473, and it was in Bruges that the celebrated Flemish printer Colard Mansion practised his trade and passed on his skills to the Englishman William Caxton. However, it was Antwerp that emerged as the major centre of printing in the Low Countries and printed books in Scotland appear to have come from there and other non-Flemish cities. For example, Archbishop William Scheves of St Andrews (d. 1497) owned books printed in Antwerp, Brussels, and Leuven, as well as Strasbourg, Cologne, Nuremberg, Pavia, and Basel.

Tapestry

Tapestries were a significant component of Flemish and southern Low Countries material culture that found their way to Scotland. It was known as 'arras' after the town of Arras in Artois, which gained a reputation in the late medieval period for the production of the highest quality tapestry. In the 1430s the Spanish nobleman Pero Tafur noted that Arras was 'very rich, especially by reason of its woven cloths and all kinds of tapestries, and although they are also made in other places, yet it well appears that those which are made in Arras have the preference.' However, fine quality tapestry was manufactured in other Low Countries centres in Flanders as well as in Brabant, Hainaut, Liège, and Tournai. After the death of the Burgundian Duke Charles the Bold in 1477, Arras was seized by the French, was subject to new taxes and manufacturing restrictions, and lost its position as the foremost producer of luxury tapestry. The term 'arras' became associated with southern Low Countries production as a whole, indicating high quality design and materials.

Tapestries were often given as diplomatic gifts by the aristocracy. In 1413, John the Fearless, Duke of Burgundy, gave Robert Stewart, Duke of Albany and Governor of Scotland, a series of tapestries purchased from Jehan Renout of Arras. The five pieces in blue and gold thread depicted a grand lady and children surrounded by flowers. The entire suite measured 200 ells in length (140 metres) and cost 200 francs. By 1413 Albany had been Governor of Scotland on behalf of James I for seven years, the king having been captured and held hostage at the English court. He had previously played a prominent role at the highest level of Scottish political life as chamberlain, guardian, and lieutenant of Scotland under Robert II and Robert III. In 1407 Albany despatched an ambassadorial mission to Flanders in order to negotiate a new staple agreement between Scotland and Bruges after a period of piracy and suspended trade. Scottish merchants were granted the right to a commissioner to defend their trading rights in Flanders, 'authorised by us [the Duke of Burgundy] and to which we are giving power and authority to pursue, require, seek, and defend the goods of those merchants and subjects'. The tapestry gift may have been intended to solidify this trade relationship by reminding Albany of the luxury products to be found in Flanders and the wealth of the Burgundian dukes.

In 1435 the exchequer of James I paid £6 10s. to 'Egidie Gremar de Arras'. The following year Egidio, or Giles, is named as a 'tapisario' making 'pannos de attrabato apud Bruges' ('cloths of arras in Bruges'). 'Gremar' may have been a rendering of the name Grenier, a family of tapestry merchants based in Tournai who sold to clients such as the dukes of Burgundy, Edward IV and Henry VII of England, and Duke Francesco Sforza of Milan. Also in 1436, the crown purchased from Flanders 'duabus tapetis cum armis domini regis' ('two tapestries with the arms of the lord king') along with a collection of precious jewels, and Giles perhaps facilitated these purchases in his role as tapestry merchant.

As elite, luxury objects, tapestries from the southern Low Countries became a ubiquitous feature of diplomatic and marital events among royalty. When Margaret Tudor arrived in Scotland in 1503 she brought with her seventy-four 'Flemmych stikks' of arras (that is, individual tapestries). John Young, the English herald and diplomat, reported that on Margaret's entry into Edinburgh 'The towne … was in many places hung with tapestries'. At the marriage ceremony at Holyrood Abbey, the queen's great chamber contained tapestry hangings representing the history of Troy and the king's chamber was adorned with tapestries depicting the story of Hercules, 'together with other histories'. The Trojan tapestry set was possibly manufactured according to the initial drawings retained by tapestry merchant Pasquier Grenier after he provided the first set to Charles the Bold. The Hercules tapestries were also Flemish, having been brought to Scotland by James's factor in Flanders, James Homyll, in 1503.

The crown's taste for southern Low Countries tapestry continued with James V who in 1532 commissioned from weaver François van Cralot of Bruges a tapestry altar frontal of fine serge and silk depicting the royal arms and mottoes as well as antique and floral designs. In February 1538 James sent a servant 'to pass in Flanders for bringing of certain tapestries', amounting to thirty-seven pieces. It is from his reign that we have the earliest comprehensive inventory for the property of the crown: by 1539 he owned no fewer than 161 pieces of tapestry.

Arras was also prevalent in Scottish ecclesiastical institutions. By 1371 Coldingham Priory possessed one piece of arras to adorn its high altar. By the late fifteenth century the collegiate church of St Salvator's in St Andrews possessed three pieces of arras for the high altar, one frontal of arras, one blue and one green lined tapestry for the high altar, and two arras cloths for the presbytery. In 1432 Glasgow Cathedral had a great arras tapestry depicting the life of St Kentigern, the patron saint of the cathedral. It is likely that such a tapestry was commissioned specially rather than made on speculation, considering the specific subject matter. In 1436 Aberdeen Cathedral held a piece of arras depicting the seven deadly sins, another of Jesus, and four others. By the mid-six-teenth century Crail collegiate church held 'a baldachin [canopy] of arras work for the provost's stall'.

Fabrics

Luxury Flemish fabrics were purchased in great quantities by the Scottish crown, both for royal use and for servants as livery clothing. The Treasurers' Accounts provide details of the types of fabrics given by the crown to its household members. Two of the most numerous types during the reign of James IV were Bruges satin and Rijsel or Lille cloth. Both were distributed to aristocratic household members and servants, who often received clothing or fabric in lieu of money payments. This identified the recipients visually as members of the household and subordinate to its head.

Satin was an expensive silken fabric and was one of the most sought after textiles for the wealthy elite. In 1471 the Scottish Parliament passed legislation restricting the wearing of silks to knights, minstrels, heralds, high-ranking burgesses, and those with £100 of annual rent. The southern Low Countries did not manufacture silks until the latter part of the fifteenth century when Bruges and Antwerp developed industries in spinning, weaving, and dyeing of silk. Up until that point the Italian city-states had dominated the European market, exporting their wares to the great commercial centres. It seems that the Bruges satin in the royal accounts is a sign of Scottish elite consumers patronising this relatively new industry in Flanders.

The crown also imported large quantities of Lille cloth. In the fifteenth century the Flemish textile industries experienced a reorientation away from cheaper, heavier cloths and towards more luxurious fabrics. Lille developed into a significant manufacturer of the light woollen fabrics of say and serge, which may have been the Lille cloth that appears so frequently in the Treasurers' Accounts. For Lent, Easter, and Whitsun in 1496 James IV was supplied with a riding gown, a side gown, a cloak, a gown 'of the new fashion', and a coat, all of Rijsel black. The king also supplied several of his servants with black and brown Lille cloth for his marriage in 1503.

For the most part the Lille cloth in the Treasurers' Accounts is described as black in colour. The dyeing of black fabrics was particularly skilful and time-consuming since it required many repeated processes to achieve a strong, dense colour. Black was therefore expensive and by the mid-fifteenth century had developed into the most fashionable colour. The Burgundian duke Philip the Good particularly favoured black for his own apparel, making the colour a symbol of wealth and sophistication, and in the diary of the well-travelled German knight, Georg von Ehingen, James II is portrayed in fashionable black attire (Figure 7.3).

Flemish fabrics were also deployed by the crown at the chivalric spectacle of the tournament, a highly ritualised display of aristocratic martial prowess. James IV staged the tournament of the Wild Knight and the Black Lady in June 1507 and again in May 1508, with themes of renewal and regeneration following the birth of a short-lived prince. These themes were represented by a Tree of Esperance or 'hope' bearing fruit, leaves, and flowers. Flemish taffeta featured extensively, having been imported in white, yellow, purple, green, and grey at a cost of £88 in total. It was used to decorate one of the pavilions or arming tents, to make coats of arms and banners, and to make the dress and 'chair triumphale' of the Black Lady. These tournaments had an international audience, with 'many gentlemen out of England, France and Denmark' in attendance. There was therefore a need to represent the Scottish crown through the most prestigious and expensive materials. This conformed with the mid-fifteenth century advice of Scottish knight Gilbert Hay, who said that the ruler 'should ever have the most notable, fairest, richest, most exotic and best made adornments, so that he should appear above and before all others in knowledge and dignity'.

Figure 7.3. James II dressed in fashionable black, from the diary of Georg von Ehingen.

Metalwork

Scottish consumers imported southern Low Countries metalwork including tableware, church furnishings and bells, and grave markers. Flanders was a notable producer of copper, bronze, and brass objects in the late medieval period, superseding Dinant and other towns in the Meuse River region to the south. Bruges and Ghent as well as Tournai were prominent exporters of metalwork. Flanders' wide international client base meant that its metal products were exported abroad, including to Scotland, for use in secular and religious contexts. Some examples of Flemish metalwork in church furnishings have already been noted in Chapter 6, but there are also instances of metal tableware being imported from the Low Countries. For the marriage of James IV and Margaret Tudor in 1503, James had his factor in Flanders buy six pitchers, six flagons, eight cases of cups (in each case six cups with covers), twenty-four plates, twenty-four dishes of white silver, six goblets with gilded covers, and chairs of state, costing a total of £703 14s.

John Young noted how during the wedding feast there were displayed 'rich dressers', on which the king's fine collection of metalwork would have been arrayed. Tableware from the Low Countries was also imported by Andrew Halyburton (see Box 4.4). For Robert Wells, Archdeacon of St Andrews, he purchased a doubly gilded silver chalice, a copper chalice with a silver cup, both gilded all over, and three cups with covers. For William Elphinstone, Bishop of Aberdeen, he bought in Bruges two doubly gilded chalices, and for James Stewart, Duke of Ross, he bought six silver goblets with covers.

Artillery

The Burgundian Low Countries were considered by medieval contemporaries to produce some of the most technologically advanced artillery. In the fifteenth century Bruges and Sluis were major centres of gun production, manufacturing great quantities of wrought iron and bronze artillery and exporting it abroad. Brussels, Liège, Mechelen, and Mons were also significant centres of production. Antwerp too was a great production and redistribution centre, manufacturing as well as trading in armaments made in such places as Tournai, Brussels, Milan, and Germany.

The earliest extant inventory for the Scottish crown's gun holdings is from 1566 so it is not possible to know how advanced these were in the fourteenth and fifteenth centuries. Guns are not known to have been manufactured in Scotland until 1473 when the Treasurers' Accounts of James III show a payment towards the repair of the Blackfriars' Priory in Edinburgh, apparently damaged while in use as a gun foundry. However, payments were made in the 1380s to artillery workers, gunners, and gun keepers at Edinburgh and Stirling Castles, for saltpetre and sulphur, and for 'an instrument called a gun'.

In 1430 James I imported from Flanders a bombard with an inscription in gold lettering:

> For the illustrious James, worthy prince of the Scots.
> Magnificent king, when I sound off, I reduce castles.
> I was made at his order; therefore I am called 'Lion'.

The identification of the bombard as a lion – or other such beasts – was deeply significant for the European aristocratic elite, for whom certain chivalric qualities were associated with particular animals. The lion, the 'king of beasts', according to a contemporary heraldic treatise, was in all things 'right glorious and right valiant', epitomising the bravery and prowess expected of the knightly class. It was a fitting symbol of the military strength of the monarchy, and the Flemish manufacturer of the bombard would have added an element of material sophistication. In 1436 James imported 'bombards, engines, and other instruments and trappings of war' from Flanders. He spent £590 8s. 2d. on these weapons in preparation for his unsuccessful siege of Roxburgh to which he took 'noble, great machines, from smaller guns to greater artillery'. It is possible that he lost some or all of these guns to the English.

The arms holdings of the Scottish crown were increased on the marriage of James II to Mary of Guelders on 3 July 1449. Mary was a great-niece of the Burgundian Duke Philip the Good, who provided James with a vast assemblage of weapons and armour transported to Scotland in five galleys. This dowry contained twenty-two iron veuglaires along with sixty-four chambers and 400 stones for them, forty-six iron culverins, and five barrels of powder for both the veuglaires and the culverins. Veuglaires were medium-sized guns used both in sieges and battles. Culverins were the smallest type of gun and were used primarily on the battlefield. From these types of guns evolved the modern handgun. These pieces were at the forefront of mid-fifteenth-century manufacture, though it is unclear whether they originated in the southern Low Countries or elsewhere.

Two great wrought iron bombards were given to James II by Philip the Good in 1457, one of which was Mons Meg. Of the 'two bombards sent by the duke of Burgundy',

Figure 7.4. The Bombard known as Mons Meg, Edinburgh Castle.

Mons Meg is now at Edinburgh Castle while the other is no longer known to exist. Mons was manufactured in 1449 in the town of the same name by Jehan Cambier, a master of artillery production who was paid the sum of £1,536 2s. The other bombard was bought from Brugeois merchant Jehan van de Velde in 1457. Philip intended it to be 'sent with other pieces of artillery to the king of Scotland, to aid him in his affairs'. The two bombards were accompanied by fifty men-at-arms on their voyage to Scotland, from Sluis to Arnemuiden then to Veere in Zeeland.

Mons Meg remained a prestigious symbol of military power and status into the sixteenth century. James IV used her for his unsuccessful siege of Norham Castle in northern England, intending to destabilise the rule of Henry VII. In July 1497 she departed from Edinburgh Castle on a specially constructed mount alongside oxen, horses, carts, and guns. Minstrels provided a musical accompaniment to the bombard, which was covered with a painted cloth. These decorative elements demonstrate Mons Meg's status as a showpiece to project publicly the military power of the king, as well as his possession of the highest quality Flemish armaments.

Clearly fifteenth- and early sixteenth-century Scotland was significantly influenced by the material culture of Flanders. It permeated the most prestigious spheres of elite society, located in royal palaces, castles and cathedrals. From art to artillery, Flemish design and production were recognised by Scots as being of a standard fitting for the most important secular and religious ceremonies, making art and artefacts one of the most significant links between Scotland and Flanders in the late medieval period.

MF/RM

8

Sport and Recreation

The relationship between medieval Flanders and Scotland was multifaceted. Trade and diplomatic links were clearly vital to Scotland's economic health, but there was also cultural exchange of a range of different sorts between the two countries. We have already seen how Scottish art and architecture drew on Flemish inspiration and example, and how Flemish luxury goods in particular were much sought after by wealthy Scottish patrons. But there were other ways in which Scots and Flemish people interacted. Jousts and tournaments were a staple of aristocratic culture in the late Middle Ages, combining dizzying spectacle with martial prowess, and the fifteenth-century dukes of Burgundy promoted knightly games for political as well as sporting reasons. A fine example of this is the tournament held in Scotland in 1449 as part of the negotiations that led to the marriage of James II to Duke Philip of Burgundy's grand-niece, Mary of Guelders, of which we have an unusually detailed account. But there were other kinds of recreational activity, less spectacular, but more enduring, in the form of tennis, curling and golf, that testify to the close links between Scotland and Flanders. Indeed, it can be argued that the quintessentially Scottish sports of curling and golf are in fact Flemish in origin.

The Tournament of 1449

The medieval tournament could be an occasion of grand spectacle, which provided entertainment and celebration of chivalric culture to be enjoyed by all those who witnessed the battle of skill and technique, as well as promoting the reputation and virtue of those who participated. Such a tournament, representing a cultural exchange between Scotland

and Burgundy, was held at Stirling in February 1449 and recorded in considerable detail because of the involvement of the great Burgundian tournament champion, Jacques de Lalain. Tournaments were held for the purpose of honing the martial skills of knights for use in actual combat, but they were also occasions for the presentation of chivalric virtue, underlining qualities of nobility in terms of deportment and valour, serving as an inspiration to those who observed the contest, and providing an opportunity for a public presentation of power and authority by those presiding over the event.

Jacques de Lalain was famed as one of the great tournament champions of the fifteenth century, and his reputation endures through recorded accounts of his life and deeds, written by Jean le Fevre and incorporated into Georges Chastellain's *Chroniques*. Lalain's early display of martial prowess had drawn him to the attention of both Philip Duke of Burgundy and Charles VII of France, and he consolidated his reputation in a number of tournaments, which established him in the world of the chivalric sporting elite. Keen to further the interests of his protégé, Philip conferred knighthood upon Lalain (although he was not admitted to the prestigious Order of the Golden Fleece until 1451).

In 1446, Lalain travelled to France, Navarre, Aragon and Castile mounting open challenges, and with the increase in his reputation his entourage would have expanded

Box 8.1. The Order of the Golden Fleece

Orders of chivalry associated with particular monarchs and royal dynasties began to emerge in the fourteenth century, the English Order of the Garter being among the earliest, founded by Edward III in 1348. Primarily designed to enhance the prestige of the founder and his descendants, Philip 'the Good' Duke of Burgundy used the occasion of his marriage to Isabella of Portugal in January 1430 to establish the Order of the Golden Fleece (*La Toison d'Or*), the centre for which was Dijon. Membership of the order consisted of twenty-four knights, was strictly Burgundian and, at least initially, could not be held with any other order. There have been various theories concerning the symbolism of the golden fleece, including a reference to the fleece sought by Jason and the Argonauts, or the fleece of Gideon soaking up the dews of heaven. Duke Philip makes none of this explicit in his foundation charter, but states that it is 'To do reverence to God and to uphold the Christian faith, and to honour and increase the noble order of chivalry'.

Figure 8.1. Jacques de Lalain from *Livre des Faits de Jacques Lalain* (*The Book of the Deeds of Jacques de Lalain*) attributed mainly to the Burgundian chroniclers Jean Le Fevre de Saint-Remy, Georges Chastellain and the Herald Charolais.

to more than 100 companions and servants. The chronicler states that Lalain returned to Lille from these endeavours to an enthusiastic welcome by Duke Philip, but 'it was not long before he took leave of the duke and took himself by sea to the realm of Scotland'. Lalain may have been tempted to try his skills against James Douglas, brother of William eighth Earl of Douglas, an opponent who had developed his own reputation as skilled in arms. Lalain's chronicler states that, although not personally present at the tournament, his account was received from eyewitnesses, including Lalain himself, and he has 'written the truth according to the report of the Scots and those of our party, so that I was able to recount it without error'. The two principals met one another and agreed terms, allowing Lalain and Douglas to choose two companions who were 'men of rank and known in arms'. For Lalain, these were his uncle, Simon de Lalain, and Hervé de Meriadec, described as a squire from Brittany, and Douglas's companions were James Douglas of Ralston (brother of Sir Henry Douglas of Lochleven) and John Ross of Hawkhead.

Although Jacques de Lalain was a renowned jouster and chivalric hero of his time, he and his companions were also men of status in the service of Duke Philip, who had been approached by the Scots for assistance in brokering a marriage alliance for their king, James II. Philip looked to the neighbouring duchy of Guelders, as Arnold Duke of Guelders had three daughters, the eldest of whom, Mary, had been sent to live at the

Burgundian court under the protection of Philip's duchess, Isabella of Portugal. Scottish ambassadors sent to pursue negotiations for James II's marriage had been fêted by Duke Philip from August to September 1448 in a lavish display of splendour and hospitality designed to impress the Scots and further plans for an alliance.

Lalain and his companions would have been empowered to conduct negotiations during their visit, and once the Burgundians had arrived in Scotland, the direct involvement of James II is clear, with the chronicler stating that 'the king of Scotland agreed to be their judge, and appointed time and place, and had the lists made ready at Stirling'. Preparations for the tournament took place in an atmosphere of feasting and entertainment, laid on to impress the Burgundian visitors, particularly as the Scottish ambassadors, returning from their visit to the continent the previous autumn, would have described the elaborate hospitality they had received in Burgundy. The eighteen-year-old James II was just beginning to take personal control of his kingdom, and seems to have been involved directly in negotiations for his own marriage. He was evidently keen to use the occasion to project an impressive presentation of Scottish royal power and prestige to these representatives of the Burgundian court.

The chronicler's account describes the ceremonial focus on the king as he 'mounted his throne', after which the Burgundians, dressed in furred robes of black velvet, arrived 'accompanied by noblemen who had come with them, and also by those whom the king had appointed to advise with them'. Following the arrival of the Burgundians in their pavilion at the tournament ground, 'they went and did reverence to the King of Scotland'. The Douglas champions were next to arrive at the entrance to the lists, accompanied by William eighth Earl of Douglas 'and other great lords, knights and other people, who, it was said, amounted to fully four or five thousand men'.

The Scots and the Burgundians were to fight in the manner of a combat of six, on foot, armed with spear, axe, sword and dagger. At the request of the Scots, the throwing of spears was forbidden, but weapons were to be sharp rather than blunted and the fight was to continue *à outrance* (to the death), or until the king ordered it to cease. Although the terms allowed each combatant to help his companions, the chronicler records a speech made by Jacques shortly before they left their pavilion: 'I pray you with all the zeal I can that you will neither aid me nor succour me in any way whatsoever, but permit me to meet such fortune, be it good or ill, as God may please to send me'. Such a speech served to underline both Lalain's supreme confidence in his own skills, and his chivalric honour. The Burgundians matched themselves with specific opponents, with Lalain against James Master of Douglas, Simon against John Ross of Hawkhead and Hervé de Meriadec against James Douglas of Ralston. The chronicler delivers a spirited and detailed match report, describing the process and outcome of the three paired combats.

The Burgundians jettisoned their lances and proceeded to engage their opponents with axes, driving them back and making them lose their lances. The chronicler's account focuses on the two principals, Jacques de Lalain and James Douglas, stressing the skill required for Lalain to turn aside the concerted effort made by Douglas to wound him in his face, exposed by his half-visor. Indeed, by seizing Douglas by the latter's own basinet with closed visor, Lalain was able to manoeuvre his opponent 'backwards to the throne of the king, twice lifting him off his feet with the intention of throwing him on the ground, and so putting him out of breath'.

There was a similar outcome in the other paired combats, with Simon Lalain withstanding the assault from John Ross of Hawkhead. The chronicler commended Ross for his great strength, but makes it clear that it was Simon's superior tactics that told against his opponent, driving Ross back the length of the lists until he 'began to weary, and to lose strength and breath'. James Douglas of Ralston and Hervé de Meriadec had a spirited encounter which saw Douglas flattened to the ground, only to rise again and continue fighting. As the chronicler points out, Meriadec had Douglas at his mercy on a number of occasions, but was unwilling to carry home his advantage, 'which was nobly done, and ought to be set down to his honour'. The account leaves no doubt that the outcome of all three combats, despite some spirited defence and attack from the Scots, was victory for the Burgundians. It could have ended very badly indeed had James II not thrown down his truncheon to end the combat.

The tournament was held on Shrove Tuesday (25 February 1449), a date traditionally favoured for tournaments as it was a celebratory occasion that preceded the penitential season of Lent. Stirling was one of Scotland's principal royal castles with extensive parkland suitable for such a public occasion and with the additional symbolic value of association with the Snowdon of Arthurian legend (promoted by the crown from at least the reign of David II). Over all this, the young king presided as the focal point of a display of Scottish royal power, presenting as attractive an image as possible to these foreign visitors, which included treating the Burgundian champions to a grand feast after the contest, and sending them home with 'honourable gifts' from the king. Shortly after the return of Lalain's party to Burgundy, Mary's father, Arnold Duke of Guelders, travelled to Brussels and sealed the marriage contract on 1 April, triggering a flurry of activity in preparing Mary for her prospective role as queen of Scotland. The departure in June of the bride for her new home was the occasion of a magnificent send-off at Bruges, with Jacques de Lalain performing in a celebratory tournament as he had at Stirling the previous February.

The tournament of 1449 may have been the first public occasion on which James II determined to vie with the Douglases for leadership of chivalric culture within the realm, and he was determined to emulate the example of his new Burgundian allies in asserting this aspect of his role. It is evident that sport and diplomacy could be comfortably combined, and the tournament of 1449 served the multiple purposes of presenting both Douglas and royal power through the dimension of chivalric culture in what may have been the opening shots in a concerted re-assertion of the Stewart crown's authority.

CM

Early Games

The Flemish impact on Scotland is evident in modern games such as curling, tennis and golf. To understand how this influence developed, we need to bear in mind the linguistic as well as cultural links between Scotland, England and the Low Countries. As outlined in Chapter 9, the Dutch, Flemish, English and Scots languages all have a common Germanic ancestry and their close relationship has resulted in remarkable phonological resemblances. While the Gaelic language has quite different Celtic roots, the distinctive Older Scots tongue spoken throughout Lowland Scotland by the later Middle Ages developed from Old English but with substantial Flemish (or Middle Dutch) influence due to the widespread migration and settlement of Flemish people in the twelfth century and after. Such influence – linguistic and cultural – is evident in the early games played in Scotland.

Curling bonspiel – *Krul bollen spel*

The game of curling or the curling bonspiel – a match between opposing teams – is considered a traditional Scottish game, and certainly the game as it is played worldwide today has its origins in Scotland. However, historians have long debated whether there was earlier Flemish influence on the development of the game. There is strong etymological evidence that this was indeed the case. English dictionaries state that the game of curling is played with stones on ice (1610s) and that a description of a similar game is attested from Flanders (c.1600). The word *curl* as a verb is derived from the metathesis or transposition of *crulle* (c.1300) from Old English or Middle Dutch *krul*. In Dutch today *krullen* means to curl (v.), i.e., to cause an object to make a curling movement or motion. The word *bonspiel* (n.) consists of two elements, the word *spiel* and the prefix *bon*. The word *spiel* as a noun is related to Old English or Middle Dutch *spilian* (v.) meaning to play, and *spil* or *spel* (n.) meaning a game. Curling historians in Scotland have discussed the origins of the word *bonspiel* and the prefix *bon* at length, but without reaching consensus. However, it is likely that *bon* is related to Old English or Middle Dutch *bolle* (n.) meaning a round (wooden) object. This is similar to the present-day English *bowl* (n.) and Dutch *bol* (n.), as used in games. In Germanic languages the letter *n* is added at the end of a word to create verbs and plurals. To play with a *bol*, therefore, is *bollen* and the plural of *bol* is also bollen. In Dutch dialects the middle letters may dissolve in the pronunciation, *bollen* becoming *bol'n* or *bo'n*. The traditional Scottish curling word *bonspiel* may then be related to the Dutch *bollen spel* and *curling bonspiel* to *krul bollen spel*. Interestingly, today *het krulbol spel* is still played in the Netherlands and Belgium (in Zeeuws-Vlaanderen) and is considered an old Flemish folk game, even protected by UNESCO as part of its national heritage.

There is additional proof that the game of curling has been influenced by Flemish (Dutch) elements. Archaeological finds suggest that, in the medieval Low Countries, various ball games were played with wooden objects. The origins of many ballgames, and stick- and ballgames, from the Middle Ages are obscured by the absence of clear documentary evidence, but edicts banning certain games being played in the streets

Figure 8.2. David Teniers the Younger, *Landscape with Peasants Playing Bowls Outside an Inn*. The wooden *bol* was rolled over land towards a target.

inside the town walls and images in Books of Hours testify to their popularity. In Netherlandish art of the sixteenth and seventeenth centuries there are many depictions of the *bollen spel*, whereby wooden bowls are rolled on flat land towards a stake as target (see Figure 8.2).

Winters in Northern Europe during the Middle Ages were particularly cold and peaked during the so-called Little Ice Age. As a result, the *bollen spel*, and the game of *colf* too, were played on ice as winter pastimes. The wooden *bol* was laid on its flat side and a wooden stick handle attached to aid in throwing it across the ice. A painting by Pieter Bruegel the Elder, *Winter Landscape* (Figure 8.3), clearly depicts this *bol* game being played on ice, while further evidence is provided by a remarkable engraving by Robert de Baudous (after a drawing by Cornelis Claesz. van Wieringen), *Winter* (1591–1618), part of a series of four engravings depicting seasonal life on the water. Here we can clearly see a group of men playing a game on ice very similar to the curling bonspiel as it is played in Scotland (Figure 8.4).

Figure 8.3. Pieter Bruegel the Elder, *Winter Landscape with Skaters and a Bird Trap* (detail). During winter the *bollen* game was taken to the frozen canals and waterways; the *bol* was laid on its flat side and pushed over the ice using an inserted wooden handle.

Figure 8.4. Robert de Baudous after Cornelis Claesz etc. van Wieringen, *Winter* (1591–1618). A game of *bollen* being played on ice during wintertime. A wooden handle is inserted in the *bol* and is pushed towards a target on the ice, while a besom is used to brush the ice. Note also the two *colf* players in the foreground.

Navita sic gelido subductâ classe Decembri HYEMS *Securus glaciem ferratâ compede sulcat.*

It is possible, therefore, that the *bollenspel* – played both on land and on ice in the Low Countries with wooden implements – was introduced to Scotland by immigrant Flemings prior to c.1500 and that this game was merged with the native Scottish (Gaelic) game of throwing *kuting* stones on ice after c.1500 to become the game we know today as curling. A wooden *bol* was perfectly round, whilst kuting stones were pluriform. The curling stone became a rounded implement.

Caitchpule – *caets spel*

Caitchpule (or tennis) in Scotland or *caets spel* in the Low Countries was originally played as a handball game and is considered a forerunner of the modern game of tennis. In England the game was referred to as tennis (or *tinnis*) but in Scotland the now almost extinct word caitchpule was used to denominate the handball game. The word tennis (in a 1400 document spelt as *tenetz*) is derived from the French imperative of *tenir* (to hold). '*Tenez*' was used as a warning required by the rules of medieval tennis before serving the ball.

Discussing the game's origins David Murison, the renowned editor of the *Scottish National Dictionary*, suggested that:

> A sure indication of the close and cordial relations existing between the Netherlands and Scotland appears in the various names for games which the Scots borrowed chiefly in the fifteenth century and in one instance at least appropriated for good: *cache*, and later the combination *cachepell*, tennis, are Middle Flemish *caetse* (*-spel*); golf (Middle Dutch *kolf*, a club, *kolven*, a game with clubs), despite the disbelief of some Scottish devotees, is too well illustrated in Flemish painting to be anything else than of Dutch origin, however it may have been developed or modified in its adopted country...

Figure 8.5. Book of Hours (June) – Adélaïde de Savoie, Duchess of Burgundy (c.1460). A game of *caets* (handball) played between two opposing teams of three players. Traditionally the roof above the gallery was used to serve the ball.

Figure 8.6. The royal tennis court at Falkland Palace, Fife.

The early hand ball game was originally an outdoor game played on the open field or, as depicted in Figure 8.5, in the streets. Traditionally the game was played between two opposing teams of three players. Court play was limited to single or double players while a cord or net was introduced for the ball to be played over as an additional obstacle. Ball games, like *caets* and *colf*, became hugely popular in the Low Countries, especially Flanders and later Holland.

Racket tennis played on courts in Europe mostly replaced the handball game played outside and was a game for aristocrats and royalty due to the exclusivity of available space and buildings. An enclosed tennis court required large dimensions and was usually attached to palace buildings or otherwise special tennis houses were built. In Scotland the construction of an open caitchpule (or tennis court) at James V's royal palace at Falkland began in 1539 and still stands today as the earliest tennis court in Britain (Figure 8.6).

In its heyday the game in Scotland was not called tennis but rather *caitche*, a term originating from the Dutch word *caets* used in the Low Countries. The game of *caets* or caitchpule may well have been introduced by twelfth-century Flemish immigrants. Most of what is known about caitchpule in Scotland relates to the sixteenth century and after, but there is reference to the game as early as the reign of Alexander III in the thirteenth century. In 1598 James VI commended 'playing at the caitch or tennis' to his

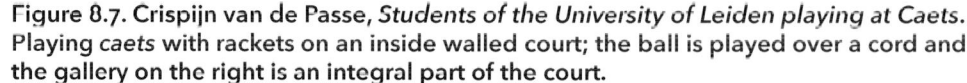

Figure 8.7. Crispijn van de Passe, *Students of the University of Leiden playing at Caets*. Playing *caets* with rackets on an inside walled court; the ball is played over a cord and the gallery on the right is an integral part of the court.

young son as a 'fair and pleasant' field game, and there are references to *caitche* being played in Perth, Stirling, St Andrews and Edinburgh.

Caitchpule remained a highly popular game at the royal courts of Scotland and England until the Civil Wars of the mid-seventeenth century from which the game never fully recovered until the introduction of the new Victorian form of lawn tennis in 1874 by Major Walter Winfield. The old game of tennis played inside walled courts has sporadically continued to this day and is better known as real tennis as opposed to lawn tennis.

Golf – *Colf*

The origin of the game is probably the most debated subject among golf historians. But who invented the game, and where, is an inappropriate question to pose as early games were not invented but rather evolved over time and were influenced by numerous cultural developments. Moreover, stick and ball games in medieval times were played in varying forms and were not governed by standard rules as is the convention today.

Golf historians have commonly focused on the comparisons and analogies between the game of golf in Scotland and the game of *colf* (also spelled *kolf*) in the Low Countries, especially during the seventeenth century in the Dutch Republic. The reason for this is the abundance of images representing the game of *colf* in popular landscape paintings and portraits by many well-known Dutch artists. The similarities between the two games in Scotland and the Dutch Republic are indeed quite striking, and there is documentary evidence to suggest that they are in fact related, leading historians to the conclusion that golf had its origins in Holland. A closer analysis, however, suggests that there is a distinct Scottish influence on the game being played by the Dutch in Holland. There is little doubt that the words *golf* (or *goff*, *gouwf*, and other spellings) and *colf* (or *kolf*) are linguistically related. But there is an issue as to whether an earlier Flemish connection gave rise to the game of golf in Scotland.

Figure 8.8. Hendrick Avercamp, *Winter Landscape on the River IJssel near Kampen*, 1615 (detail). A group of colfers playing on ice during wintertime in the northern Low Countries surrounded by arbiters and helpers. Clearly visible are a long nosed jointed wooden club and a leather stitched ball, both common in Scotland. The ball is teed up on some snow. Players in Holland would play with a single club only, whereas in Scotland players would have on average four clubs to use, carried by a caddie.

A starting-point for addressing this possibility is to look at the game of *colf* played in the northern Low Countries. With the founding of the Dutch Republic, following the fall of the city of Antwerp in 1585, large numbers of people from Flanders and Brabant fled the southern Netherlands and settled in northern towns and cities. This included the upper crust of Flemish society consisting of wealthy merchants and bankers, intellectuals and artists. This influx of Flemings substantially influenced cultural development in the north, including an increase in popularity of games such as *caets, bollen* and *colf.*

At the same time substantial numbers of Scots also settled in the Dutch Republic, either attracted as students to the University of Leiden, the now famed bulwark of religious and intellectual freedom in Europe; as mercenaries fighting for the Dutch against their Habsburg enemies; or as merchants trading in such Dutch ports as Veere and Rotterdam. It is not surprising therefore to find evidence in paintings and in literature of Scottish influence on the game of *colf* as played in the northern Low Countries. The development and popularisation of this Dutch game of *colf* benefited from cross-fertilisation with the traditional version of the game already being played in Scotland.

It is possible that golf, like *bollen* and *caitche*, was originally introduced to Scotland by twelfth-century Flemish settlers. Certainly, there is sufficient linguistic and phonological proof that the Scots word *golf* derives from the Middle Dutch *colf* used by Flemish immigrants at the time.

The early game of golf in Scotland was probably played in various forms. From illustrations in fourteenth-century Flemish Books of Hours we can discern two basic forms of stick and ball games by the name of *colf*: one with two opposing teams with a number of players contesting a single ball (similar to today's shinty in Scotland); and the other, as seen in Figure 8.9, with two or more individual players playing their own ball towards a set target (similar to today's golf or croquet games). Another interesting illustration from the late fifteenth century is in a Book of Hours illuminated by Simon Bening, whose father was from Scotland, that depicts three *colf* players each playing their wooden balls on land towards a hole in the ground (see Figure 8.10). The fourth man is probably the person acting as neutral arbiter and pointing at the inn where the innkeeper stands in the doorway waiting to serve beer after the game when the wagers are settled. Arbiters were customary and necessary because of the heavy gambling habits of the players.

Another illustration of *colf* in a similar Book of Hours depicts a player in full swing and another attempting to stroke his ball into a hole. In the background the contours of the town of Antwerp are visible (Figure 8.9). The game is played on land and contradicts the assumption by some Scottish golf historians that the game was originally played on ice over short distances towards a post as target. Clearly the early game of *colf* was

Figure 8.9. Book of Hours, Flemish School, sixteenth century. Two groups of three colf players and two accompanying arbiters. Two players are in full swing, another is playing towards the hole. In the background is the city of Antwerp.

played on land and not on ice as later became customary. It is also clearly a long game requiring a full swing at the ball. And finally, the ball is played into a hole as a target. At first the ball was made of wood, but this was replaced by a leather ball stuffed with hair, a cross-over from the game of *caets* or caitchpule. It is possible that this cross-over was first made in Scotland where golf had become increasingly popular whereas in the Low Countries *caets* was still the dominant game. The earliest written record of golf being played in Scotland is the Act of Parliament of 1458 banning it (and football) as distractions from military practice. That the legislation was renewed in 1471 and again in 1491 attests to golf's continuing popularity in the face of stern official disapproval.

Although played by royalty in Scotland – Mary Queen of Scots is believed to have enjoyed it – golf had not yet made it to royal status in England. However, James VI's accession to the English throne in 1603 saw his court move from Edinburgh to London and with it a large retinue of Scottish nobles, gentlemen and merchants. As a result, the Scottish game of golf was introduced to England, first played on Blackheath beside the royal palace at Greenwich. Continuing commercial links between Scotland, England

Figure 8.10. *Colf* players, Flemish Book of Hours (September) illustrated by Simon Bening (c.1520). Three players playing wooden *colf* balls towards a hole as target overlooked by an arbiter and the innkeeper in the background.

Figure 8.11. Adriaen van der Velde, *Colf players near Haarlem* (detail). The player on the left is dressed in a Scottish kilt. The two onlookers would normally be arbiters as the wagers could be substantial. The clubs are traditional Dutch one-piece *colf* clubs made of ash with a leaden cover over the clubhead as additional swing-weight.

and the Low Countries, especially the Dutch Republic, ensured that the Scottish and Dutch versions of the game, both having strong Flemish roots, adapted to and adopted from one another. In Scotland, including the Scottish enclave in England, golf became the favoured game of a new class of wealthy gentlemen and burgesses – just as it did in the Dutch Republic. This is clearly visible in numerous Dutch paintings portraying players wearing kilts or using jointed clubs as was normal in Scotland as opposed to the single piece *colf* club used in the Low Countries (see Figure 8.11). Confusingly the numerous Dutch paintings with *colf* scenes have led to the belief by some historians that the game of *colf* in Holland was the origin of golf in Scotland, whereas its true origins lie much earlier among Flemish migrants from twelfth-century Flanders settling in Scotland in the newly founded burgh towns.

RB

PART III

ASSIMILATION AND ABSORPTION

9

Language

The lasting impact of the Flemish on the Scots language goes far beyond the embedding of some Flemish-derived words in the Scots vocabulary. The divergence of the sister languages of Scots and English from their common roots is not only concurrent with, but can be to no small extent attributed to, the first influx of Flemish immigrants to Scotland, and their subsequent influence on the language and culture of those parts of the country in which they settled.

However, teasing out the precise derivations of words is a complex task: Scots and English, after all, like Dutch and Flemish, are Germanic languages that were brought to the British Isles by the invasion and settlement of peoples from Northern Europe. These Germanic peoples established the Anglo-Saxon kingdoms of the sixth and seventh centuries, out of which England would finally emerge in the tenth century. Early Scots is thought to have derived from the dialect of Old English spoken in the Anglo-Saxon kingdom of Northumbria. Though Northumbrian English had worked its way across the border sometime before the seventh century and established itself principally in small pockets in the south and east of Scotland, the language took several hundred years to diverge fully into the distinct variety we now describe as Scots. This shift mirrored the emergence of what we now describe as Standard English from the English dialect spoken in the Anglo-Saxon kingdom of Mercia. The exact chronology is difficult to determine, but in the main it is agreed that whilst the establishment of Early Scots can be pinned down to the thirteenth century, the process began a century earlier.

The divergence of a language variety requires the establishment of a distinct lexicon, invariably incorporating 'loan words' acquired via trade and immigration. The twelfth century marks the beginning of a discernible shift away from Northumbrian

English, which also coincides with Henry II's expulsion of the Flemish from England in 1154. When these Flemish moved across the Scottish border they settled in significant numbers in the south and the east of Scotland. These are areas in which English had been the primary language, and Scots shortly would be. There can be little doubt that this influx, and the easily importable vocabulary of Flemish terms relating to industry and trade, contributed significantly to the formation of the Scots language. Indeed, the broader economic and cultural impact of the Flemish on Scotland had no small role to play in the wider changes which were to see Scots, rather than Gaelic, established as the language of status and of the state in Scotland.

The establishment of the early Scottish burghs was also a critical factor in the development of the Scots language. To the linguistic mix of Norse-influenced Northern Middle English, French and Gaelic, Flemish speakers added a substantial number of words. The words *guild* and *kirkmaister* are examples of how linguistic influence was reflected in burghal terminology. The Flemish would also have added their weight to the restoration of non-palatalised forms of words like *kirk* that in English became *church*. Palatalisation refers to a way of pronouncing a consonant in which part of the tongue is moved close to the hard palate. Old Norse is usually given as the source of these non-palatalised forms, but as often happens more than one influence was at work and Flemish had a supporting role.

The Flemish tongue is essentially a form of Dutch and this leads, in terms of linguistic analysis, to a difficulty in isolating the influence of the Flemish people and their language on Scots from that of the Dutch. The Flemish language, naturally, has a somewhat complicated ancestry of its own. The significance of West Flanders and, later, Brabant as centres of literature in the thirteenth and fourteenth centuries resulted in Flemish becoming in many ways the *de facto* dialect of status within the Low Countries, such that Middle Dutch and Flemish were almost entirely indistinguishable from one another. Attempts have been made to disentangle the relative impacts of these two people groups. In the process of compiling *A Dictionary of the Older Scottish Tongue* and the *Scottish National Dictionary* — now available as the online *Dictionary of the Scots Language* (www.dsl.ac.uk) — a huge body of data on the Scots language was brought together. From this data, David Murison, editor of the *Scottish National Dictionary* from 1946–76, did painstaking work in extracting and analysing the influence of Dutch and Flemish.

The Flemish influence on the Scots language is felt particularly in fields where there were significant areas of contact. As might be expected, the two most important related to trade and cloth. From trade, we have *cran* for *crane*, and perhaps the most evergreen of the Scots borrowings, *callant*, originally derived from the Flemish word *caland* for *customer*, but eventually acquiring its now common colloquial meaning of a person, an individual, a lad. Another successful borrowing pertained to the Scottish and continental expectation that craftsmen submit a sterling example of their work in order to gain membership of a trade-guild, a piece that would be called a *maisterstick* in Scots, from the Flemish *meesterstuck*. In England, where that particular tradition of peer evaluation did not exist, the word underwent a slight change, and became the English word 'masterpiece'. Also from trade, *plack*, a word for a small coin, which is still in circulation in colloquial Scots, and *coft*, in the sense of *bought*, which in certain parts of the country is still to be overheard in everyday conversation. Somewhat less durable were the Scots borrowings from the Flemish in the field of textiles, a large number of which have now fallen completely out of use. Amongst the various loanwords for materials and garments which entered the Scots language, *cortrik*, *mutch* and *lapkin* are possibly the most immediately recognisable.

But there were a number of other areas worthy of note: agriculture, weights and measures, coinage, games, war and weapons. As argued in Chapter 8, *cache* or *caitch*, the Scots word for a form of tennis, and *gowf*, the word for a popular game involving the striking of a ball with clubs, almost certainly owe their linguistic origins to the Flemish, as does another traditional Scottish pastime, *crooning*, and the frequent locale for that pastime, the *howff*, or pub. Of particular interest, given the seafaring histories of the Low Countries, is the sheer volume of maritime terminology and vocabulary which entered the Scots language via the Flemish. The Scots 'makar' or poet Gavin Douglas (1474–1522), whose provostship of the collegiate church of St Giles in Edinburgh would certainly have brought him into contact with the sizable Flemish community nearby, was particularly reliant on such borrowings for his 1513 work *Eneados*, the first full translation of Virgil's *Aeneid* into any Germanic language. The nautical lexicon of the Flemish proved invaluable to Douglas in chronicling the wanderings of Aeneas around the eastern Mediterranean. *Bel* for *bubble* and *helmstok* for *tiller* are amongst the numerous Flemish loanwords preserved for us through Douglas, though the self-explanatory *scone* is no doubt by far the most celebrated.

There is also a miscellaneous set of other Flemish-rooted words that have embedded themselves in Scots. *Crag*, the Scots word for *neck*, and *bucht*, a sheep-pen, are particularly noteworthy additions which fall into this category. Murison painstakingly distinguished between the Flemish linguistic influence in the fourteenth, fifteenth, sixteenth, seventeenth and eighteenth centuries. The table overleaf has been extracted from Murison's work.

The words in Table 9.1 do not include Flemish-rooted words that made their way into both the English and Scots vocabulary. The focus here is solely on the impact on the

Table 9.1. Examples of the Flemish influence on the Scots language

Trade

Century	Scots word	Flemish word	English meaning
14th	cran	craen	A crane for lifting
15th	wissel	wissel	Change of money
16th	calland	caland	A customer
16th	maisterstick	messterstuck	A skills test for joining a guild

Cloth

Century	Scots word	Flemish word	English meaning
14th	cortrik	Cortrik	A kind of black velvet made at Kortrijk (Courtrai), Flanders
15th	birges	Bruges	A kind of satin material, derived from Bruges, Flanders
15th	eik	iecke	The grease of wool
15th	ryssil	Ryssel	A woollen stuff derived from Rijsel (Lille), Flanders
16th	ley	Leie	A kind of cloth/canvas, likely from the name of the River Leie, Flanders

Agriculture

Century	Scots word	Flemish word	English meaning
15th	bucht	bocht	A sheep pen
15th	ferrow cow	verrekoe	A cow not in calf
15th	slipe	slijp	A sledge
16th	cavie	kevie	A chicken coop
16th	roddiken	roode	The fourth stomach of a ruminant
17th	kesart	kaesborde	A cheese vat

Weights and Measures

Century	Scots word	Flemish word	English meaning
15th	grotken	grootken	A gross

Coinage

Century	Scots word	Flemish word	English meaning
15th	plack	placke	A copper coin
15th	rider	rijder	A gold coin
15th	steke	stik	A coin/piece of money

Table 9.1. Examples of the Flemish influence on the Scots language (*continued*)

Games

Century	Scots word	Flemish word	English meaning
15th	cache	caetse	Tennis

War and Weapons

Century	Scots word	Flemish word	English meaning
16th	crannikin	kraaniken	A part of a crossbow
16th	flas	flasch	A powder-flask
16th	fyane	fijan	Enemy

Miscellaneous

Century	Scots word	Flemish word	English meaning
14th	crag	kraghe	The neck
14th	slop/slap	slop	A gap in a wall
15th	smook	smuuken	Smoke
16th	scaf	schaeven	To scrounge
16th	scone	schoon	A flour cake/scone
16th	plot	ploten	To pluck wool or feathers
17th	cud	kodde	A cudgel
18th	loy	loi	Sluggish/lazy
18th	swack	zwak	Active/nimble
18th	winze	wensen	A curse

Scots language. From the linguistic interchange between Britain and the Low Countries generally comes a whole host of notable Scots words — *wagon, mannekin, brandy* and, perhaps most ubiquitously of late, *rant* — whose precise ancestry it is impossible to be sure about, except that they came from roughly there to roughly here.

The heyday of the economic relationship between Scotland and Flanders was the fourteenth and fifteenth centuries, so it is not surprising that many of the words pertaining to trade and cloth date to this period. By the same token, the more troubled sixteenth century saw the transmission to Scotland of Flemish words relating to war and weapons. In the earlier period, the transmission mechanism was primarily through Flemish traders and immigrant Flemish weavers domiciled in Scotland. In the later period, the influence may have come through Scottish mercenaries fighting in Northern

Europe and bringing words back to Scotland. Though some limited interchange between the two languages continued beyond the sixteenth century, after the Reformation, and with the printing of Bibles in English, the Scots language began to fall out of fashion, and by the eighteenth century had come to be seen as provincial and unrefined. Borrowing from other languages became much more infrequent, and rarely escaped whichever regional dialect of Scots they first entered. It is worth noting that a similar fate befell the Flemish tongue within this time frame, precipitated by much the same social and political catalysts, with the various dialects of Dutch gradually being subsumed into the larger national language.

It is difficult to separate out the influences of the Germanic languages on Scots. The Scandinavian languages, Low German, Dutch, and Flemish, have all played their parts, and it is not always clear whether a Scots word comes from one or more of these languages or whether it was there in Old English from the start. When one adds in the complication of influences from other forms of English, and the second-hand borrowings which are implicit in this, the scale of the task seems to be beyond us. However, the work of Murison in separating out words of Flemish origin and relating them to defined fields of activity and the century when they were borrowed amply demonstrates the economic and linguistic contribution of the Flemish to Scotland.

AF/CR/TC

Surnames

Surnames can provide important information about people, such as where they came from, where they settled, and what they did. Most Flemish incomers to Scotland in the eleventh and twelfth centuries would have come without a hereditary surname — that is a surname passed down from father to son. The only exception would have been the Flemish knightly class, some of whom would have adopted such names by this stage. However, later incomers, mainly merchants and skilled craftsmen, would typically have had hereditary surnames. Some of these immigrants had or adopted surnames that over time have come to be viewed as typically Scottish and as a result their Flemish roots have been obscured. This chapter examines how surnames came to be formed and reviews attempts that have been made to identify the Flemish origins of families associated with Scotland.

Hereditary Surnames

At the time of the Norman Conquest of 1066, and the first influx of Flemish settlers to Britain, individuals were identified by 'by-names' rather than surnames. These were names that related to place of origin, occupation, ethnicity or nationality and sometimes peculiar personal characteristics. It was out of these by-names that hereditary surnames began to develop in the twelfth and thirteenth centuries, first among landowners and then more widely among other social groups. The surnames that evolved can be grouped into various classes (see Box 10.1). Locational surnames include a wide range of types of place, including ethnic or national designations such as Fleming, English or Scot. Such

> **Box 10.1. Surname Classes**
> Most surnames fall into one or other of four classes based on:
> 1. *Location* (known variously as locative, toponymic, territorial, landed) e.g., Wood, Sutherland, Scott.
> 2. *Family* (patronymic, fealtic) e.g., Wilson, Robertson, MacDonald (Gaelic).
> 3. *Occupation* (trade, office) e.g., Smith, Taylor, Hunter.
> 4. *Personal characteristics* (nicknames, descriptors) e.g., Noble, Brown, Campbell (Gaelic *cam beul* or 'crooked mouth'), Cruickshank ('bow-legged').

surnames accounted for up to 50% of all surnames in many areas. While members of the elite typically adopted locational surnames, those of lower social status were more likely to adopt surnames based on family relationships or occupation.

A number of prominent Scottish families with possible Flemish origins acquired their surnames in England before migrating north to Scotland, though subsequently those names have been taken as distinctively Scottish. A good example of this is the Lindsay family name. A Flemish noblemen Gilbert de Ghent accompanied William in the Conquest of England in 1066 and was rewarded with extensive lands near Lincoln and in the surrounding Lindsey area. As a result, he was also known as Gilbert de Lindsey and this was the name carried by his offspring, Walter and William, when they settled in the Borders of Scotland. Sir Walter is thought to have accompanied David Earl of Huntingdon when he came north to claim the Scottish throne as David I in 1124. The 'de Lindsays' first acquired lands at Ercildon (or Ercildoune) in Roxburghshire, now known as Earlston, on the banks of the Leader Water, but subsequently the main branch of the family established itself in Glenesk, Angus, around 1358. The various branches of the Lindsay family played a prominent role in Scottish history thereafter, acquiring the earldoms of Crawford and Balcarres that are still in their hands, while the surname itself became widespread, its English and Flemish origins long forgotten.

There are a number of other Scottish families that can, with varying degrees of certainty, be traced back to Flanders via England. The Graham family that came north from Grantham in Yorkshire (also known as Granham or Graham in the medieval period) may have had Flemish roots. The founder of the Graham family in Scotland is believed to be William de Graham (c.1080–1127) who is said to have come north from England to Scotland with David I in 1124. Recent DNA testing of males in Scotland with the surname Graham — using the methodology explained in Box 10.2 — revealed that a large number of them carried the same rare genetic signature indicative of descent from William de Graham. Other families with possible roots in Flanders include the Oliphants, who came to Scotland from what was originally Holy Ford (later Olifard and Oliphant) in Northamptonshire, and the Spaldings who took their name from a town in Lincolnshire before settling in Glenshee, Perthshire.

As well as names derived from England, twelfth-century Flemish settlers in Scotland also adopted what proved to be hereditary surnames taken from the lands they were granted. As we saw in Chapter 3, the various branches of the descendants of Freskin de Moravia adopted their names from the lands they held in the north of Scotland. Thus the Sutherland family took its name from the Old Norse 'south land', the land south of Scandinavia or the Norse territories of Orkney and Shetland, while the Murray surname was an adaptation of the place-name, Moray. Similarly, in 1160, Berowald the Fleming was granted land by Malcolm IV including the area called Innes and his descendants took Innes as their family name. Another example is the Douglas family that probably took its name from the Douglas Water in South Lanarkshire, a tributary of the River Clyde.

The origins of William de Douglas (living 1174), first Lord of Douglas are unclear, but also known as the son of Arkenbald or Erkenbald (Archibald in Scots), he was most likely of Flemish ancestry. William married Margaret de Kerdale, sister of Freskin de Kerdale, grandson of Freskin de Moravia. William's son Archibald de Douglas appears to have spent a considerable time in Moray as episcopal charters of his brother Bricius de Douglas show. Genetic testing of documented descendants of Douglas Earls of Morton back to the 1400s and others of their distant cousins shows that all descend from William de Douglas. These Douglas test takers match documented descendants of the Sutherlands of Forse, extant descendants of William first Earl of Sutherland, reputedly great grandson of Freskin de Moravia. The common shared male ancestor of these two noble lineages was c.1100.

A more general adoption of hereditary surnames seems to have occurred in the fourteenth century. A list of merchants from Flanders working in Scotland in the mid-fourteenth century is indicative of this trend (Box 10.3). The names with the earliest dates are probably by-names: for example, Taskyno, and possibly Lancio de Castro and Clays de Tore. However, over time, the names take on the more familiar first name and hereditary surname format, such as Johanni Raynerson, Johannis Wolcopper, Petri Machenarum. Few, if any, of these particular surnames are found in Scotland today. As merchants many of them would have been in Scotland only temporarily while any that stayed may have yielded lines of descent that in due course petered out. Finally,

Box 10.2. Methodology for genetic evidence

Lineage and surname research uses the male specific Y-chromosome as it is passed from a father only to his sons (so called Y-DNA). Firstly, individuals are identified who have documented descent from Flemish elites. Such test takers tend to have titles, are representatives of their chiefly line or are cadets of the direct line. The ancestry of each test taker must descend unbroken in the male line back to the reputed progenitor (ie., no break in descent by female inheritance or illegitimacy). A DNA sample is collected using buccal cells from the cheek inside of the mouth.

The sample is processed using accurate genome sequencing technologies known as 'Next Generation Sequencing'. Such tests are used by both geneticists and genetic genealogists (those who combine both documentary and genetic evidence). The test extracts and analyses values for large sections of the Y-chromosome, in order of 12 million plus base pairs (base pairs link the two stands of the DNA helix together). The result for each test taker is compared with other individuals who have tested. Differences in the sequence that are shared by individuals, if deemed stable, are named and become known as SNP 'markers' (Single Nucleotide Polymorphism). Within a lineage a new SNP marker is formed approximately every 125 years and can be used to identify branching between male cousins and even brothers. Such markers are added to the genetic tree for the Y-chromosome and placed according to their relationship with other markers, for example whether they are older or younger in formation.

The frequency, distribution and age of markers can be overlaid with historical evidence so as to infer the migration and development of a lineage including the adoption of fixed surnames by different descendants. A lineage that has been resident within the British Isles for 3000 years will differ significantly from a lineage that arrived only 800 years ago, in terms of its genetic diversity, its distribution, its frequency and the surnames borne by test takers. An individual who cannot document his ancestry beyond the late seventeenth century or later can therefore take a Y-DNA test to see if he matches individuals who do have a documented descent. If he matches on specific markers then he can confirm linkage to a Flemish elite and even identify from which branch of a family he descends.

> **Box 10.3. Flemish merchants in Scotland**
>
> Taskyno (Berwick, 1327), Lamberto Povlyn (Edinburgh, 1328), Beydyno Wlf and Lancio de Castro (Inverkeithing, 1328), Clays Onterlotis (Perth, 1328), Clays de Tore (Berwick, 1329), Johanni Raynerson and Johanni de Hayel (1329), Johannis Wolcopper (1329), Petri Machenarum and Petri Dafhalle (Berwick, 1331), Cristiano Clerico (1343), Petro Buste (1360), Ade Metten Eye (1361, 1362, 1364), Pauli Metten Eye (1361), Jacobo Paulo Meteney (1366), Johanni Pres (1364), Johanni Ondcorne (1364), Dionisi de Munt (1367)
>
> *Source:* Exchequer Rolls of Scotland

some names may have adapted over time. The name Ondcorne, for example, may have become Oldcorn, a name still recognisable today. Flemish as well as other non-Scottish surnames were often changed over time to ones that rolled more easily off the Scottish tongue. The Belgian town of Liege (in French) is Luik (in Flemish) and this could well have become a locational surname which, in turn, was adapted to become Luke.

The Surname Fleming

The surname Fleming is just one of a number of names that Flemish people either brought to Britain or adopted later when they had settled in the country. However, Flemish people without the surname Fleming were likely much more numerous than those with it. Nonetheless, the name Fleming itself is of special interest to us because it indicates the nationality of its original bearers, i.e., natives of Flanders. The *Oxford English Dictionary* dates the earliest example of the noun Fleming to c.1430, but as a by-name, in the form of the Latin *Flandrensis* ('of Flanders') and the Anglo-Norman *Le Fleming* (from the Old French *flamenc*), it occurs much earlier. As a hereditary surname it is in use in Scotland by the late thirteenth century.

   The sixty Flemish knights who joined William the Conqueror's army in 1066 were often identified by these Latin and French by-names, presumably given to them in Normandy as they would have been meaningless in Flanders. The first people to adopt the surname Fleming in Britain appear to have been the twelfth-century grandsons of Erkenbald Flandrensis from Rouen in Normandy, a companion of William's who was given extensive lands in Cornwall and Devon. While some genealogists have argued that most people with the surname Fleming are descendants of Erkenbald, this does not bear serious scrutiny. Rather the evidence indicates that a number of the early Flemish settlers — both knights carrying the by-name *le Fleming* and later migrants of lower social status — took the Fleming surname that subsequently became hereditary. This is supported by DNA evidence that demonstrates the multiple genetic origins of people bearing the surname Fleming. Although the results are still preliminary, the evidence indicates that little or no matching Y-DNA (DNA that is carried through the male line in a family) among those who have tested (see Box 10.2).

This would support the view that the Fleming surname has multiple origins in perhaps several dozen different progenitors. These would include the twelfth-century knights and their descendants who took the name of Fleming, but were otherwise unrelated, and later migrants who adopted the name but were again unrelated to any other people with the name Fleming. Interestingly, genetic evidence also suggests that some lineages now bearing the surname Fleming were resident in Scotland (or Britain more generally) about 800 years ago — in other words, earlier than the earliest migrations of individuals from Flanders. The descendants of these early Scots may have adopted the name Fleming as they resided and worked on the land of a landowner named Fleming. They may also have adopted the name as an occupational surname while working on the specialised weaving equipment developed in Flanders and known as the 'Fleming loom'.

Non-elite immigrants included servants in noble households and skilled workmen such as weavers, traders and merchants. A major research project on 'England's Immigrants, 1330–1550' (www.englandsimmigrants.com) has compiled a database of over 64,000 names of people known to have migrated to England between 1330 and 1550. Of the 21,538 people for whom a place of origin was recorded, 1,178 came from Flanders (5.5%). Of these, the main occupations that were recorded were servant (237), shoemaker/souter (20/20), tailor (26) and weaver (20). There are 264 people with the surname Fleming, more than 20% of the total number from Flanders, indicating that they, or an ancestor, had adopted the surname rather than it being inherited from a single person. The recorded occupations of those with the surname Fleming were servant (50), labourer (5), corviser (2), husbandman (2) and pattenmaker (2). The large number of servants bearing the name may indicate that these were people who had taken the surname Fleming from their master.

The database of the 'People of Medieval Scotland, 1093–1371' research project (www.poms.ac.uk) records fifty-seven people with the surname Fleming between 1140 and 1314. These include Mainard the Fleming, grieve of St Andrews (c.1150); Everard Fleming who owned property in Perth (c.1198); Berewald Fleming, his son John and grandson Walter, who established their family in Moray in the late twelfth century and adopted the locational name Innes (see Chapter 3); Michael Fleming, sheriff of Edinburgh and clerk to Kings William I and Alexander II; William Fleming, burgess of Dumbarton (c.1272); and Malcolm Fleming, made Earl of Wigtown in 1341 (whose family history is traced in detail in Chapter 12 below). The mix of landholders and burgesses reflects the nature of the Flemish migrant population detailed in previous chapters: land-hungry members of the social elite and merchants and craftsmen with highly exportable skills.

Fleming Place-names

The name Fleming can also be found in a number of place-names in different parts of Scotland. In some, but not all such instances, the place-name signifies where a settlement of Flemish people may have occurred. In technical language, the proper name by which a people or ethnic group is know is an *ethnonym*, and an ethnonym is sometimes found in place-names designating genuine settlements of ethnic groups as opposed to place-names that derive from a single individual bearing the same name. In other words, the term Fleming in a place-name may indicate a Flemish settlement (a genuine ethnonym) or may simply be based on a local landowner with the surname Fleming. Distinguishing between the two is extremely difficult. Only two current Scottish place-names can be said, with any degree of confidence, to have an ethnic origin: Flemington in Ayton parish in the former Berwickshire, and Flemyland in Dalry, Ayrshire. Three others, no longer in existence but identified on Map 10.1, might well also count as ethnic: Fleming-Beath in Beath, Fife; Flemingis-land in Kettins, Angus; and Flemingtoun in Roxburghshire. In the former Cumberland, just south of the border with England, there are three more possible ethnonyms: Flimby and Flamiggs near Cockermouth, and Fleming Hall near Gosforth.

All of these place-names are designated as 'probable' ethnonyms on Map 10.1, but there are a number of others that rank as 'possibles'. These include Fleminghill in Kilmarnock parish, Ayrshire, and five of the places called Flemington, in Aberlemno in Angus, Petty in Inverness-shire, Cambuslang and Dalziel in Lanarkshire, and Newlands in Peeblesshire. Likewise, the former settlement of Fleemington in Lochwinnoch, Renfrewshire, Towart-Fleming (now Toward Taynuilt) in the parish of Dunoon and Kilmun, Argyll, fall into this category. Finally, crossing the border into England, the inlet Fleming Halse near Carlisle in Cumberland is also a 'possible'.

Map 10.1. Flemish ethnicity in place names.

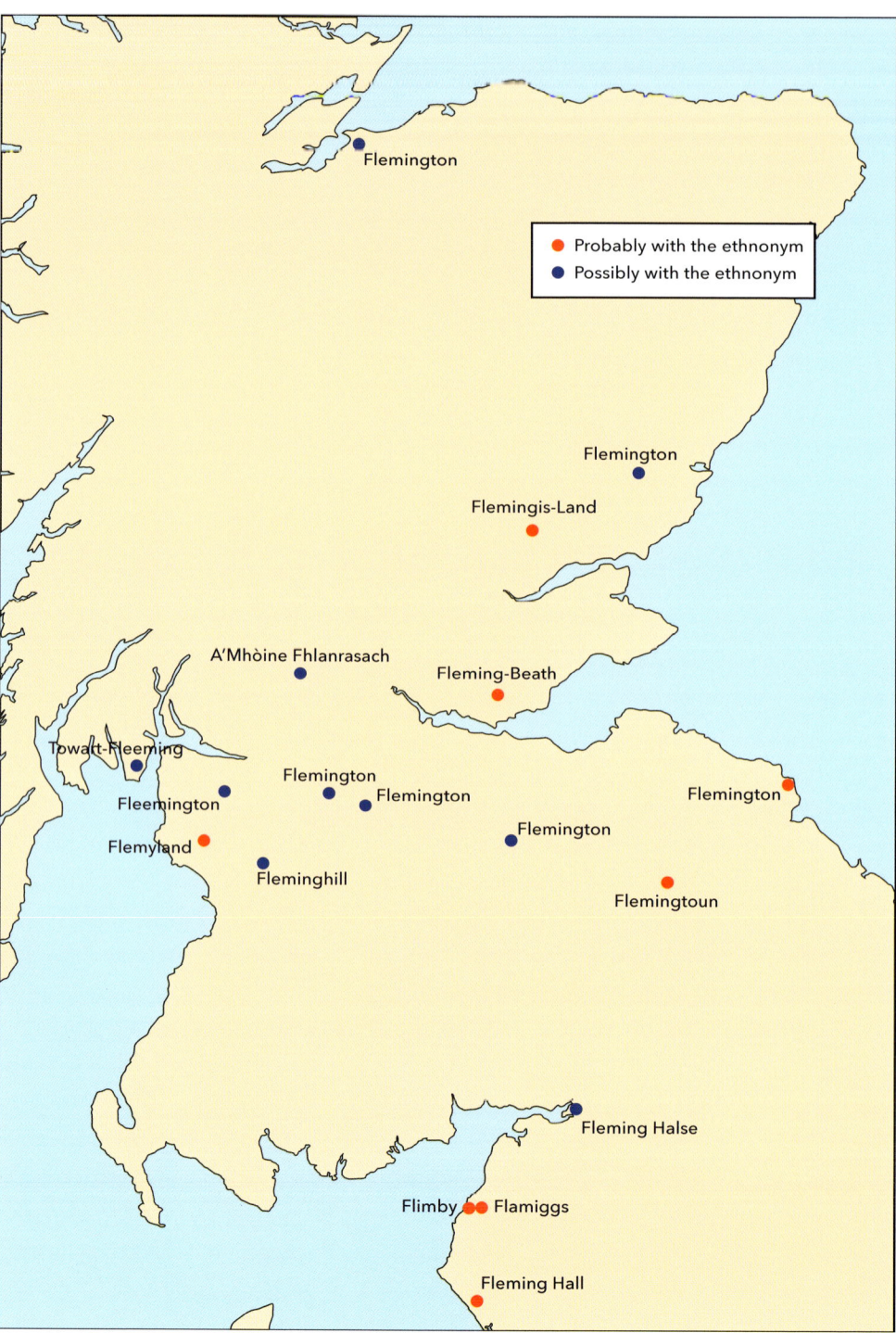

Identifying Flemish Origin Families in Scotland

There are two books that contain a wealth of information on Scottish families with possible Flemish roots. The earliest is George Black's seminal work, *The Surnames of Scotland: Their Origin, Meaning and History* (1946). While not specifically concerned with Flemish origin families, he identified some fifteen surnames with possible Flemish roots. These are set out in column 1 of Table 10.1. Column 2 lists a wider range of names based on Beryl Platts' *Scottish Hazard: The Flemish Nobility and their Impact on Scotland* (1985). Her focus was exclusively on the elite and, primarily using heraldic evidence, she identified a wide range of Scottish families whose coats of arms and other heraldic devices were similar to those common in Flanders. While an important contribution to raising awareness

Table 10.1. Families found in Scotland with possible Flemish roots.

George Black	Beryl Platts	Additional sources	
Blaw	Abernethy	Aide	Henman
Bonar	Anstruther	Armstrong	Holm
Cant	Baird	Air	Houbron
Clink	Balliol	Ayres	Junker
Crawfurd	Boswell	Bailey	Justice
Crab	Brodie	Bart	Kemp
Douglas	Bruce	Beal	Kessen
Fleming	Cameron	Beaton	Kettle
Frisken	Campbell	Bell	Luke
Harrower	Comyn	Bennie	Morran
Innes	Crawfurd	Beveridge	Mortimer
Leslie	Douglas	Binning	Mutch
Murray	Erskine	Bishop	Peacock
Mustard	Fleming	Clemmet	Petrie
Younger	Fraser	Clow	Plenderleith
	Graham	Cornelius	Prain
	Hamilton	Cousin	Pundler
	Hay	Cox	Roche
	Innes	Danks	Roy
	Leith	Dewar	Rutherford
	Leslie	Dowie	Smout
	Lindsay	Enzell	Spalding
	Lochore	Erskine	Stein
	Montgomerie	Flockhart	Sturman
	Murray	Frame	Sutherland
	Oliphant	Frizall	Swankie
	Seton	Furlong	Vermont
	Stewart	Gentleman	Waddell
	Stirling	Grote	Wingate
		Hally	Woodall
		Hazel	Wyles

of the place of Flemish families in medieval Scotland, the validity of her approach has been questioned by historians and doubt hangs over some of her conclusions.

In addition to these sources, the 'Scotland and the Flemish People' project (www. flemish.wp.st-andrews.ac.uk/) garnered a range of miscellaneous information on possible Flemish origin families that was published as blogs over its five year life span. Some of this remains speculative, but the names have been included nonetheless in column 3 of Table 10.1. In principle, where conventional historical research proves inconclusive, it should be possible to use DNA analysis to test each name against a control group of people from Flanders in order to validate a Flemish root. However, as outlined in Chapter 1, the fluidity of the borders of Flanders, the mobility of the peoples who inhabited it over time, and the extinction of male lines make it difficult in practice to identify a control group of men with deep origins there. Improved sampling of male lines in Flanders and DNA from archaeological samples (Ancient DNA) will to some extent ameliorate this.

There are some families — Sutherland and Murray for instance — that have well attested family trees that go back to Flanders and there can be high degree of confidence that they, and the Fleming family itself, have Flemish roots. Other families such as the Douglases that can find a close DNA match with a male from one of these three families can also claim a Flemish origin.

GE/AM/AF/PM

11

Scotticisation

Previous chapters have touched on the rapidity with which the Flemish migrants to Scotland became assimilated into the economic, social and cultural fabric of their host country. It is also worth noting that there is little evidence to suggest that the incomers were met with widespread hostility. As we saw in Chapter 3, unlike the Norman Conquest of England, the process by which Flemish and other settlers 'colonised' Scotland did not involve the wholesale appropriation of lands belonging to the indigenous population. It was a much more gradual process extending well over a century and marked more by peaceful integration and absorption than by tension and conflict. This chapter examines these processes in more detail. Inevitably, because of the nature of the surviving evidence, we know more about the ways in which elite Flemish individuals and families became part of a wider Scottish noble class. However, some attempt can be made to comment on the ways in which Flemish people were absorbed into the early burgh communities and how their later compatriots — sometimes religious refugees — were received in Scotland.

The coming of the Flemish elite to Scotland was linked to parallel changes in Wales and Ireland in the century after the Norman Conquest of England. In these lands too, colonisation, urbanisation, radical changes in Christian worship and political change, were the hallmarks of what was an era of revolutionary transformation. In Wales and Ireland, as in Scotland, populations from the Low Countries, which contemporaries often lumped together under the label 'Flemings', formed an identifiable group within the French and Germanic-speaking settlers in Britain. In the twelfth century these new Flemish populations existed in such numbers, local concentrations or distinctiveness as to receive special notice as a separate group within eastern Ireland, south-west Wales — where, as we have seen, Pembrokeshire was regarded as a Flemish colony — and of course Scotland.

However, by the opening decades of the thirteenth century, this separate Flemish identity had disappeared in Scotland and elsewhere in Britain. Instead they had become assimilated into wider populations and social groups. Where they can be identified by their lines of descent or by the use of names — most obviously *Flandrensis* or Fleming, which linked them to a family origin in the Low Countries — the records convey no sense that they were members of a defined ethnic or linguistic group, different from other inhabitants of their region or the land. In effect, as we saw in the previous chapter, these terms were developing into surnames without necessarily retaining any ethnic or linguistic distinctiveness. The process by which this Flemish identity became blurred and lost significance was, however, fundamentally different in Scotland compared to the other lands of these islands. In Ireland, Wales and, indeed, England, people whose families had originally come from the Low Countries were incorporated into a single Anglo-French colonial society. In south Wales, Rees Davies calculates that a distinct Flemish identity did not survive more than four generations and by the early thirteenth century they were 'fully Anglicised' in language and custom. In Ireland, the change may have been quicker. Those colonists of Flemish origins were regarded as English in legal terms, enjoying the benefits of this status relative to the Gaelic Irish.

Davies has described this as part of 'the Anglicisation of the British Isles', but recent work by Dauvit Broun and Matthew Hammond has demonstrated that such terminology is unhelpful for the understanding of twelfth- and thirteenth-century Scotland. The period after 1150 saw the erosion of references to distinct 'nations' or peoples within the kingdom. For example, royal charters ceased addressing the inhabitants of the kingdom as English, French and Scots and spoke instead of all the king's 'good men'. However, unlike Wales and Ireland, those of Flemish descent were not absorbed into an Anglicised or Anglo-French community which was geographically, legally and politically distinguished from (and set in opposition to) a native population. Instead of remaining part of a 'colonial' society, Scotland's Flemish incomers were assimilated into a Scottish community that was not internally defined according to ethnic origin or linguistic practice. Amongst the aristocratic class, Broun and Hammond identify this as the result of Scotland's kings both fostering and intervening forcefully to impose a single aristocratic elite in their lands.

By the early thirteenth century the Scottish nobility was a group defined by intermarriage, shared cultural values and a common loyalty to the king, rather than by labels of 'native' or 'Anglo-French'. Parallel changes in urban populations are more speculative but equally important. In Wales and Ireland, boroughs remained centres of English population and legal superiority. As a result, they were regarded with hostility by native populations throughout the medieval period. In Scotland, initial ethnic distinctions seem to have broken down rapidly. North of the Forth, interactions between English-speaking burgesses and local Gaelic-speaking populations broke down, rather than entrenched, distinctions based on initial differences of ethnicity and language. Scots could clearly gain access to the urban community in a way denied the Welsh and Irish. As part of this relative fluidity, burgesses of Flemish origin merged into a single burgh population. The famous reference to the Flemings of Berwick dying in defence of their Red Hall during Edward I's storming of the burgh in 1296 refers not to a distinct and permanent Flemish community within the urban landscape. Rather the Hall, like the Germans' White Hall, was the local residence for merchants based in their home country who were on trading ventures in Scotland.

How far is it possible to trace this process of assimilation? Without being able to enter the heads of the descendants of Flemish settlers, it is hard to gauge how they identified with either their ancestral or current homes. However, there is some tentative evidence that can be put forward with regard to those noble families whose naming practices were examined in Chapter 10. As we saw there, the twelfth and early thirteenth centuries was a formative era for the naming of families amongst Anglo-French lineages. Many of the Flemish (and other) nobles who acquired estates in Scotland during the twelfth century found it natural to identify themselves and their offspring with the name of their new holdings. The Biggar and Crawford families in Lanarkshire indicate this practice as, more tellingly, does the choice made by William son of Erkenbald (or Arkenbald) to adopt his territorial designation as Lord of Douglas as a surname. By just after 1200 William's numerous sons were all being referred to as 'de Douglas'. The Douglas surname — which points to an identity with a lordship in Lanarkshire — suggests a family identity based solely on their position in Scotland.

Most of the first William Douglas's younger sons pursued careers, not in Clydesdale, but in the north of Scotland. This migration followed the election of Bricius de Douglas as bishop of Moray in 1203. It brought the Douglases who served in the church of Moray and, in the case of Alexander Douglas, as sheriff of Elgin, into close association with their kinsmen there who were descended from Freskin the Flemish lord of Duffus. This conjunction throws into relief a different approach to naming. In the opening twenty years of the thirteenth century, the current lord of Duffus was named in charters as William son of William *Freskyny*. His cousin who held lands in Sutherland was named Hugh *Fresekin* in a royal charter of c.1211–1214. These lords seemed to be developing a surname derived from the personal name of a common and pivotal ancestor. However, by the late 1220s this naming approach had changed. In 1226 the new lord of Duffus,

William's son, was naming himself in a charter as Walter *de Moravia* and applying the same name to his dead father. *De Moravia*, Anglicised to Murray, became the name by which the family was subsequently known. At about the same time, Hugo Freskin's son, William, issued a charter that referred to him as lord of Sutherland rather than using any link to Freskin. His descendants would instead use Sutherland as their surname.

What do such choices tell us? They probably indicate the recognised value of adopting a family name which provided clear identification with one principal lordship or region and which fostered a sense of shared kinship. They served, whether deliberately or not, to Scotticise these lineages, removing any evidence of origins beyond the kingdom. It created a sense of a single aristocratic elite if descendants of incomers like *de Douglas*, *de Moravia* and *de Biggar*, could stand alongside native lords such as *de Strathbogie*, *de Mar* and *de Dunbar* without any sense of ethnic difference. This should make us think about those individuals who continued to use Fleming, *Flandrensis*, as their names. The adoption of this surname may result from personal choice that reflected a conservative desire to retain a sense of geographical origins. It could also indicate families or individuals who had arrived in Scotland at the very end of the twelfth century and were less integrated into their new home. Alternatively, it might have been used by families that, unlike the Douglases and Murrays, lacked a sufficiently defined geographical focus to their lands to provide a surname based on Scottish landholdings.

While it should caution us against drawing simple conclusions, it is in fact hard to see any sense of difference between those named as Fleming and their peers in later thirteenth century Scotland. Like Inglis or Wallace, originally signifying English and Welsh identity respectively, the name seems to have lost any ethnic significance.

For the Murrays, who chose a name reflecting identification, not with a single fief, but with a whole province, the change of name may have represented an assertion of leadership across a wide area. William Sutherland may initially have been making a similar point. His father had been granted Skelbo and other estates in Sutherland, but, as mentioned above, it was William who adopted the title of lord of Sutherland in the 1220s. During the next decade this standing was heightened by King Alexander II's elevation of William to the rank of earl. The earls possessed a special status in thirteenth-century Scotland as the only group of the nobility to hold a title which distinguished them formally from the wider baronage. The creation of William as Earl of Sutherland followed that of Fearchar as Earl of Ross. While Fearchar seems to have been a member of a local lineage, bearing a Gaelic name, William's ancestry was very different. His promotion to the ranks of the earls, often regarded as a group of provincial rulers whose history was entwined with that of the Scottish kingdom, demonstrated that concerns of ethnicity were meaningless to Alexander II. Instead what shaped his choices of Fearchar

Box 11.1. The 'Good' Sir James Douglas

While the Douglases had established themselves in Scotland in the late twelfth century, it was during the first War of Independence (1296–1328) that the foundations of the family's subsequent prominence in Scottish aristocratic society were laid. This was largely due to Sir James Douglas (c.1286–1330) who, following Robert Bruce's seizure of the throne in 1306, joined the embattled king in the guerrilla campaigns waged against the English king and his Scottish supporters, quickly becoming his right-hand man. His military exploits and loyalty to King Robert became the stuff of legend and Sir James emerged as a key figure in John Barbour's epic poem, *The Brus*, written in vernacular Scots in the 1380s. Both Barbour and other near contemporary accounts tell of how, on Robert's death in 1328, Sir James fulfilled the king's dying wishes by embarking on a pilgrimage to the Holy Land carrying his heart in a silver casket. Sir James never reached his intended destination, the Holy Sepulchre in Jerusalem, but was killed fighting Muslims in Spain in 1330. Nonetheless, his heroism earned him the soubriquet 'the Good', while his loyalty to King Robert earned him and his family extensive land-holdings, many of them once belonging to the king's enemies, the Comyn and Balliol families.

RM

and William as earls over provinces which were far from the king's normal residences, and had been sources of hostility to royal government, were the ability and resources of these nobles to control outlying regions of the kingdom.

Names and titles indicate the absorption of lordly dynasties of Flemish descent into the Scottish aristocratic melting pot. Two or three generations seem to have been sufficient to turn families like the Douglases, Murrays and Sutherlands into Scottish lords. The agreement in 1250 for the marriage between the son of William (II) Lord of Douglas to the sister of Hugh Abernethy, a junior branch of the family of the earl of Fife, and of clear native stock, shows shared legal and cultural expectations in the alliance. Such a match had lost any meaning in terms of social or cultural assimilation, but represented just another amongst multiple bonds linking different families within the Scottish aristocratic world. Events from the 1290s onwards, when the Wars of Independence tested the strength of aristocratic identification with a separate, sovereign Scottish realm, equally revealed no ethnic distinction in support for Scotland's status. The two Andrew Murrays, father and son, Malcolm Fleming the guardian of the young King David Bruce, and the 'Good' Sir James Douglas and many of his name would reflect the identification of these families of Flemish ancestry with the Scottish kingdom.

As for the skilled workers who came to Scotland in later centuries, it is probable that they too were quickly absorbed into local society. Fewer in number and arriving still more gradually than the knightly class, they appear to have been assimilated into burgh society with relative ease. As we saw in Chapter 4, many were recognised for the special skills they brought with them, becoming burgesses and occupying leadership positions in commerce, politics and the church. Likewise, in the late sixteenth century, the Flemish refugees who had fled religious persecution in their homeland and who were encouraged to bring their skills to Scotland, appear to have settled into the burgh communities without difficulty or hostility. Sharing the same Protestant faith as their host communities, locals and emigrés both lived and worshipped as a single community.

MB

12

The Fleming Family: A Case Study

In the last decade of the thirteenth century the male line of the Flemish family which had started with Baldwin of Biggar's settlement in Clydesdale approximately 150 years earlier came to an end when Sir Nicholas of Biggar died leaving a widow and two daughters as his heirs. We cannot say with certainty what immediately followed but it seems that a member of another family, possibly also with Flemish roots, married one of the daughters and, in doing so, acquired the Biggar lands. That family carried the name *Fleming*. This chapter offers an account of the fluctuating fortunes of this Fleming family over the next five centuries, from the Wars of Independence, when their allegiance to the Bruce dynasty was rewarded by elevation to the earldom of Wigtown, to the time of the Jacobites, when the death of Charles, twelfth Lord Fleming and seventh Earl of Wigtown, brought the line to an end. It is a case study of adaptation and survival that shows how the Fleming surname came to be interwoven with the history of Scotland.

'Let the Deed Shaw': The Flemings and the Earldom of Wigtown, 1306–1382

A portrait of a man in armour holding a gory head in his hand with the words 'Let the Deed Shaw' is reported to have been in the Fleming family home at Cumbernauld until 1845. The painting appears no longer to exist but the central figure in it was reputed to be Sir Robert Fleming, companion to Robert Bruce, and the severed head to be that of the Red Comyn, murdered by Bruce in Greyfriars Church, Dumfries, on 10 February 1306. Fleming tradition contends that after Bruce stabbed Comyn he told his companions waiting outside: 'I doubt I have slain Comyn'. One of these companions, Roger Kirkpatrick, allegedly responded: 'Doubt? then I'll mak siccar', and with that he entered the church to ensure the Red Comyn was dead. Kirkpatrick was accompanied by Robert Fleming who supposedly hacked off Comyn's head before holding it aloft, shouting: 'Let the Deed Shaw'. This became the Fleming family motto.

Fact and fiction come together in this version of events. All the fourteenth- and early fifteenth-century chronicles agree that Comyn suffered a two-stage death, but none of them specifically names Fleming as being present or validate the claim that Comyn's head was severed from his body. Yes, Fleming may well have been one of the unnamed supporters of Bruce present at Greyfriars, but equally it might have been a later fabrication designed to cement Fleming's place in history as a committed Bruce supporter.

We know very little about this Sir Robert Fleming. Nineteenth-century genealogists would have us believe that he was rewarded for his support of Bruce with lands previously held by Comyn in Lenzie within the barony of Kirkintilloch, and that he was the father of Malcolm Fleming, the first Earl of Wigtown. Unfortunately, as with the nature of Sir Robert's support for Bruce and the timing of his death, there are no existing records to substantiate this. A further mystery, as Table 12.1 indicates, is how the Fleming family also acquired the barony of Biggar around this time.

Sir Robert probably died closer in time to Bruce's coronation in 1306 than the battle of Bannockburn in 1314, and the main beneficiary of Bruce's largesse was probably not Robert Fleming himself but his eldest son Malcolm. His fortunes were very much tied to those of the two Bruce kings, Robert I and his son David II, and by the time Robert I died in 1329 Malcolm was a substantial baron, his lands extending beyond Kirkintilloch to properties in the Lennox, Carrick and Wigtownshire, and his responsibilities to those of keeper of Dumbarton Castle and sheriff of Dunbartonshire. As steward of the royal household, his status was enhanced further by his proximity to the king. Following Robert's death, Malcolm's role within the royal household continued and he was considered a 'foster-father' figure to David who was only five when his father died. Greater rewards and responsibilities were eventually to come Malcolm's way as a result of this relationship.

David II's reign had a troubled beginning as Edward Balliol pressed his claim to the throne on the grounds that he was the son of John Balliol, the Scottish king deposed in 1296. Edward had himself crowned at Scone in September 1332 and had the support of the English king Edward III. Ten months later, David's prospects deteriorated further when Edward inflicted a heavy defeat on the Scots at Halidon Hill; Malcolm Fleming was one of the few fortunate to escape with his life. Malcolm then returned to Dumbarton Castle where he provided a safe haven for the young king and his wife until May 1334 when it was decided to send them both to France for their own safety.

Table 12.1. The Fleming family, 1306–1382.

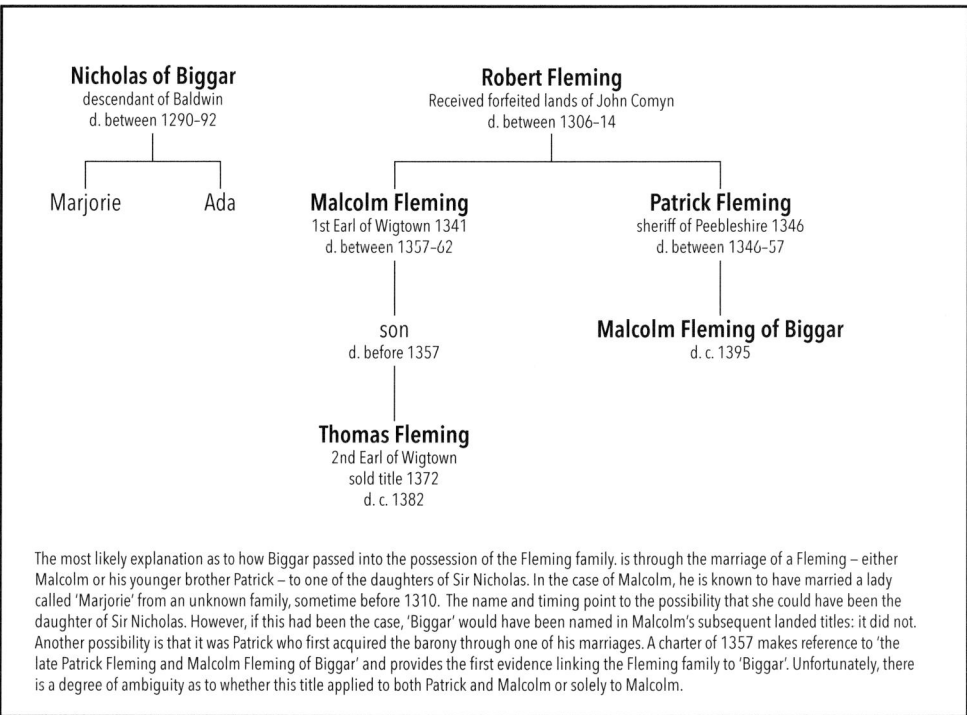

The most likely explanation as to how Biggar passed into the possession of the Fleming family. is through the marriage of a Fleming – either Malcolm or his younger brother Patrick – to one of the daughters of Sir Nicholas. In the case of Malcolm, he is known to have married a lady called 'Marjorie' from an unknown family, sometime before 1310. The name and timing point to the possibility that she could have been the daughter of Sir Nicholas. However, if this had been the case, 'Biggar' would have been named in Malcolm's subsequent landed titles: it did not. Another possibility is that it was Patrick who first acquired the barony through one of his marriages. A charter of 1357 makes reference to 'the late Patrick Fleming and Malcolm Fleming of Biggar' and provides the first evidence linking the Fleming family to 'Biggar'. Unfortunately, there is a degree of ambiguity as to whether this title applied to both Patrick and Malcolm or solely to Malcolm.

Seven years passed before the seventeen-year-old David returned to Scotland in May 1341. He immediately rewarded Malcolm for his loyalty and military abilities with the hereditary earldom of Wigtown. It was an area which had formerly given support to the Balliols, and even after Bannockburn had retained a degree of independence. The young king hoped Malcolm would bring this potentially troublesome south-west region under control.

There is no doubt that Malcolm Fleming was very much part of the king's inner circle and enjoyed David's confidence, but a heavy Scottish defeat by the English in 1346 at Neville's Cross in Durham resulted in both men being taken prisoner. The king was taken to London while a wounded or ill Malcolm was held in Northumberland until he was sufficiently well to be transferred south. That did not happen. A few months later, and much to the annoyance of Edward III, Malcolm escaped after having successfully bribed one of his captors.

Unfortunately for Malcolm, the following ten years were as unkind to him as the previous twenty-five had been rewarding. He no longer had the ability to impose himself as a military leader, possibly owing to wounds sustained in battle, illness or, quite simply, the ageing process. A consequence of this was that he lost control of his south-west territories in Galloway and Carrick to Balliol supporters.

Malcolm also paid the price for remaining firmly allied to David over the ransom terms for the king's release. This brought him into conflict with Robert Stewart, the king's nephew and heir, whose immediate interests as Governor of Scotland seemed best served by prolonging the king's stay in England. At one stage, a frustrated David proposed a succession-release plan based on a younger son of Edward III being named as heir instead of Robert, and Malcolm supported this when Parliament discussed it in 1351. In this Malcolm was very much in the minority and his stance only served to alienate him further from the increasingly powerful Robert Stewart.

Within two years Malcolm suffered the consequences when Robert removed him from the keepership of Dumbarton Castle. This in turn contributed to a drop in income and it became clear during the last years of Malcolm's life that, in addition to being sidelined by Robert Stewart, he was beginning to experience some financial problems. His death most likely occurred within three to four months of David's return to Scotland in September 1357 and certainly no later than 1362; he was succeeded by his grandson Thomas, one of the hostages held at Northumberland as part of David's ransom.

The exact date of Thomas's release is unknown, but it is thought to have been about 1366 by which time the title had been vacant for at least four years. It was clear to David that Thomas was not the man to provide the sort of political and military leadership his grandfather had once done so successfully. It may have been that Thomas suffered from some disability and was physically unfit to do so, and, for that reason, when David granted the restored earldom of Wigtown to Thomas in 1367, he did not include the critically important regality powers previously associated with the title: without them, Thomas was earl in name only.

The unexpected death of David II in February 1371 and the succession of Robert Stewart as Robert II did nothing to improve Thomas's position. Twelve months later he decided to extricate himself from Wigtownshire and sell the earldom for £500 to Archibald, third Earl of Douglas, otherwise known as Archibald the Grim. However, while Robert was not in a sufficiently strong position to challenge Archibald over this questionable transaction, he did withhold the title of earl.

The sale of the earldom completed the Fleming family's fall from the highest echelons of noble society to its minor ranks within the space of thirty-one years. For Thomas, his actions did not resolve his financial problems. By the time he died ten years later he seemed only to have retained Fulwood, north of Stewarton in Renfrewshire, the other estates having been sold to ease his financial difficulties. During this period of steep decline, it fell to Sir Malcolm Fleming of Biggar, a nephew of the first Earl of Wigtown, to recover what he could of them.

Feuds, Forfeiture, and Good Fortune, 1382–1542

Sir Malcolm concentrated his efforts on recovering possession of the Fleming lands in the barony of Lenzie and by 1382 was largely successful in achieving this. He was also appointed keeper of Dumbarton Castle by David II from 1364 until 1369 and subsequently, during the reign of Robert II, held the same position at Edinburgh Castle from 1374 until 1388.

At the same time, his son Sir David Fleming became a close ally of Robert II's son and heir, the Earl of Carrick. By 1384 the earl had built up a sufficiently strong power base to oust his elderly father from power and make himself guardian. How willing a participant the king had been in this new arrangement is unclear; there is evidence to suggest that it amounted to a palace coup in which Sir David Fleming played an active part by giving his support to Carrick. Whatever the circumstances, the measures taken to sideline Robert II met with the approval of the General Council when it convened in November 1384.

Eventually, in 1390, Carrick succeeded to the throne as Robert III, but endured a troublesome reign, often brought on by his own physical frailty. When unable to carry out his duties, his ambitious brother, the Duke of Albany, frequently acted as guardian-lieutenant. However, in 1402, the king felt able to resume his personal rule and elevated Sir David to a position of influence at the heart of government, along with Henry, Earl of Orkney and Lord of Roslin, and Henry Wardlaw, Bishop of St Andrews. Fleming was to take on the role of diplomatic envoy and negotiate hostage terms for the nobles taken prisoner by the English after the defeat of the Scots at Humbleton in September 1402, including Archibald, fourth Earl of Douglas. He also acted as one of the guardians for Robert's heir, James.

Fleming met with some early success after negotiating an eleven-month truce with the English king Henry IV. Almost immediately Robert III rewarded him with a grant of lands in the earldom of Carrick. But trouble was not far away. An English rebellion against Henry IV, led by Henry Percy, Earl of Northumberland, and Lord Thomas Bardolph, was supported by Fleming. When it failed, both Percy and Bardolph were granted refuge in Scotland under the care of Fleming and Orkney. For a less scrupulous man this would have provided an ideal bargaining tool: the return of Archibald, fourth Earl of Douglas, in exchange for Percy and Bardolph. Fleming,

Table 12.2. The Fleming family, 1382–1524.

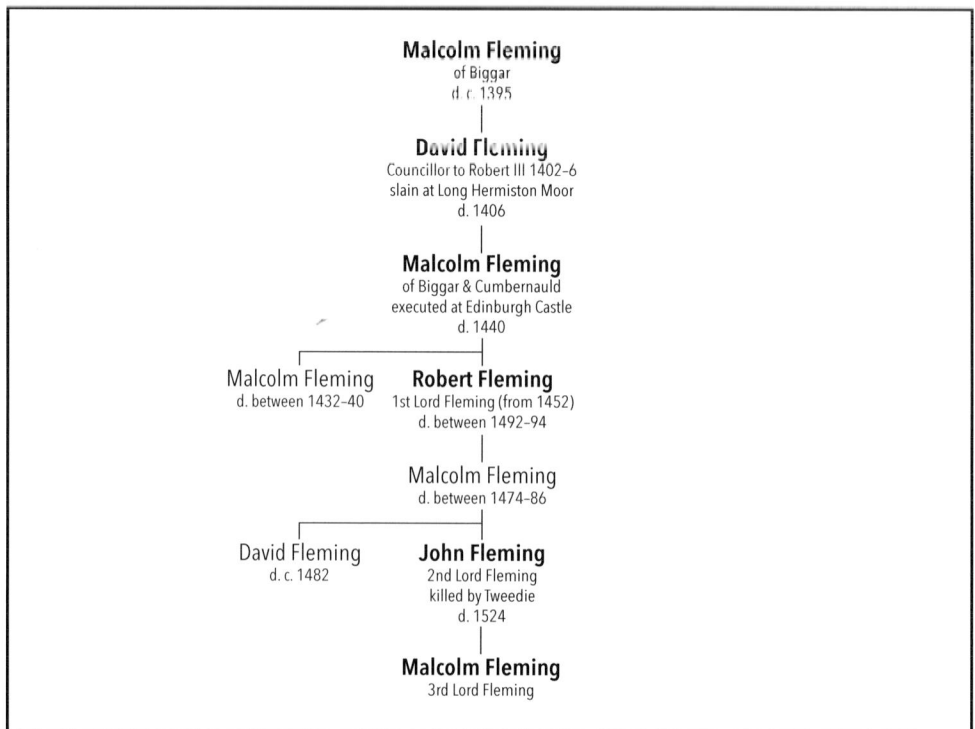

however, decided to allow them to take refuge in Wales to spare them execution at Henry IV's hands.

This may well have been the last straw for James Douglas of Balvenie, brother of the hostage, Earl of Douglas. In addition to Fleming's failure to secure his brother's release, James must have been alarmed by the king's decision to grant Fleming the lands and barony of Cavers in Roxburgh, an area considered to be the preserve of the Douglas family, and also by Fleming's appointment as sheriff of Roxburgh. An unexpected opportunity to reassert Douglas authority presented itself on 14 February 1406.

In a risky plan designed to promote the authority of Prince James, the twelve-year-old son of Robert III and heir to the throne, Fleming and Orkney headed off into the heartland of Douglas territory with James as their figurehead. The response from James Douglas and his supporters was to leave Edinburgh in pursuit of them. At Long Hermiston Moor the two sides met and Sir David Fleming was killed after some heavy fighting. Orkney managed to take the heir to the throne to the Bass Rock in the Firth of Forth where they remained until rescuers arrived by ship. Unfortunately, as they headed for safety in France they were intercepted by English pirates with the result that James became a prisoner of Henry IV for the next eighteen years. Following these grave misfortunes in which David Fleming, the king's closest counsellor, had died, and James, the king's son and heir, had been taken prisoner, the unhappy king himself passed away in April 1406.

It was not until 1424 that James I returned to Scotland, but his personal rule was dramatically cut short by his assassination in 1437 and the accession of his young son, James II. In another development, the powerful fifth Earl of Douglas died in 1439 and was succeeded by his son William, a precocious teenager who had turned to Malcolm Fleming, David's son and successor, for guidance and support. Both these developments were to come together in what became known as the 'Black Dinner'.

This took place on 24 November 1440 when James II was aged only nine and held under the care of Alexander Livingston, keeper of Stirling Castle, and Sir William Crichton, Lord Chancellor and custodian of Edinburgh Castle. An invitation to attend a banquet at Edinburgh Castle was enthusiastically accepted by William Douglas who brought with him his younger brother, David, and also Malcolm Fleming. Tradition has it that during the meal a bull's head was placed on the table, a sign that the guests were to be executed and, on the orders of Crichton, the Earl of Douglas and his brother were taken outside and beheaded. Malcolm, possibly because he was a witness to this event, suffered the same fate days later, but with one significant difference, whereas Fleming's lands were forfeited, Douglas's were not.

It became clear that the man pulling Crichton's strings was James Douglas of Balvenie, the grand-uncle of the executed Douglas boys who now inherited the earldom from his grand-nephews and was the sole beneficiary of Crichton's actions. This was the same man who had slaughtered Malcolm's father in 1406 and now, due to his obese appearance, fully justified his other name 'James the Gross'.

Not surprisingly, Malcolm Fleming's son Robert was incandescent with rage about a judgement he rightly considered 'false and rotten'. He instigated legal proceedings to remove the charge of treason against his father and, most importantly, recover his forfeited lands. At Linlithgow Cross on 7 January 1441 he lodged his complaint, but the sheriff-depute decided the matter was outside his jurisdiction and should be presented to the justiciar for south of the Forth. Undeterred by the fact that the person who held this position was the Fleming family nemesis, James the Gross, now seventh Earl of Douglas, Robert's case was heard on 13 February. Not only was the new earl conciliatory in consenting to Robert recovering his father's forfeited lands, but he agreed to a marriage arrangement, not an uncommon practice in settling contemporary feuds, between Fleming and his third daughter, Janet.

Robert Fleming's fortunes were to be transformed further after James II came of age in 1449. In 1451 he granted Biggar a charter to hold weekly markets and annual fairs, allowing it to develop into a thriving market town. The following year Robert was one of seven barons created parliamentary peers by the king, the first Lord Fleming. This was part of James II's strategy to build up parliamentary support through patronage. While the title did not bring additional lands, it did formally recognise Robert's position as one of the more important barons, receiving summonses to Parliament that lesser barons or lairds did not receive.

Robert held his title for forty years, and managed to outlive both James II, fatally wounded during the siege of Roxburgh Castle in 1460, and James III, killed at Sauchieburn in 1488 during a rebellion against him. During the minority of James III, Robert faced some anxious times when Gilbert Lord Kennedy pursued the recovery of lands of Kirkintilloch in Fleming's barony of Lenzie. When the dispute was due to be heard at the justiciary court at Dumbarton on 15 April 1466, Fleming elected not to attend in person as he believed Kennedy was to be accompanied by a large number of armed supporters. The court ruled in Kennedy's favour. However, for reasons unknown, the lands – of more strategic than financial importance – were restored to Fleming shortly after.

Towards the end of his life the first Lord Fleming appeared unable to manage his affairs and a series of court actions were taken against him. When he eventually died sometime between 1492 and 1494, his eldest son having predeceased him, it was his grandson, John Fleming, who succeeded to the title.

The second Lord Fleming had the good fortune to avoid the catastrophic Scottish defeat at Flodden in 1513 where three bishops, eleven earls, fifteen lords and many thousands of ordinary people, perished along with their king, James IV. At the time Fleming was with the Scottish fleet on a diplomatic mission to France. The death of so many of Scotland's political elite combined with the beginning of a new royal minority – James V succeeded his father as a one-year old infant – provided opportunities for men of Fleming's status to come to the fore. He became a member of the Council; was made lord chamberlain; and acted as an envoy in negotiations with France.

His untimely death in 1524 came while he was out hawking with close family and friends in the border lands of Drumelzier, not far from Biggar. There he found himself unexpectedly confronted by a large assembly of men led by John Tweedie of Drumelzier. The feud between the Tweedies and the Flemings had its roots in the Tweedies' desire to secure the marriage of Catherine Frizzel, heiress of Fruid in Tweedsmuir, to James, the eldest son and heir of John Tweedie. But Catherine may already have been married to one of Fleming's illegitimate sons and perhaps it was this news that provoked John

Tweedie into brutally killing the second Lord Fleming and taking captive three of his party until Catherine was delivered to Drumelzier.

Such feuds were not uncommon for the time. In this case we know the immediate response of Malcolm, the new Lord Fleming, was to send Catherine to Drumelzier in order to secure the safe release of the three men. Malcolm then sought justice regarding the safe return of Catherine and the killing of his father. On neither account did he achieve immediate success despite offering in marriage one of his sisters as an alternative to Catherine.

The Tweedie dispute dragged on until 1530 when the Lords of Council met and ruled that John Tweedie should fund a chaplaincy in the church of Biggar to hold masses and pray for the soul of the murdered second Lord Fleming. While the marriage between Tweedie and Catherine was accepted, some of her land was to be transferred to Malcolm. In addition, John Tweedie and all the others guilty of Fleming's slaughter had to leave the country within three months and endure a period of exile. This outcome may appear relatively lenient by today's standards but in the sixteenth century the killing of a rival during a feud was not uncommon.

The Flemings and Mary Queen of Scots: 1542–1579

The last five years of Malcolm's life were nothing if not eventful. In 1542 he found himself one of several Scottish lords captured and escorted to the Tower of London when the Scots suffered defeat at the hands of an English army at the Battle of Solway Moss. James V died three weeks later from a fever, leaving the country to face an uncertain future as his heir, Mary Queen of Scots, was only six days old. It was a situation that provided an opportunity for the English king Henry VIII to use his hostages to good effect.

Three months later Malcolm was released on condition that he advanced the English king's marriage plans for his son Edward to wed the Scottish queen. This included the removal of Mary to England where she would be brought up at the English court. At first Fleming seemed an enthusiastic supporter of the marriage but, much to Henry's annoyance, later changed his mind and transferred his loyalties to the queen mother, Mary of Guise, who favoured a French marriage for her daughter.

Henry VIII's death in January 1547 did not put an end to England's 'Rough Wooing' of Scotland. Later that year, in September, the Scots suffered another disastrous defeat at the Battle of Pinkie – a defeat made worse for the Fleming family as Malcolm and two of his sons-in-law were amongst the many thousands of Scots to lose their lives.

However, there were some compensations. Malcolm's marriage to Lady Janet, the illegitimate daughter of James IV by his mistress the Countess of Bothwell, had helped to secure his position at James V's court, and did the same for five of his children at the court of Mary Queen of Scots following his death. Illegitimacy was no impediment to being welcomed into the royal household, and when it was decided in 1548 to send the infant Mary to France for safe-keeping, Janet Fleming was entrusted to accompany her as her governess. Her time in France was rudely cut short when in 1550 she scandalised the French court by unashamedly broadcasting she was expecting a child by the French king, Henry II, and was ordered to return to Scotland. But Lady Janet was well liked by the Scottish queen who welcomed her back to France ten years later with her illegitimate son Henry of Valois.

Lady Janet's own eldest son, James, fourth Lord Fleming, travelled to France on several occasions and in 1550, at the instigation of Mary of Guise, was part of a group feted with presents in what appeared to be an attempt to secure his allegiance to the French side. Some eight years later James returned as one of the commissioners sent to represent Scotland at the wedding of the fifteen-year-old Scottish queen to François, heir to the French throne. Tragically, like three others, James died in mysterious circumstances after the wedding celebrations. As always, rumours of foul play abounded, but a letter from Mary to her mother in Scotland suggested a virulent epidemic as the more likely cause. John, the younger brother of James, became the fifth Lord Fleming.

For the Scottish queen, her years in France were largely happy ones, partly due to the bond she developed with Lady Janet's youngest daughter, Mary Fleming, who was close in age. She became one of the queen's celebrated Four Maries, the others being Beaton, Seton and Livingston, who attended the queen as maids-in-waiting. Their lives were inextricably linked and when the queen's husband Francis died from an ear infection they returned with her to Scotland where she began her personal rule in August 1561.

In terms of language, religion and culture, the queen must have felt like a stranger in her own country, particularly since Parliament had declared Scotland to be Protestant in 1560 and she had been raised a Roman Catholic. In these circumstances she turned to families she already knew and trusted, like Lords Seton, Livingston and Fleming, all brothers of her dependable ladies-in-waiting, the Four Maries.

In the case of John Fleming, it quickly became clear that the close bond of mutual trust and friendship which his sister enjoyed with the queen extended to him. She visited him at Cumbernauld within a year of her return to Scotland and the following May insisted on hosting his wedding feast at Holyrood. For her part, the queen was impressed by John's intelligence and commitment to her service and, in keeping with family tradition, rewarded him with the office of lord chamberlain.

Evidence of Fleming's commitment to the queen's cause came in the summer of 1565 when he and his brothers-in-law, Atholl and Livingston, joined the queen's side in response to an abortive rebellion sparked by her controversial marriage to Lord Darnley. This became known as the 'Chaseabout Raid' because no pitched battle took place, but it was effectively a victory for Mary. Again, in the next year, Fleming joined Seton, Livingston, Bothwell and Huntly in safely escorting the pregnant queen and Darnley to Dunbar after the murder of Mary's Italian secretary, David Rizzio, at Holyrood.

It was not long before Fleming grew openly to detest Darnley, but despite this, he had nothing to do with Darnley's murder at Kirk o' Field in 1567. However, he appeared to support Mary's fateful decision to marry the prime suspect of the crime, Fleming's cousin, the Earl of Bothwell, and was one of the few lords to attend the wedding. The marriage crystallised opposition to Mary and now included Fleming's brother-in-law, the Earl of Atholl. At Carberry Hill both sides met but rather than spill more blood the queen decided to hand herself over to the lords who opposed her. In the aftermath of Carberry Hill, Fleming and Seton accompanied Bothwell northwards before leaving him to make his escape.

Following the queen's enforced abdication Fleming refused to attend the coronation of her son, James VI, in July 1567. An increasing number of nobles began to give their support to Mary and turn against the Earl of Moray, Mary's illegitimate half-brother who had been appointed regent. This was evident in the large army she assembled after her dramatic escape from Lochleven Castle in 1568. Fleming left Dumbarton Castle to join her at Langside near Glasgow where they observed the humiliating defeat of her army by Moray's men. It is from this point on that his actions in support of the deposed queen separate him from many other Marian supporters.

Following the defeat at Langside, Fleming accompanied Mary on her flight to England from where he was entrusted with a mission seeking military assistance from France. However, this was thwarted by the intervention of Elizabeth of England. Fleming returned to Scotland in 1569 after attending the inconclusive first 'trial' of Mary as one of her commissioners. Back in Scotland he concentrated on turning Dumbarton Castle into an impregnable Marian fortress, well aware of its strategic importance, dominating the Clyde and providing access to French overseas supplies.

At one stage there was a suggestion that his half-brother, Henry of Valois, son of Lady Fleming and Henry II, might be approached to lead a French expedition which would use Dumbarton as a base. This did not happen. However, French support did come in the way of two great ships which arrived in Loch Ryan, Wigtownshire, led by Thomas Fleming, brother of John Fleming of Boghall. This was enough to persuade

Table 12.3. The Fleming family, 1524-1579.

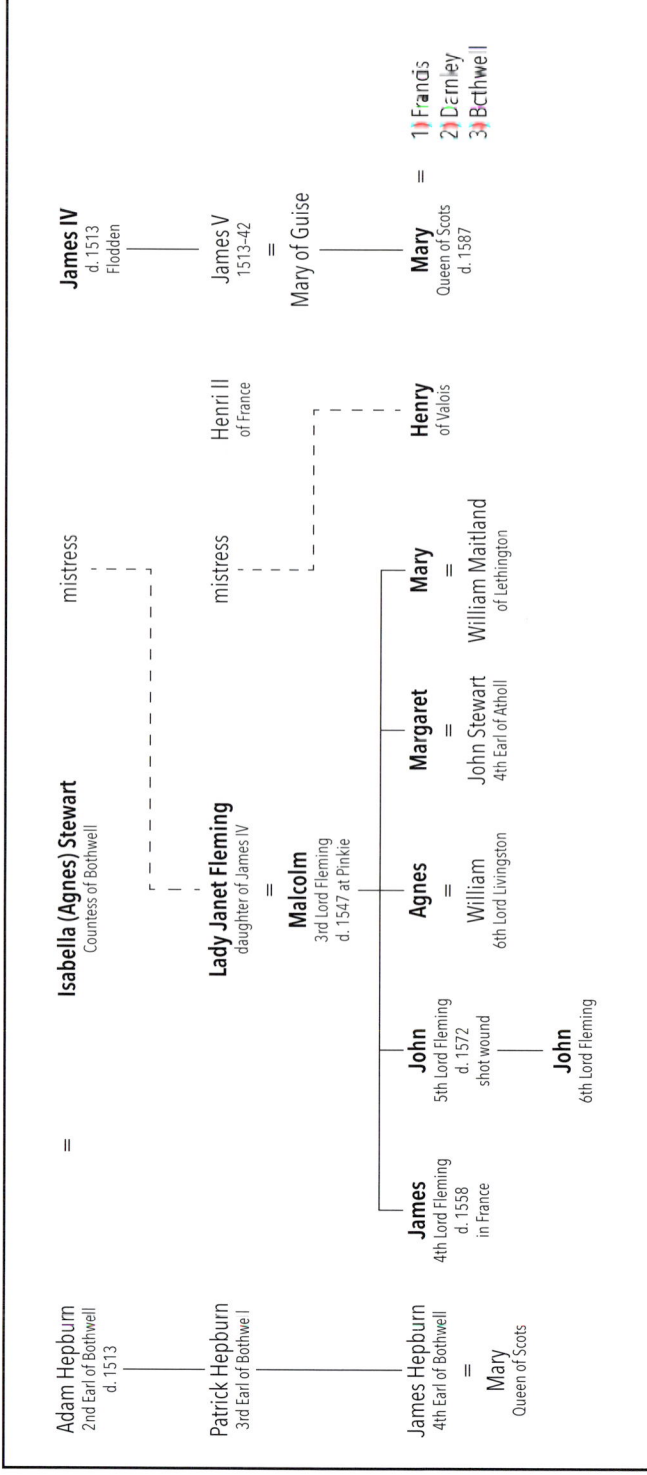

The table illustrates the presence of the Fleming network at the court of Mary Queen of Scots. Margaret Fleming was married to the Catholic Earl of Atholl and was reputed to have been one of the queen's highest ranking servants. She wanted to visit Mary at Tutbury but was refused by Elizabeth I. Agnes Fleming was married to Lord Livingston, a Protestant lord devoted to the queen. Agnes stayed with the queen at Bolton and Tutbury castles but on her return to Scotland she was imprisoned for two months at Dalkeith Castle by the regent Morton for allegedly communicating messages from the queen to her Marian supporters. Mary Fleming, the belle of the Four Maries, married in 1567 the queen's Secretary, William Maitland. No member of the Fleming family was present at the execution of the queen in 1587.

the fifth Lord Fleming to refuse to surrender Dumbarton Castle to the regent Moray despite the forfeiture of his lands and Mary's seemingly hopeless position.

Eventually, after holding the castle for six years, it was taken in a daring raid involving a former soldier of the castle, hell-bent on revenge for Fleming ordering the whipping of his wife for an alleged theft. However, Fleming escaped to France where he secured money from Charles IX of France. On his return in 1572 to Edinburgh Castle, the last remaining Marian stronghold, he met his death in bizarre circumstances. An accidental shot from a French soldier ricocheted into his leg; he remained in Edinburgh castle until a litter carried him to Boghall Castle in Biggar where he died and was buried.

As Table 12.3 illustrates, Fleming support for Mary extended to other family members, both during and after her personal rule. But support for the failed Marian cause came at a heavy price. In 1570, Fleming's estates were forfeited and taken over by the crown; at Cumbernauld the forest deer and rare white cattle were destroyed and at Biggar tenants were forced to pay large sums of money. At least there was some comfort for the fifth lord's wife, Lady Elizabeth Ross, who was treated with great consideration by the Regent Lennox following the taking of Dumbarton Castle in 1572 and granted some means of supporting herself and her family.

Elizabeth outlived her husband by a few years but in her will she referred to her only son, John, as 'laird of Biggar'. Following her death, John and his four sisters were brought up by the fourth Earl of Atholl and his wife, Margaret Fleming, sister to their father. It was not until 1579 that an Act of Parliament was passed restoring most of the forfeited lands and the title of sixth Lord Fleming to the ten year-old John.

The Fleming Earls of Wigtown: 1579-1747

John Lord Fleming was a similar age to James VI, the son of Mary Queen of Scots, who did not begin his personal rule until 1585. Three years later the king appointed the sixth Lord Fleming principal usher of the king's house, a position which gave him an important role at court. Nonetheless, although one of Scotland's thirty-three lords, he was not an earl, of whom there were thirteen in 1589, and thus not in the highest echelon of noble society. That changed after 1603 when, on the death of Elizabeth I, James VI of Scotland succeeded to the throne of England and took to London several of his favoured Scottish nobles, including the sixth Lord Fleming.

It was at Westminster that in 1606 James granted the earldom of Wigtown to Lord John Fleming, one of eighteen created between 1605 and the king's death in 1624. Unlike the first creation of the title which stipulated an obligation to provide five knights' service, the recreated title carried no military obligation. Nor did it provide a return of the lands previously held during the first creation. This was undoubtedly a disappointment to Fleming as throughout most of the sixteenth century the family had retained a vested interest in Whithorn Priory and a plan had been drafted which would have resulted in the return of the lands of Galloway previously given to Malcolm Fleming by David II.

When the first earl died in 1619 his son John succeeded to the earldom and, like his father before him, became a member of the Privy Council in what proved to be difficult times.

Religious conflict dominated Scottish politics for most of the seventeenth century and was to prove a challenge for the Fleming family. After the Union of the Crowns in 1603 royal interference in ecclesiastical affairs created severe tensions as successive monarchs sought to 'anglicise' the Scottish Presbyterian kirk by imposing both bishops and a more ritualised form of worship. It is difficult to say where the second Earl of Wigtown stood on this as he was first and foremost a monarchist, having spent some time at the court of Charles I. However, like the rest of the Scottish nobility, he signed the National Covenant in 1638 following Charles I's imposition of an English-style Prayer Book on his reluctant Scottish subjects.

The response from Charles I was to reassert his authority over Scotland by force. John Lord Fleming, the second Earl of Wigtown's son, supported the Covenanting cause by raising and equipping troops at his own expense. In what became known as the Bishops' War, the king's army was quickly defeated and Charles I was forced into a humiliating settlement in the summer of 1641.

But even before then, the second earl clearly shared the unease of his cousin, James Graham, Marquis of Montrose, about the anti-monarchical direction the Covenanting movement appeared to be taking. In August 1640, at the instigation of Montrose, Wigtown agreed to hold a meeting at his Cumbernauld home for those concerned about the rumoured ambitions of the Covenanting leadership, in particular the Earl of Argyll. From that meeting, twenty nobles, including Montrose and Wigtown, signed a secret bond promising mutual support.

Montrose's next step was to meet secretly with Charles I and switch his support from the Covenanting side to the king's. Not surprisingly, by 1643 Wigtown was receiving requests from Charles I to call upon his friends, vassals, tenants and dependents to do the same. Nonetheless, Wigtown was not prepared actively to commit himself, possibly because he was aware of the potential risks it posed to the security of his estates. Given what subsequently happened to his eldest son, and indeed to Montrose himself, this turned out to be a wise move.

Figure 12.1. John, 2nd earl of Wigtown.   **Figure 12.2. The Marquis of Montrose.**

His son, John Lord Fleming, joined Montrose's forces and was at Philiphaugh, near Selkirk, in 1645, when Montrose's unlikely run of victories came to an end; his heavily outnumbered troops were crushed by a Covenanting army. Montrose was urged to escape and sought safety abroad. John also escaped but remained in Scotland where he was called upon to answer for his actions. Initially he was subjected to a hefty fine of £6,400, but he claimed he was in no position to pay as he had not been reimbursed for the £20,000 he had borrowed to equip his Covenanting regiment during the Bishops' War. After careful scrutiny his case was accepted; he was fortunate to get off so lightly.

John eventually succeeded to the earldom when his father died in May 1650, the year after the English Parliament executed Charles I and created a republic under Oliver Cromwell. Montrose returned from exile to lend his support to the deposed king's son, Charles II, and it was the third Earl of Wigtown's younger brother, Sir William Fleming, who acted as a go-between the two men. Unfortunately for Montrose, his return ended in defeat, betrayal, and a sentence of death which was duly carried out on 21 May 1650. It was eleven years before Montrose was given a proper funeral; the Earl of Wigtown, as one of Montrose's closest living relatives, played a prominent part as he followed behind the coffin as it made its way to its final resting place at St Giles Cathedral in Edinburgh.

The third Earl was succeeded by his eldest son, John (1665–68), and then John's brother, William (1668–81). In the 1660s, the restoration of the monarchy promised to bring an end to religious strife but all it did was to change its nature. Charles II re-established episcopacy in Scotland in 1662 with the agreement of Parliament. About a third of Scottish ministers could not accept these changes and started holding their services in buildings other than churches. These meetings, or conventicles as they were called, were declared illegal. This created a particularly difficult situation for William with regard to his sister-in-law, Anna Kerr, the Dowager Countess of Wigtown. She was firmly committed to the Covenanting side and was arrested in 1672 for attending two field conventicles at the house of Boghall. Anna was fined 4,000 merks (a merk or mark was 13s 4d) and payment was to be made to Sir William Sharp who was then to deliver the money to William, Earl of Wigtown. Perhaps this family connection made him a particularly suitable choice in 1674 to consider the conditions of those imprisoned for attending conventicles! By the time of his death in 1681 the religious strife between Presbyterians and Episcopalians was no nearer to being resolved.

John and Charles, the sons of William, were the last two earls of Wigtown. At the time of their father's death John was about eight years-old and Charles a couple of years younger. An important figure in their formative years was James Drummond, fourth Earl of Perth, who was appointed their guardian in 1684, the year before James VII and II succeeded his brother Charles II as an openly Catholic monarch. Perth was a loyal supporter of the new king and in 1685 converted to Catholicism. This may have been a key factor in Charles entering the Roman Catholic seminary at Douai in 1689 where he trained to become a priest. His elder brother, John, sixth Earl of Wigtown (1681–1744), may also have spent time in France and, following the king's overthrow in 1688–89, attended the exiled Jacobite court.

The sixth Earl was back in Scotland when the issue of the union of the Scottish and English Parliaments came to the fore following the accession of Queen Anne in 1702. Sympathetic to the Jacobite cause, John was an outspoken critic of the Act of Union in 1707 and supportive of the first of the four major uprisings aimed at the restoration of the Stuart monarchy that immediately followed. The earl's younger brother, Charles Fleming, was dispatched from France to Scotland early in 1708 to communicate details of the imminent arrival of the nineteen-year-old son of the deceased James II. James Stuart, known as the Old Pretender, intended to arrive at the Firth of Forth with French naval support and proclaim himself king. However, on his arrival, he found there were no pilots to guide the French fleet and no sign of support from the mainland. A numerically superior English fleet appeared causing the French commander – much against the wishes of James – to flee north and then return to Dunkirk.

Table 12.4. The Fleming family, 1579–1747.

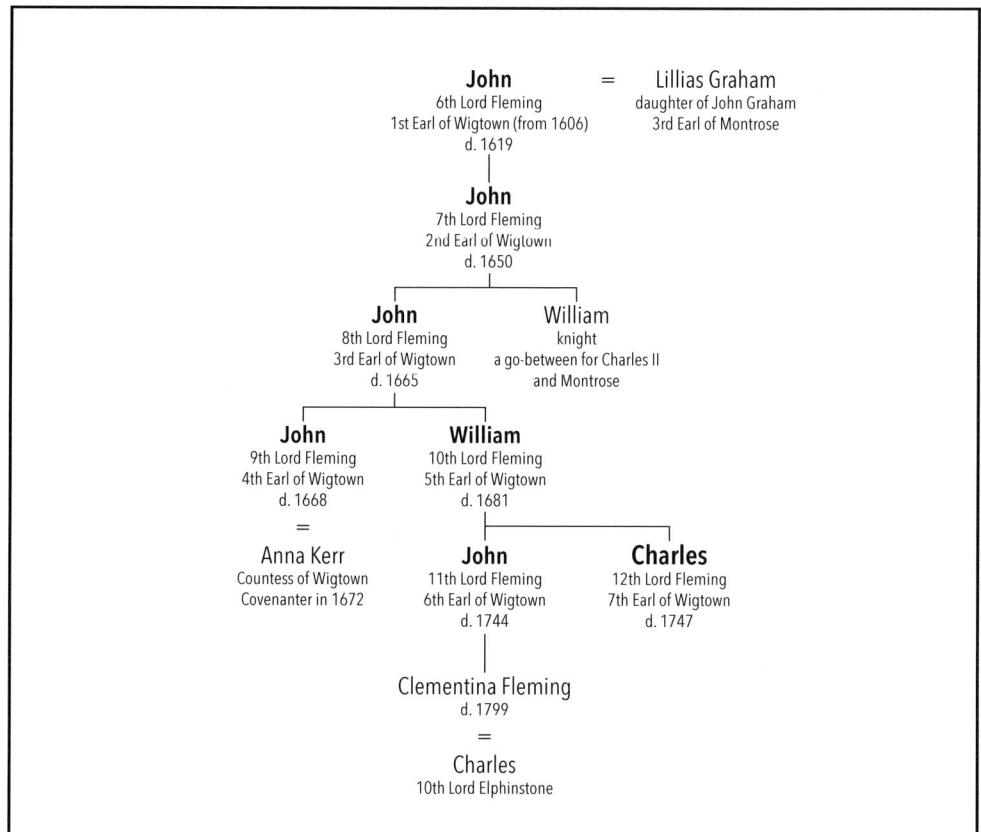

When it came to the 1715 Jacobite Uprising, the sixth earl, well known for his continued Jacobite leanings, was duly summoned to appear in Edinburgh to give assurances of his loyalty to the government side and to pay bail. He did not comply and consequently was apprehended and imprisoned in Edinburgh Castle; there he remained for ten months, an angry and frustrated man, unable to participate in the rebellion. By the late 1720s, however, he appears to have abandoned his support for the Jacobite cause. As a trustee of a group set up to advise the Old Pretender, he probably came to accept the view of its leader, George Lockhart of Carnwath, that Jacobitism had become a lost cause and any thoughts of an uprising in 1727 should not be entertained. Certainly, by 1736 the government was sufficiently confident of Wigtown's change of allegiance to have him appointed as the king's Chamberlain of Fife. His loyalty was never put fully to the test as he died the year before the last and most dramatic of the Jacobite Uprisings in 1745.

Towards the end of his life John was concerned about the future of the title. The sixth earl's three marriages, the third to the daughter of Lockhart of Carnwath, had failed to produce a son, and there was no prospect of his unmarried brother and heir, Charles, doing so. In these circumstances, the title would pass to John's daughter Clementina who was married to the son and heir of the ninth Lord Elphinstone. John did not want the peerage of Wigtown to be merged with any other title and ensured this legally with a new deed of entail in 1741. As a result, after Charles, seventh Earl of Wigtown and twelfth Lord Fleming, died in 1747, his niece Clementina inherited the estates, but not the title, which became extinct. After Clementina's husband became Lord Elphinstone in 1757 she disposed of some of her lands. She lived until 1799 when her second grandson, Charles, assumed the name Fleming and took possession of the estates. Unfortunately, he fell heavily into debt and was granted permission by an Act of Parliament in 1826 to sell the lands to pay off his creditors.

This case study of the Fleming family illustrates how their fortunes were interwoven with some of the defining moments in Scottish history from the fourteenth-century Wars of Independence through the reign of Mary Queen of Scots to the Jacobite Rebellions of the eighteenth century. It is a notable story of baronial survival and resilience. There is a certain irony in that, having survived a series of challenges that threatened its very existence – most notably the loss of the earldom and sale of heritable lands in the fourteenth century and forfeiture in 1440 and 1570 – the line effectively came to an end as a result of the failure of the sixth Earl of Wigtown to produce a son and heir. The family was remarkably fortunate that during its five centuries of existence succession had not been an issue: on twelve occasions a son succeeded the father; on a further two occasions it passed to a grandson; on an additional three it passed directly to a brother; and only once did it pass to a male cousin. Furthermore, on the occasions when the head of family suffered an untimely or violent death – as in 1406, 1440, 1524, 1547 and 1558 – there was a young male to take his place. The survival of noble families like the Flemings owed much to this sequence of good fortune in producing male heirs. On the single occasion when this did not occur, the lineage came to an end.

CLR

Conclusion

What's in a surname? Answering the question with which we began has turned out to be much less straightforward, and much more intriguing, than might have been anticipated. A history of notable Scottish Flemings would focus on such luminaries as Sir Alexander Fleming (1881–1955), the Nobel Prize winning scientist from Ayrshire, whose pioneering work on antibiotics has seen him ranked only behind Robert Bruce and William Wallace in popular polls of the greatest Scots of all time. Trailing in his wake one would no doubt find Ian Fleming (1908–65), the creator of James Bond, whose family hailed from Dundee and made a major impact on the city's development (see box below). However, for all that individuals carrying the surname Fleming have achieved status and celebrity, it was never the intention that this book should focus solely on the bearers of one particular name.

Flemings of note in Dundee

Descendants of Flemish migrants associated with Dundee include a notable and ultimately very successful family carrying the surname Fleming. John Fleming (1806-1873) of Kirkmichael in Perthshire had two surviving sons, Robert (1845-1933) and John (1847-1925). Both became well known in Scotland, John as head of one of the most prominent timber importers and suppliers, and Robert as one of the founders of the financial trusts in Dundee. Robert, who also became an international financier of note, was the author Ian Fleming's grandfather. Both sons were major philanthropists in Dundee.

Rather, as its title makes clear, the goal was to explore the relationship between Scotland and the Flemish people, a relationship that takes us well beyond the Fleming name itself to the fluid borders of the medieval county of Flanders and the heterogeneous peoples who inhabited it and who were identified as Flemish by their contemporaries. There is much in this book that will give genealogists and family historians pause for thought, and some new evidence has been presented about the lineages of a range of families that claim Flemish ancestry. Indeed, this is the first time that elements of history, genealogy and DNA analysis have been brought to bear in a comprehensive way on the Flemish presence in Scotland. However, this genealogical material has been firmly set within broader historical contours and contexts. In these wider perspectives, the history of the 'Flemings', especially in the Middle Ages, is deeply interwoven with the history of Scotland, bound up with the causes and consequences of the migration of Flemish people from Flanders to Scotland and the economic and social ties that resulted from this.

It is not known what proportion of the Scottish population is of Flemish descent – one estimate, almost certainly exaggerated, has put it as high as a third – but it is undoubtedly greater than the very marginal place that Flemish immigrants are allotted in standard histories of Scotland. As with the 'Norman' Conquest of England, so the terms used to characterise the twelfth-century 'Normanisation' of Scotland downplay the role played by Flemish knights and mercenaries, merchants and craftsmen, in processes that transformed both Scottish urban and rural life. This is perhaps not entirely surprising. After all, as we have seen, whether we think of geography, language or ethnicity, Flanders and the Flemish are not easily defined and, unless specifically referred to as such, Flemish settlers in Scotland are not easily distinguished from Anglo-Norman ones. Moreover, both then and subsequently, while the numbers were significant, they were not overwhelming, and this no doubt contributed to the apparent ease with which they were assimilated into local Scottish communities. The Flemish artisans, often religious refugees, who settled in Scottish towns in the late sixteenth century worshipped together with their hosts and appear to have been quickly absorbed into burgh society. In this they were following the example of their forebears who had done so much to populate and develop those same towns in the twelfth and thirteenth centuries but whose ethnic roots and identities were eroded and forgotten within generations. Likewise, the Flemish knightly class that was at the cutting edge of migration and settlement in the twelfth century, and from which many prominent Scottish noble families claim descent, abandoned their Flemish identity over the ensuing century, becoming part of a broader noble class defined, not by ethnicity, but by allegiance to the Scottish crown.

As this suggests, these Flemish incomers were highly adaptable and often highly skilled individuals whose knowledge and expertise proved crucial to Scotland's social and economic development. Indeed, a leading theme of this book has been the critical importance of the economic ties between Scotland and Flanders throughout the Middle Ages. On the back of the wool trade, and the insatiable demand of the Flemish textile industry, there developed a much wider range of commercial and cultural ties between the two regions and a constant flow of traffic across the North Sea from Scotland's east coast ports to Bruges, Middleburg and Veere. In cultural terms, the traffic was largely one-way: the dukes of Burgundy, and the trading emporia of Flanders that enriched them, set standards and produced goods that Scots sought to emulate as well as purchase. The influence of Flemish cultural and artistic taste is impossible to miss in fifteenth and sixteenth century Scotland. Yet it is evident also in earlier castle building, in the design and furnishing of churches, in the crowsteps and pantiles of the fishing villages around the Forth, and even in military hardware. The impact of the Scots on the development of Flanders can probably be measured exclusively in terms of wool, woolfells, fleeces and fish. The impact of Flanders and the Flemish on Scotland has been far more profound and multifarious.

Focusing exclusively on one ethnic group inevitably highlights their importance and achievements at the expense of others. Scotland, as was noted at the outset, is a mongrel nation made up of a wide mix of ethnicities whose interactions over time have shaped and reshaped the country and its people. The Flemish who came to Scotland between the twelfth and sixteenth centuries have left indelible traces on the Scottish landscape, its language and culture as well as its social and political identity. They are an important but too often neglected part of the rich historical tapestry that has made Scotland what it is today. In identifying those threads of the tapestry that lead back to medieval Flanders, we hope this book has revealed some of the richness and importance of this centuries-old relationship.

RM/AF

Author Profiles

MB: *Michael Brown* is professor of Scottish History at the University of St Andrews. His books include *James I* (Edinburgh, 1994), *The Black Douglases* (East Linton, 1998), *The Wars of Scotland, 1214–1371* (Edinburgh, 2004) and *Disunited Kingdoms: Peoples and Politics in the British Isles, 1280–1460* (Harlow, 2013).

RB: *Robin Bargmann* holds a master's degree in commercial law from Leiden University. He spent his professional life in international commercial banking, but is a well-known golf historian and author of *Serendipity of Early Golf* (2010).

TC: *Thomas Clark* is a poet and translator who works extensively in the area of Scots language. His translated works include *Beowulf*, Martial's *Epigrams*, and his first poetry collection, *Intae the Snaw*. He is Scots language editor at *Bella Caledonia*.

DD: *David Dobson* is a Research Fellow at the University of Edinburgh and an Honorary Research Fellow at the St Andrews Institute of Scottish Historical Research. His research interests focus mainly on the Scottish Diaspora and his publications include *Scottish Emigration to Colonial America, 1683–1783* (1994, 2004); *Scottish Trade with Colonial Charleston, 1683–1783* (2009); and over 115 historical and genealogical source books (Baltimore 1983–2013).

AE: *Amy Eberlin* was awarded a PhD from the University of St Andrews in 2016 as part of the 'Scotland and the Flemish People' project. Her doctoral research focused on trade and the Scottish mercantile elite in the fourteenth and fifteenth centuries. She now works at the University of Stirling.

EE: *Elizabeth Ewan* is Professor of History and Scottish Studies at the University of Guelph, Ontario, Canada. She works on medieval and early modern Scottish urban, gender, and crime history and has published extensively in these fields.

GE: *George English* is a director of the Family History service Research Through People (www.researchthroughpeople.co.uk). He has worked extensively on religious persecution in the Low Countries as well as undertaking genealogical and historical research. His research has been published in the United Kingdom, the United States and Europe.

RE: *Robin Evetts* has a PhD in Art History from the University of St Andrews and was formerly a Senior Inspector of Historic Buildings with Historic Scotland. He maintains his interest in the history and protection of St Andrews and is a Trustee of a number of local and national historic building related organisations.

AF: *Alexander Fleming* is an economist by training and occupation and holds two doctorates, including an Honorary LLD from the University of St Andrews. A sponsor of the 'Scotland and the Flemish People' project, he has contributed substantially to the research undertaken into the Flemish presence in Scotland.

MF: *Morvern French* completed her PhD at the University of St Andrews in 2016 as part of the 'Scotland and the Flemish People' project. Her research focused on the trade in luxury goods between Flanders and Scotland in the late Middle Ages. She now works at Historic Environment Scotland.

RF: *Richard Fawcett* spent most of his career working in the Inspectorate of Ancient Monuments of Historic Scotland, where he was involved in the conservation and presentation of many of Scotland's most significant medieval buildings. He recently retired from teaching in the School of Art History at the University of St Andrews where he was a professor.

JI: *John Irvine* is a genealogist and local historian and is a former Chairman of the Local History Forum. He has written articles for local history journals on a wide range of topics. He has also published widely in the genealogy field and has researched the genealogy of both illustrious Dundee locals and the common man.

AM: *Alasdair Macdonald* is a Teaching Fellow and Lead Tutor in the department of Genealogical Studies at the University of Strathclyde. He is currently researching the origin and linkage of male lineages in the British Isles using Y-chromosomal DNA.

CM: *Christine McGladdery* is a senior teaching fellow in Mediaeval Scottish History at the University of St Andrews, and has published the recently fully revised monograph, *James II* (Edinburgh, 2015).

PM: *Peadar Morgan* completed his PhD at the University of St Andrews in 2013. His doctoral research focused on the names of the many ethnicities appearing in the past and present place-names of Scotland and the Border counties of England.

RM: *Roger Mason* recently retired as professor of Scottish History at the University of St Andrews. He has published widely in the field of late medieval and early modern Scottish History and was director of the 'Scotland and the Flemish People' project.

SM: *Silke Muylaert* is a graduate of Ghent University and recently completed a PhD at the University of Kent on the foreign churches in England during the Elizabethan period, for which she received the Huguenot Scholarship in 2015.

EO: *Eljas Oksanen* is a researcher for the Portable Antiquities Scheme in London, and an honorary research associate at the Institute of Archaeology, University College London. He has a PhD in history from the University of Cambridge that focused on the relations between Flanders and the Anglo-Norman world in the Middle Ages, now published as *Flanders and the Anglo-Norman World, 1066–1216* (2012).

MP: *Matthew Price* is currently Conservation Officer for Fife Council. A Chartered Surveyor and former post-graduate in European Urban Conservation at Dundee, he has wide experience of the conservation of traditional buildings over a career that includes periods with the Scottish Lime Centre, Scottish Civic Trust and the City of Edinburgh. He has published a number of articles on Scottish vernacular buildings.

CR: *Chris Robinson* retired from her post as Director of Scottish Language Dictionaries in 2015. She has taught for many years at the University of Edinburgh and the University of the Highlands and Islands. Her main interests are the Scots language and Middle English.

CLR: *Charles L. Rigg* is a history graduate of the University of Edinburgh and a Director and Trustee of Biggar Museum Trust. He is a member of the museum curatorial team and in that role played a part in interpreting the significance of the collection for the newly-opened Biggar and Upper Clydesdale Museum. He has a special interest in the twelfth-century incomers to Upper Clydesdale and in the Flemings of Biggar and Cumbernauld.

ER: *Elizabeth Rawlings* is a retired headteacher. She is a researcher and historian and is responsible for local genealogical studies for individuals, local history groups and Heritage Llangwm. This included the medieval research into the De la Roche family beginning with Godebertus Flandrensis (born Pembroke Castle 1195).

CJT: *Chris Tabraham* is an archaeologist and historian who spent his forty-year career as Inspector of Ancient Monuments for Historic Scotland, retiring as its Principal Historian. One of the foremost authorities on Scottish castles, he has directed excavations at several, and published numerous books and articles about them, and Scottish history in general.

Select Bibliography

What follows is by no means comprehensive, but will provide the interested reader with a starting-point for further research. Where the same book is relevant to more than one chapter, it is cited only on the first occasion of its relevance.

Chapter 1: Flanders and the Flemish

Paul Arblaster, *A History of the Low Countries* (2nd edn, London, 2012).

Wim Blockmans and Walter Prevenier, *The Promised Lands: The Low Countries under Burgundian Rule, 1369–1530*, trans. E. Fackelman, ed. E. Peters (Philadelphia, 1999).

J. C. H. Blom and E. Lamberts (eds), *History of the Low Countries* (new edn, New York and Oxford, 2006).

Alastair Duke, 'The Elusive Netherlands: The Question of National Identity in the Early Modern Low Countries on the Eve of the Revolt', *BMGN - Low Countries Historical Review*, 199 (2004), 10–38.

Ludo Milis, *Religion, Culture and Mentalities in the Medieval Low Countries*, ed. J. Deploige, M. De Reu *et al.* (Turnhout, 2005).

David Nicholas, *Medieval Flanders* (London and New York, 1992).

Eljas Oksanen, *Flanders and the Anglo-Norman World, 1066–1216* (Cambridge, 2012).

Els Witte, Jan Craeybeckx and Alain Meynen, *Political History of Belgium from 1830 Onwards* (Brussels, 2009).

Chapter 2: Flanders and Scotland

Caroline Barron and Nigel Saul (eds), *England and the Low Countries in the Late Middle Ages* (Stroud/New York, 1995).

Michael Brown, *The Wars of Scotland, 1214–1371* (Edinburgh, 2004).

Jane Dawson, *Scotland Re-Formed, 1488–1587* (Edinburgh, 2007).

David Ditchburn, *Scotland and Europe: The Medieval Kingdom and its Contacts with Christendom, 1214–1560* (East Linton, 2001).

J. Arnold Fleming, *Flemish Influence in Britain* (2 vols, Glasgow, 1930).

Alan Macquarrie, 'Anselm Adornes of Bruges: Traveller in the East and Friend of James III', *Innes Review*, 38 (1982), 15-22.

Grant G. Simpson (ed.), *Scotland and the Low Countries, 1124–1994* (East Linton, 1996).

Peter Stabel, *Dwarfs among Giants: The Flemish Urban Network in the Late Middle Ages* (Leuven/Apeldoorn, 1997).

Katie Stevenson, *Power and Propaganda: Scotland, 1306–1488* (Edinburgh, 2014).

Chapter 3: Flemish Migration I: Knights and Mercenaries

England

R. Allen Brown, 'The Battle of Hastings', in J. France (ed.), *Medieval Warfare, 1000–1300* (Aldershot, 2006), 145-70.

R. H. George, 'The Contribution of Flanders to the Conquest of England (1065–1086)', *Revue belge de philologie et d'histoire*, 5:1 (1926), 81–99.

K. S. B. Keats-Rohan, *Domesday People: A Prosopography of Persons Occurring in English Documents, 1066–1166*, volume I, *Domesday Book* (Woodbridge, 1999).

Renée Nipp, 'The Political Relations between England and Flanders', in C. Harper Bill (ed.), *Anglo-Norman Studies XXI: Proceedings of the Battle Conference 1998* (Woodbridge, 1999), 145–174.

Johan Verberckmoes, 'Flemish Tenants-in-Chief in Domesday England', *Revue belge de philologie et d'histoire*, 66:4 (1988), 725–75.

Wales

Elizabeth van Houts, 'The Ship List of William the Conquerer', in R. Allen Brown (ed.), *Anglo-Norman Studies X: Proceedings of the Battle Conference 1987* (Woodbridge, 1988), 159–83.

Benjamin Heath Malkin, *The Scenery, Antiquities and Biography of South Wales* (London, 1804).

Henry Owen, 'The Flemings in Pembrokeshire', *Archaeologia Cambrensis*, 5th series 12 (1895), 96–106.

Henry Owen, *Old Pembroke Families in the Ancient County Palatine of Pembroke* (London, 1902).

Mary Salmon, *A Source-Book of Welsh History* (Oxford, 1927).

Lauran Toorians, 'Wizo Flandrensis and the Flemish settlement in Pembrokeshire', *Cambridge Medieval Celtic Studies*, 20 (1990), 99–118.

Gerald of Wales, *The Journey through Wales and The Description of Wales*, ed. Lewis Thorpe (Harmondsworth, 1978).

Llangwm Heritage Project: http://www.heritagellangwm.org.uk.

Scotland

G. W. S. Barrow, *The Anglo-Norman Era in Scottish History* (Oxford, 1980).

G. W. S. Barrow, *Scotland and its Neighbours in the Middle Ages* (London, 1992).

A. A. M. Duncan, *Scotland: The Making of the Kingdom* (Edinburgh,1975).

Alexander Grant, 'Lordship and Society in Twelfth-Century Clydesdale', in H. Pryce and J. Watts (ed.), *Power and Identity in the Middle Ages: Essays in Memory of Rees Davies* (Oxford, 2007), 98–124.

Richard Oram, *Domination and Lordship: Scotland 1070–1230* (Edinburgh, 2011).

Richard Oram, *David I: The King Who Made Scotland* (Stroud, 2004).

Richard Oram, 'David I and the Scottish Conquest and Colonization of Moray', *Northern Scotland*, 19 (1999), 1–19.

R.L. Graeme Ritchie, *The Normans in Scotland* (Edinburgh, 1954).

Lauran Toorians, 'Flemish Settlement in Twelfth-Century Scotland', *in Revue belge de philologie et d'histoire*, 74 (1996), 659–93.

Lauran Toorians, 'Twelfth-Century Flemish Settlement in Scotland', in Grant G. Simpson (ed.), *Scotland and the Low Countries 1124–1994* (East Linton, 1996), 1–14.

'The People of Medieval Scotland, 1093–1371' (www.poms.ac.uk).

http://flemish.wp.st-andrews.ac.uk/2014/11/21/exploring-the-relationships-among-some-key-flemish-families/

http://flemish.wp.st-andrews.ac.uk/2015/03/20/the-barony-of-kerdale-and-its-links-with-some-key-moray-families/

http://flemish.wp.st-andrews.ac.uk/2015/10/16/the-flemish-in-moray-part-one/

http://flemish.wp.st-andrews.ac.uk/2015/10/23/the-flemish-in-moray-part-2/

http://flemish.wp.st-andrews.ac.uk/2016/02/26/the-murray-sutherland-and-douglas-families-were-they-related-and-were-they-flemish/

http://flemish.wp.st-andrews.ac.uk/2016/01/29/the-lightsome-lindsays-roots-and-branches/

http://flemish.wp.st-andrews.ac.uk/2015/10/29/the-family-of-innes-of-morayshire/

Chapter 4: Flemish Migration II: Merchants and Craftsmen

Marcel Backhouse, *The Flemish and Walloon Communities at Sandwich during the Reign of Elizabeth I, 1561–1603* (Wetteren, 1995).

George Black, *The Surnames of Scotland: their Origin, Meaning and History* (New York, 1946).

J. J. Blyth, *Burntisland: Early History and People* (Kirkcaldy, 1948).

A. J. Campbell, *Some Fife Apprentices and Freemen, 1524-1899* (St Andrews, n.d.).

S. Cowan, *The Ancient Capital of Scotland* (London, 1904).

David Dobson, *Mariners of the Lothians* (St Andrews, 1993).

David Dobson, *Directory of Seafarers of the East Neuk, 1580–1800* (St Andrews, 2008).

Elizabeth Ewan, 'Crab, John', *Oxford Dictionary of National Biography* (Oxford, 2004).

J. Ferguson, *Linlithgow Palace* (Edinburgh, 1910).

Michael Fry, *Edinburgh: A History of the City* (London, 2009).

C. E. Green, *East Lothian* (Edinburgh, 1907).

J. Harrison, *History of the Monastery of Holy Rood and the Palace of Holyroodhouse* (Edinburgh, 1919).

Cosmo Innes (ed.), *The Ledger of Andrew Halyburton* (Edinburgh, 1867).

J. C. Irons, *Leith and its Antiquities* (Edinburgh, 1897).

South Leith Records, 1588–1850 (2 vols, Edinburgh, 1911–1925).

Thomas McGowran, *Newhaven on Forth* (Edinburgh, 1985).

A. J. Mackay, *History of Fife and Kinross* (Edinburgh, 1896).

N. D. Mackay, *Aberfeldy, Past and Present* (Aberfeldy, 1954).

Paula Martin, *Cupar: The History of a Small Scottish Town* (Edinburgh, 2006).

Alexander Maxwell, *Old Dundee prior to the Reformation* (Dundee, 1891).

Alexander Patterson, *The History of Crieff* (Edinburgh, 1912).

Andrew Pettegree, *Foreign Protestant Communities in Sixteenth-Century London* (Oxford, 1986).

W. Stephen, *History of Inverkeithing and Rosyth* (Aberdeen, 1921).

James Wilkie, *The History of Fife from the Earliest Times to the Nineteenth Century* (Edinburgh and London, 1924).

Chapter 5: Castles

P. Dixon and C. J. Tabraham, 'Fortifications', in Keith Stringer and Angus Winchester (eds), *Northern England and Southern Scotland in the Central Middle Ages* (Woodbridge, 2017), 327–350.

G. Haggarty and C. J. Tabraham, 'Excavation of a Motte near Roberton, Clydesdale, 1979', *Transactions of the Dumfriesshire and Galloway Natural History and Antiquarian Society*, 57 (1982), 51–64.

H. Owen, 'The Flemings in Pembrokeshire', *Archaeologia Cambrensis*, 5th series XII (London, 1895), 96–106.

Grant G. Simpson and Bruce Webster, 'Charter Evidence and the Distribution of Mottes in Scotland', in R. Liddiard (ed.), *Anglo-Norman Castles* (Woodbridge, 2003), 223–44.

C. J. Tabraham, 'Norman Settlement in Upper Clydesdale: Recent Archaeological Fieldwork', *Transactions of the Dumfriesshire and Galloway Natural History and Antiquarian Society*, 53 (1977-8), 114–28.

C. J. Tabraham, *Scotland's Castles* (2nd ed., London, 2005).

Chapter 6: Towns and Churches

Town Planning

Ronald G. Cant, 'Burgh Planning and early Domestic Architecture: The Example of St Andrews (c.1130-1730)', in Deborah Mays (ed.), *The Architecture of Scottish Cities* (1997), 1–12.

Anne Turner Simpson and Sylvia Stevenson, *Historic St Andrews* (Scottish Burgh Survey, 1981).

Robert N. Smart, 'The Sixteenth Century Bird's Eye View Plan of St Andrews' (1974), in *Three Decades of Historical Notes* (St Andrews Preservation Trust, 1996).

Ronald G. Cant, *St Andrews, The Guide and Handbook of the St Andrews Preservation Trust* (1982).

Church Architecture

Richard Fawcett, 'Architectural Links Between Scotland and the Low Countries in the Later Middle Ages', in E. de Bièvre (ed.), *Utrecht, Britain and the Continent* (British Archaeological Association Transactions XVIII, Leeds, 1996), 172–82.

Marjan Buyle, Thomas Coomans, Jan Esther and Luc Francis Genicot, *Architecture Gothique en Belgique* (Editions Racine, 1997).

John G. Dunbar, *Scottish Royal Palaces* (East Linton, 1999).

Richard Fawcett, *The Architecture of the Scottish Medieval Church, 1100–1560* (New Haven and London, 2011).

Local Architecture

J. Bell, *Broomlees Tile Works* (Elie and Earlsferry History Society, 2005).

G. Emerton, *The Pattern of Scottish Roofing* (Historic Environment Scotland, 2000).

Stuart Eydmann, 'Pantiles', in Moses Jenkins (ed.), *Building Scotland: Celebrating Scotland's Traditional Building Materials* (Edinburgh, 2010), 143–155.

F. Bennett and A. Pinion, *Roof Slating and Tiling* (Shaftesbury, 1935; rpt. 2000).

Matthew Price, 'Crowsteps in Fife', *Context: The Journal of the Institute of Historic Building Conservation*, 128 (2013), 32–35.

G. L. Pride, *Dictionary of Scottish Building* (Edinburgh, 1996)

R. J. Naismith, *Buildings of the Scottish Countryside* (London, 1987).

Liz Whitfeld, *Rural Buildings of the Lothians: Conservation and Conversion* (Edinburgh, 2000).

Chapter 7: Arts, Artefacts and Artillery

Accounts of the Lord High Treasurer of Scotland, ed. T. Dickson *et al.* (13 vols, Edinburgh, 1877–1978).

A Collection of Inventories and Other Records of the Royal Wardrobe and Jewelhouse; and of the Artillery and Munitioun in some of the Royal Castles. M.CCCC.LXXXVIII.– M.DC.VI., ed. Thomas Thomson (Edinburgh, 1815).

Kelly DeVries, 'A 15th-century weapons dowry: the weapons dowry of Duke Philip the Good of Burgundy for the marriage of Mary of Guelders and James II of Scotland in 1449', *Royal Armouries Yearbook*, 6 (2001), 22–31.

The Exchequer Rolls of Scotland, ed. John Stuart and G. Burnett (23 vols, Edinburgh, 1878–1908).

Claude Gaier and Claude Blair, 'The Origin of Mons Meg', *The Journal of the Arms and Armour Society*, 5 (1965–7), 425–31.

Andrea Thomas, *Glory and Honour: The Renaissance in Scotland* (Edinburgh, 2013).

Chapter 8: Sport and Recreation

Robin K. Bargmann, *Serendipity of Early Golf* (n.p., 2010).

L. St John Butler and P. J. Wordie, *The Royal Game*, Falkland Palace Real Tennis Club (Kippen, 1989).

David Ditchburn, 'Rituals, Space and the Marriage of James II and Mary of Guelders, 1449', in F. Andrews (ed.), *Ritual and Space in the Middle Ages, Proceedings of the 2009 Harlaxton Symposium* (Donington, 2011), 179–96.

Olive Geddes, *A Swing Through Time: Golf in Scotland 1457–1744* (Edinburgh, 2007).

David Hamilton, *Golf: Scotland's Game* (Kilmacolm, 1998).

Jonathan Israel, *The Dutch Republic: Its Rise, Greatness and Fall, 1477–1806* (Oxford, 1995).

Christine McGladdery, *James II* (Edinburgh, 2015).

David B. Smith, *Curling: An Illustrated History* (Edinburgh,1981).

Chapter 9: Language

Dictionary of the Scots Language (2004). Scottish Language Dictionaries Ltd.: http://www.dsl.ac.uk.

Caroline Macafee, 'The History of Scots to 1700', in *Dictionary of the Scots Language* (2004). Scottish Language Dictionaries Ltd: http://www.dsl.ac.uk.

David Murison, 'The Dutch Element in the Vocabulary of the Scots', in A. J. Aitken *et al.* (ed.), *Edinburgh Studies in English and Scots* (London, 1971).

Chapter 10: Surnames

George F. Black, *The Surnames of Scotland: their Origin, Meaning and History* (New York, 1946).

F. Lawrence Fleming, *Exploring the True Heritage of the Fleming Family Name* (n.p., 2018).

David Hey, *Family Names and Family History* (London and New York, 2000).

Beryl Platts, *Scottish Hazard: The Flemish Nobility and their Impact on Scotland*, Vol 1 (London, 1985).

George Redmonds, Turi King and David Hey, *Surnames, DNA & Family History* (Oxford, 2011).

http://flemish.wp.st-andrews.ac.uk/2015/10/02/the-waddell-family-a-search-for-possible-flemish-roots/

http://flemish.wp.st-andrews.ac.uk/2015/05/22/surname-formation-in-britain/

http://flemish.wp.st-andrews.ac.uk/2015/05/29/the-formation-of-the-fleming-surname/

http://flemish.wp.st-andrews.ac.uk/2015/04/02/the-frame-family-weavers-from-flanders/

http://flemish.wp.st-andrews.ac.uk/2015/04/17/the-cant-family-and-the-strathmartine-trust/

http://flemish.wp.st-andrews.ac.uk/2014/09/19/the-armstrong-family-and-its-possible-flemish-origins/

http://flemish.wp.st-andrews.ac.uk/2014/09/12/dowie-a-scottish-surname-with-flemish-roots/

Chapter 11: Scotticisation

Dauvit Broun, 'A Second England: Scotland and the Monarchy of Britain in *The First English Empire*', in S. Duffy and S. Foran (eds), *The English Isles: Cultural Transmission and Conflict in Britain and Ireland, 1100-1500* (Dublin, 2013), 84–102.

Matthew Hammond, 'Domination and Conquest: The Scottish Experience in the Twelfth and Thirteenth Centuries', in *ibid.*, 68–83.

Rees Davies, *The First English Empire: Power and Identities in the British Isles, 1093–1343* (Oxford, 2000).

Chapter 12: The Fleming Family: A Case Study

Fleming Family 1306-1382

Alexander Grant, 'The Death of John Comyn: What Was Going On?', *Scottish Historical Review*, 82 (2007), 176–224.

Richard Oram, 'The Making of an Earl: Malcolm Fleming', *International Review of Scottish Studies*, 42 (2017), 1–35.

Richard Oram 'The Breaking of an Earldom: The Decline of Malcolm and Failure of Earl Thomas', *International Review of Scottish Studies*, 42 (2017), 36–58.

Michael Penman, *Robert the Bruce King of the Scots* (New Haven and London, 2014).

Michael Penman, *David II, 1329–71* (Edinburgh, 2005).

Fleming Family 1382-1524

Stephen Boardman, *The Early Stewart Kings: Robert II and Robert III, 1371–1406* (East Linton, 1996).

Michael Brown, *The Black Douglases: War and Lordship in Late Medieval Scotland, 1300–1455* (East Linton, 1998).

Alexander Grant, 'The Development of the Scottish Peerage', *Scottish Historical Review*, 57 (1978), 1–27.

F. J. Grant (ed.), *Charter Chest of the Earldom of Wigtown, 1214–1681* (Scottish Record Society, 1910).

Fleming Family 1524-79

J. Bain (ed.), *Calendar of the State Papers relating to Scotland and Mary Queen of Scots, 1547–1603* (Edinburgh, 1898).

Gordon Donaldson, *All the Queen's Men: Power and Politics in Mary Stewart's Scotland* (London, 1983).

I. M. M. MacPhail, *Dumbarton Castle* (Edinburgh, 1979).

Rosalind Marshall, *Queen Mary's Women* (Edinburgh, 2006).

R. C. Reid (ed.), *Wigtownshire Charters* (Scottish History Society, 1960).

Alison Weir, *Mary, Queen of Scots and the Murder of Lord Darnley* (London, 2008).

Fleming Family 1579-1747

E. J. Cowan, *Montrose: For Covenant and King* (Edinburgh, 1975).

W. Hunter, *Biggar and the House of Fleming* (Edinburgh, 1862).

G. V. Irving, *The Upper Ward of Lanarkshire: Described and Delineated* (Glasgow, 1864).

M. M. Meikle, 'The Invisible Divide: The Greater Lairds and Nobility of Jacobean Scotland', *Scottish Historical Review*, 91 (1992), 70–87.

J. B. Paul, (ed.), *The Scots Peerage* (Edinburgh, 1904–14).

Daniel Szechi, *George Lockhart of Carnwath 1689–1727: A Study in Jacobitism* (East Linton, 2002).

Conclusion

André Maurois, *The life of Alexander Fleming* (New York, 1959).

Bill Smith, *Robert Fleming 1845–1933* (Haddington, 2000).

Picture Credits

We are grateful to the following for permission to reproduce the images listed below:

Figure 3.1: William of Normandy and Eustace of Boulogne at the Battle of Hastings, Bayeux Tapestry.

Figure 4.1: Jean Froissart's *Chroniques* (1410), National Library of the Netherlands, The Hague, KB, 72 A 25.

Figure 4.2: Bishop William Elphinstone by 'William of Bruges', University of Aberdeen.

Figure 4.3: James VI by Adrian Vanson, ©National Galleries of Scotland (licensor SCRAN).

Figure 6.1: John Geddy, Map of St Andrews, ©National Library of Scotland, MS 20966 (licensor SCRAN).

Figure 6.6: Hugo van der Goes, Trinity Altarpiece, ©The Royal Collection – 2001, Her Majesty Queen Elizabeth II (licensor SCRAN).

Figure 6.7: St John's Kirk chandelier, Perth Museum and Art Gallery, Perth & Kinross Council.

Figure 6.8: R. W. Billings, *The Baronial and Ecclesiastical Antiquities of Scotland*, vol. 1 (Edinburgh, 1847).

Figure 7.1: Dean Brown's Book of Hours, ©National Library of Scotland, MS 10270 (licensor SCRAN).

Figure 7.2: James IV's Book of Hours, Vienna, Österreichische Nationalbibliothek.

Figure 7.3: Diary of Georg von Ehingen, Stuttgart, Württembergishe Landesbibliothek, Cod. Hist. qt. 141, S 97.

Figure 7.4: Mons Meg, ©Crown copyright reproduced courtesy of Historic Environment Scotland (licensor SCRAN).

Index